AN INTRODUCTION TO
ANCIENT PHILOSOPHY

AN INTRODUCTION TO
ANCIENT PHILOSOPHY

A. H. ARMSTRONG

1981

LITTLEFIELD, ADAMS & CO.
TOTOWA, NEW JERSEY

First published in 1947 by
Methuen & Co. Limited
11 New Fetter Lane
London EC4P 4EE

Second Edition 1949
Third Edition 1957
Reprinted 1977

First published as a Littlefield, Adams Quality Paperback in
1981 by Littlefield, Adams & Co. 81 Adams Drive, Totowa,
N.J. 07512

Library of Congress Cataloging in Publication Data

Armstrong, A. H. (Arthur Hilary)
    An introduction to ancient philosophy.

    Bibliography: p.
    Includes index.
    1. Philosophy, Ancient—History. 2. Neoplatonism—
History. 3. Alexandrian school, Christian—History.
4. Augustine, Saint, Bishop of Hippo. I. Title.
B171.A78   1981   180'.9   81-3731
ISBN 0-8226-0418-3   AACR2

Printed in the United States of America

Contents

PAGE

PAGE

Critical Introduction

THE survival in print for nearly twenty years of a book of this kind is flattering to the author's vanity and beneficial to his pocket. But it raises some problems when he is confronted, at that distance of time from the original publication, with the demand for yet another edition. Nobody whose mind has not completely atrophied can read what he wrote twenty years ago without a certain discomfort. In the third edition in 1957, I did try to remove what seemed to me the major misrepresentations and errors of judgement and to do something to bring the book up to date. But there still remains a good deal, both in particular statements and in general tone and emphasis, which I should like to correct. The simplest way of doing so, both for my publishers and myself, is to follow the example of St. Augustine and the great contemporary Augustinian scholar H. I. Marrou, and write a short *Retractatio*, a critical survey or review of the book as I now see it. I shall begin with some general observations about the book as a whole, and go on to comment on a number of particular passages which seem to me to need revision.

The book grew out of a series of lectures delivered in 1943 at the London headquarters of the Newman Association, a society of Roman Catholic university graduates. It bears the stamp of what is now a rather old-fashioned sort of Roman Catholic one-sidedness and complacency. This is less marked than it might have been, because even at the time when the lectures were given I was not exactly a rabid Aristotelian Thomist, and I did something in the revisions of the third edition to make it less neo-scholastic in tone. But there still in places clings about it the musty smell of a period when educated Catholics could still talk about the Perennial Philosophy (meaning Thomism), a period of inward-looking narrowness from which, by the grace of God, the Church has been slowly and painfully emerging during the period which this book has been in print. The change which the writing of this "retractation" represents, is, fortunately, not just in the mind of its author. This narrowness and bias show themselves in the book in various ways. The occasional rather superficial inuendoes about contemporary philosophy can easily be disregarded; there are very few of them. More serious is the failure to show any sign of realizing that contemporary philosophy has important criticisms to offer of some of the traditional positions described with approval. I still do not regard myself as qualified by training or temperament to discuss those criticisms, and it is not a necessary part of my business as a historian of ancient philosophy to do so, but I should at least hàve shown some awareness of their existence. But the most serious evidence of narrowness is to be found in the whole planning of the book. It was written on the assumption that the only really important and interesting movements of thought deriving from ancient Greek philosophy in the mediaeval period were those of the Latin West. Ancient and early Christian thóught are considered in it much too much from the point of view of their relevance to Western mediaeval philosophy. This is not defensible except on the basis of a Western European provincialism from which historians, of all sorts, are now emancipating themselves. During the greater part of the Middle Ages Byzantium and the world of Islam were more culturally advanced and influential than the Latin West. The movements of thought stimulated by the inheritance of Greek philosophy in the Greek-speaking Christian East and the Moslem world were at least as important and interesting as those of Latin Christendom, and the book should have been written with them continually in mind, with Greek philosophy considered as the source of its whole great complex inheritance, and not simply of Western scholastic philosophy. Much, however, which is said in it about the relationship of Greek philosophy and Christian thought applies to the Greek East after Origen as well as the Latin West, and still seems to me to have some truth in it (though the contrast between pagan and Christian is at times rather overdone): so its provincial Latinism does not make the book's treatment of this topic valueless.

Another limitation of outlook apparent in the book needs mention, if not perhaps apology. It is very much a "Cambridge" book. I wrote in the original preface, and repeat now with the same conviction "Anythihg that is good in the method of this book and the manner of its approach to the ancient philosophers is principally due to the teaching and example of the late Professor F. M. Cornford": and I also expressed a gratitude which I still feel to Dr. A. L. Peck of Christ's College, Cambridge, for reading the book in typescript and making some valuable suggestions and corrections. This Cambridge approach to the history of ancient philosophy is particularly apparent in the chapters on Plato. The account there given of his metaphysics, perhaps rather too clear-cut and simplified even for an elementary introduction, is based very much on Cornford, with some modifications in the third edition influenced by some recent Continental writers. I am by no means convinced that this Cambridge approach to Plato is a wrong one. But I am much more aware than I was that other interpretations of the baffling evidence of the Platonic Dialogues have a good deal to recommend them, and in particular those current in the University of Oxford. Anyone who wants to explore these alternative ways of looking at Plato would be well advised to start with the books of I. M. Crombie included in my book list.

I now come to individual passages which need revision.

Ch. I. 1. p. 1

The Hellenistic distinction between the Ionian and Italian schools, adopted here, is too sharp and formalized. Early Pythagoreanism was probably influenced, especially in its cosmology, by Ionian philosophy, and in the fifth century it is certainly not possible to make this sort of clear-cut distinction between the attitudes of philosophers in the Eastern and Western halves of the Greek world. But what is said about the distinctive religious outlook of the Pythagoreans is substantially true.

Ch. I. 4–5. pp. 6–7

The earliest evidence for the existence in the Greek world of Orphic beliefs, practices or writings dates from the fifth century B.C., and does not now seem to me sufficient to support the positive assertion made here that Pythagoras and the early Pythagoreans were deeply influenced by an Orphic movement already well established when Pythagoras came to Croton. I do not think that it is possible to be certain which of the two groups influenced the other.

Ch. II. 3. p. 12

Xenophanes was of more importance than is here suggested. His conception of the all pervading God, who directs all things by the power of his thought, was a powerful and original one, and, with his attacks on the anthropomorphism and immorality of the traditional religion, did a good deal to determine the future course of Greek philosophical theology, which, on the whole, continued to assert with increasing emphasis that God was, in the words of Xenophanes "in no way like mortals in body or thought" (Fr. 23), and eventually influenced Christian theology in a non-anthropomorphic direction.

Ch. II. 7. p. 16

Discussion of Anaxagoras's theory of matter continues vigorously. The account given here still seems to me fairly likely to
approximate to his meaning, with the following important additions. Anaxagoras believed in the infinite divisibility of matter;
even an infinitesimally small quantity of anything contains an
infinite number of parts; and, because there is "a portion of
everything in everything" these include some parts of everything
else; one can never isolate a smallest particle of any substance in
a pure state. But matter tends to coagulate into "seeds," particles
which are still infinitely divisible and complex, but in which one
kind of thing enormously predominates; and these "seeds" are
the basic units from which Mind forms the world.

Ch. II. 8. p. 18

I should have mentioned that Diogenes of Apollonia is possibly
the originator of, and certainly one of the first' thinkers to put
forward, the type of teleological explanation mentioned on p. 30
(and in the next note).

Ch. III. 5. p. 30

I was altogether too uncritical here in my approval of ancient
Greek and traditional Christian teleology (though what I say
about its historical importance is true). Any genuine theist is
bound to believe that God directs the world with the utmost
wisdom and goodness. But he is not, I now think, committed to
believing that it is possible to read off God's purposes from an
inspection of physical structures and processes or the course of
history, to explain in detail why everything is ordered for the
best, or that it is desirable to try to do so. It seems to be true that
the rapid advance of science only began when scientists in the
seventeenth century gave up asking "Why?" "For what purpose
did God make things this way?" and limited themselves to the
question "How?" I have now little sympathy with the type of
thinking which led Epictetus (I. 16) to conclude that shaving was
against the natural law because beards were clearly intended by
Providence to distinguish male from female.

Ch. IV. 4. pp. 42–3

Plato seems in his later years to have himself considered the tripartite psychology too sharp and crude a dividing up of man, and to have abandoned it by the time he wrote the *Statesman*. He continued to maintain the distinction of rational and irrational in the soul, and to insist that reason should rule in man, but his conception of the irrational became wider and more flexible.

Ch. VI. 3. p. 57

What is said at the bottom of the page about Plato's realization that the rule of the Philosopher King is not a practical possibility, and the consequences he drew from it, needs more emphasis. Plato's latest political reflections in his last work, the *Laws*, on the need to establish the rule of law and subordinate the holders of office and authority strictly to it, and on the necessity of a "mixed constitution" (with a democratic element) and a system of checks and balances to keep those in authority from abusing their power, form the most permanently fruitful and influential part of his political thinking.

Ch. IX. 1. p. 97

This account of the subject of First Philosophy in Aristotle is altogether too dogmatic and over-simplified, even for a book of this kind. It conceals the fact that there are radical inconsistencies in Aristotle's statements about First Philosophy, and that it is extremely dubious whether he ever thought of it as the study of being as such in the sense of abstract being, being in general. (For these inconsistencies and the problems which arise from them the reader who is sufficiently seriously interested should consult, in the first instance, P. Merlan, *From Platonism to Neoplatonism*. Ch. VII, *Metaphysica Generalis* in Aristotle?). Readers will however note that, after making polite noises about being as such, I proceed in this chapter to discuss Aristotle's First Philosophy, not as general metaphysics but as theology, the study of the highest and most completely real beings; and this is probably the right approach in a book of this kind, in which it would be inappropriate to enter, as Merlan does, into the complexities of Aristotle's wrestling with his Academic inheritance.

Ch. X. 3. p. 103

I should have mentioned that the doctrine of the Mean probably has a Platonic origin. *Statesman* 284 D seems to point forward to it.

Ch. XI. 7. p. 129

The view that Alexander the Great preached or practised a doctrine of the Brotherhood of Man, vigorously advocated by the late W. W. Tarn, has been generally abandoned by scholars.

Ch. XIII. 4. p. 146

There is no evidence whatever for the view that there was an esoteric dogmatic teaching in the Sceptical Academy, and respect for the authority of St. Augustine should not have led me to mention it.

Ch. XIII. 7. p. 153

The reference to "Persian dualism" here is misleading. Orthodox Zoroastrianism saw the world as a battleground between the powers of good and evil. But its view of the physical universe and the way man should use its good things is more positive and cheerful than that of any other great religion. Its dualism is very far removed from the pessimistic dualism of the Gnostics, though an extreme form of the latter does appear in Manichaeism, which is more a Zoroastrian than a Christian heresy.

Ch. XV. 1. p. 168

Tertullian was, so far as I know, the only Christian theologian in the main stream of tradition who asserted that *God* was material. But later, in fifth century Gaul, there were theologians, Faustus of Riez and Cassian, who maintained that, though God was incorporeal, there were no incorporeal creatures, and, in particular, the human soul was material. Their motive seems to have been to stress the difference between God and creatures as strongly as possible and to exclude all possibility of an infiltration into Christian thought of the Neoplatonist doctrine of the divinity of the soul.

Ch. XV. 4. p. 174

The account of Origen given here probably makes him a more systematic thinker and a less orthodox Christian than he was in reality. Like most modern accounts of his thought, it is very much influenced by versions of his teaching given by violent and prejudiced opponents, and by the sixth century condemnations initiated by Justinian, which are primarily directed against the

"Origenism" of that period, and do not necessarily describe accurately Origen's owe thought.

H. Crouzel in his *Origène et la Philosophie* (see booklist) has argued very forcibly against taking these later, biassed accounts of Origen's teaching too seriously.

Ch. XVII. 2. p. 191

The statement that the Logos in the late treatises of Plotinus on Providence is "a new distinct principle" now seems to me to be clearly wrong. As Bréhier long ago saw, the term *Logos* in these treatises does not refer to a distinct hypostasis, but to the living formative and directive pattern, derived from Intellect through Soul, which gives the material universe all the unity and order of which it is capable.

Ch. XVII. 3. p. 192

I do not now think that Plotinus ever simply identified man's higher self with his archetype in the Divine Mind, though his soul can certainly become completely conformed to, and live entirely on the level of, Mind.

Ch. XVII. 4. p. 195

It no longer seems to me probable that the passage in III. 2. 9 is an allusion to Christianity. It is part of a general attack on a supine and superstitious religiosity which expects the gods to get men out of troubles which they have brought upon themselves by their folly or wickedness.

Ch. XVIII. 2. p. 200

The theological preoccupations of the later Neo-Platonists affected their philosophy less than is suggested here. They fitted myths, cults and oracles into their philosophical system by allegorical interpretation and strained exegesis of the sacred texts (in this they were not very different from their Christian contemporaries): they did not, on the whole, force their philosophical reasoning into conformity with their religious data.

Ch. XVIII. 3. p. 203

Something should have been said here about the remarkable doctrine of divine love (*Eros*) developed by Proclus. It was, perhaps, their abandonment of the doctrine that man's true self "did not come down," their humbler view of man's place in the universal scheme, which led the later Neo-Platonists to feel more need than Plotinus for a doctrine of loving divine care and help to enable man to attain his true end. Divine *Eros* in Proclus is a great unifying force which spreads down from above through the vast complexities of his universe, holding it together and drawing its members back to their source and goal: it inspires both gods and good men to descend and work for the perfection and salvation of those less good than themselves. This doctrine, though it may owe something to Christian influence, seems to me to be an authentic development of elements already present in the thought of Plato himself and the later Platonic tradition.

Ch. XVIII. 4. p. 204

The difference between the Neo-Platonists of Alexandria and the other schools was probably less than is stated here. Connections between the Alexandrian and Athenian schools were close, and it is probable that the Alexandrians did hold the full metaphysical doctrine of post-Iamblichean Neo-Platonism, though they were certainly on easier terms than other pagan Neo-Platonists with their Christian contemporaries.

Ch. XIX. 3. p. 207

Marius Victorinus is much too summarily dismissed here. The great edition of Henry and Hadot in the series *Sources Chretiennes* (Paris 1960) has for the first time made his thought really accessible and intelligible, and has revealed him as an important and interesting philosophical theologian in his own right, with a distinctive (but perfectly orthodox) approach to the mystery of the Trinity in terms of the Neo-Platonic triad of Being, Life and Intelligence.

Ch. XIX. 5. p. 212

The description here of Plotinus's view of creation as "an automatic reflex action of the Divine contemplation" is not adequate. A better account of it is given in Ch. XVI. 6.

Ch. XIX. 6. p. 215

Augustine's theory of time was probably influenced by

Plotinus's view of it as "the life of the soul in motion," expounded in the treatise *On Eternity and Time* (III. 7).

Ch. XIX. 8. p. 220

Augustine was probably more responsible for later deformations and exaggerations of the Christian doctrine of grace and predestination than is suggested here.

I

The Beginnings of Greek Philosophy. Milesians and Italians

1. PHILOSOPHY in the sense in which the word was generally understood in the ancient world may be defined as the search after the truth about the nature of the universe and of man, a search which the ancient philosophers (with certain exceptions) believed could result in the attainment and sure knowledge of the truth sought. Certainly philosophy must be either a search after attainable truth or a solemn game played with words to the advantage of those who are paid in our Universities for playing it, but of nobody else. In the ancient world, too, the need of marking off philosophy from theology and science, which might require a more precise and elaborate definition, was not yet felt. This search after truth is one which might be undertaken for more than one reason, and in fact the philosophy of the West has a two fold beginning in different quarters of the Greek world and under the impulse of different desires. The first beginning came among the Ionians, round about 600 B.C., and its driving impulse seems to have been that which Aristotle sets as the beginning of all philosophy, wonder, curiosity about the nature of things, the desire to know for its own sake. The basic Ionian question is "I wonder why things are as they are and happen as they do? How curious the world is." In the second beginning, in the Greek cities of South Italy during the second half of the sixth century, the desire behind the search for truth was different. It was the desire for deification, for likeness to God so far as is possible, for escape from the mortal life and return to that divine existence from which the soul was believed to have fallen. The basic Italian, Pythagorean question is "How may I deliver myself from the body of this death, from the sorrowful weary wheel of mortal existence, and become again a god?"

2. The Greek city-states of Ionia, on the coast of Asia Minor, at the time of the first beginning of Greek philosophy, were probably the richest and most highly civilized of the Greek communities. They also seem to have been distinguished by an attitude of religious detachment and indifferentism. There was, of course, no sort of secularism or militant anti-religious attitude.

To suppose anything of the sort would be a grotesque ana-chronism. The temples of the gods in Ionia were splendid and their public cult carried out duly and worthily of the wealth and artistic achievements of the cities. But Ionia was the country of origin of the Homeric poems, in whose dealing with the gods religious awe was reduced to a minimum, and it was not easy to take the all too human deities of Homer very seriously as the mysterious rulers of the mysterious universe. Those cults, too, in which more primitive but deeper religious feelings found ex-pression in mainland Greece, fertility-cults and the worship of the dead in all its forms, do not play much part in Ionia, and the Dionysiac worship, with its remarkable derivative Orphism (of which we shall see more when we turn to Italian philosophy) does not seem at this time to have reached the Asia Minor coast. So we find that the Ionian philosophers are remarkably detached from the traditional religion, which is not to say that they were not very deeply affected by certain primitive Greek ways of looking at the world which also find expression in the traditional myths. Nor does their detachment from religious considerations and avoidance of religious explanations of the universe entitle them to be considered scientific thinkers. But the relation of their way of thinking to science and also to mythology will be better considered after a short survey of what is known about what they actually taught.

This early Ionian philosophy is represented by a succession of three men, Thales, Anaximander and Anaximenes, all from Miletus, at that time the richest and most powerful of the Ionian cities. Hence the group collectively are sometimes called the Milesians. The first, Thales, by tradition one of the "Seven Wise Men" of Greece, seems to have written nothing and our scanty knowledge of his teaching depends on a tradition which goes back no further than Aristotle, and though the other two each seem to have written a work in prose, these works have perished, and Aristotle is again our earliest source for their teaching. Our knowledge of it therefore is uncertain and frag-mentary, and the fragments which we have were preserved by later writers whose interests and ways of asking and answering philosophical questions were not at all those of the Milesians themselves. There do, however, seem to be a few things about the three men's personal interests and activities and about the picture of the universe which they put forward of which we can be fairly certain. First of all, they were much concerned with those technical skills which along with magic and astrology formed the substance of the ancient priestly wisdom of Babylonia and Egypt, and which the Ionians introduced into the Greek world, mainly from Babylonia. They were practical astronomers, land-surveyors and geographers. Thales predicted eclipses, Anaximander is said to have invented the sundial, made the first map, and been responsible for several important astronomical discoveries. They were greatly interested in the "meteora", the phenomena of the regions above the surface of the earth, the weather and the movements of the heavenly bodies. One of the most interesting features of the Milesian picture of the universe is the way in which these philosophers explain the origin and nature of the heavenly bodies in terms of the processes of the weather. In this they are thoroughly opposed to that way of thinking about the eternal, impassible, transcendent world of the stars which became dominant in later Greek philosophy, passed from it to medieval Christendom, and received its finest literary expression in the symbolical setting of Dante's "Paradiso."

3. Practically all that we know about the philosophy of the Milesians concerns their cosmogony, their account of how the world came into being. They postulate as the first reality a single living stuff, indefinite in extent and character, from which the world and all things in it develop spontaneously. Thales called this "moisture" or more accurately "the moist" (to hugron), moisture being the principle of life according to simple observation and primitive common sense. Anaximander called it the "Apeiron," a word which means either "indefinite" or "unbounded" rather than "infinite." He may have thought of it as spherical like the Orphic world-egg; for later Greek geometers the sphere was "apeiron." Anaximenes called it air or breath. It appears that, like many other ancient philosophers, he held that the life of the universe resembled that of man, with air, the breath of life of which the human soul is made, for its principle. This stuff they call "divine" by which they probably mean no more than that it is living and everlasting, two characters which it must have if it is to be for them a sufficient explanation of the cosmic process. Their thought is far too primitive to make any distinction between spirit and matter, life and body, force and mass. This hylozoism, philosophy of the "living stuff" is not yet very far from primitive animism, the belief that everything that

moves and changes or shows any sort of activity does so because it is alive.

From this primal living stuff, they appear to have thought so far as we can tell, the universe as we know it came into being by a process conceived in terms of the phenomena of weather and climate in which they were so interested, a process like that of the rising and dissipation of clouds and storms over the sea off Miletus. They conceived it as a separating-out and recombining in different forms of the Opposites, elements of contrary character, "the hot," "the cold," "the wet," "the dry." Anaximenes reduced the whole process to one of rarefaction and condensation. The Opposites are not to be thought of as qualities or abstractions. That would be a gross anachronism. The distinction between substance and quality comes far later in the history of philosophy. They are things, stuffs; the cause of heat is the presence in the hot object of a portion of "the hot," of moisture the presence of "the wet" and so on. The whole of this process of separating out and combination, the forming and eventual dissolution of earth and sea and the strange structures of cloud and fire which Anaximander imagined to explain the phenomena of the heavenly bodies was governed by a law or rhythm of balance and retribution which the Milesians called by the very traditional name of Dike, Justice.

This account of the universe presents very obvious analogies to the old Greek myths about the origin of the gods and the world of which an easily accessible example is to be found in Hesiod's "Theogony." The primal living stuff is reminiscent of Chaos, Night or Erebus, the primordial realm of darkness and void or confusion from which the first cosmic gods, Heaven and Earth, came forth. Dike, Justice, which regulates the cosmic process, is very like the traditional idea of Fate, the power behind the gods and stronger than they which is the real ruler of the world. Even the symmetrical Pairs of Opposites (a very persistent conception in Pre-Socratic thought) may have been to some degree unconsciously suggested by the sexual pairs of gods who are responsible for the successive generations of the Theogonies. And in general Milesian, like all later Greek philosophy, conforms to the great basic assumptions of Greek traditional religion and cosmology; that the universe was born, not made: that the gods or powers, whatever they may be, are within the universe and subject to its law. There is no place in genuinely Hellenic thought for omnipotence or a transcendent Creator in the Christian sense. Yet there are important differences between mythology and Milesian philosophy. The Milesians do not put forward their stories about the universe as handed down from immemorial antiquity or told by inspired poets, but as their own conclusions. Their first principle does not, like Hesiod's, mysteriously come to be but exists eternally (a most important change). Instead of the personification (often vague enough) and personalities of the old myths we have descriptions of the various entities of the cosmic process in common-sense terms derived from every-day observation, and the process itself is conceived impersonally and in terms of natural and necessary movements. This does not, however, mean that the Milesians were scientific thinkers. Their method of producing great sweeping highly elaborated accounts of the universe and its coming into being, unsupported by reasoned argument, on the basis of a few unsystematically observed facts is really closer to the myth-maker than to the true scientist. It is of course a method which we all of us, even scientific workers outside their own field, use every day in our ordinary thinking and conversation. Perhaps the modern interpreters of the thought of the Milesians would have understood them better if, with all due care to avoid anachronism, they had thought of them as more like ordinary men of our time. They certainly seem closer to our experience than any other group of Greek philosophers. They were unreligious without being antireligious, interested and expert in the new technical skills without being really scientifically minded, curious about natural phenomena, deeply influenced without knowing it by traditional ideas, inclined to sweeping generalization and jumping to conclusions on insufficient evidence—and finally very interested in the weather!

4. The decline of Ionia began with its conquest by the Persians in 546 and culminated in the destruction of Miletus in 494 B.C. During the latter part of the sixth century the centre of the intellectual life of Greece moved to the splendid and powerful city-states of "Great Greece," South Italy and Sicily. These were colonies, that is fully independent daughter cities retaining some ties of religion and mutual help (as a general rule) with the parent state, of the cities of mainland Greece. Here Pythagoras emigrated from Samos, and here about 530 he founded the Pythagorean Brotherhood, at Croton in South

Italy. This new philosophical school, the "Italian" school which Pythagoras inaugurated, is very different from Milesian cosmogony, and has a very different spiritual background. In place of the unenthusiastic state religion of Ionia and the normal poetic mythology of the type familiar to us in Hesiod there lies behind Pythagorean philosophy the strange religious movement known as Orphism. The Orphic movement appeared in Greece in the sixth century B.C. In our scanty evidence about it we hear of purification-rituals, of small groups of devotees living an ascetic life, and of a voluminous literature circulating under the names of Orpheus, the legendary singer whom the Orphics took for their prophet, and another legendary singer Musaeus. Orphism had a widespread influence, whose precise bounds are not easy to determine, and lasted to the end of classical paganism, and it is difficult to be at all positive about the content of the earliest literature and the beliefs of the earliest groups of devotees. But it appears that the Orphic books contained cosmogonies like Hesiod's, but more fantastic and with some unusual features (notably the World-Egg), and some of them at least a sacred story of much more religious importance and profounder implications, the myth of the generation of man from the ashes of the Titans who had devoured Dionysus Zagreus, the god whom the Orphics worshipped. Thus man is a blend of divine and earthly nature, and the purification and release of the divine element is the end to which the Orphic way of life is directed. The soul, it seems, to the Orphics (and this is a new idea in the Greek world) was an immortal god imprisoned in the body and doomed, unless released by following the Orphic way of life, to go round the wheel of reincarnation in an endless succession of lives, animal and human (so that all living things are akin, and to kill an animal is to murder one of one's own family). By ritual purifications, by an ascetic life of which the most important feature was abstinence from animal flesh, and by knowledge of the correct magic formulae to use on the journey after death, the Orphics hoped to win release from the body and return to the company of the gods. The next world was to them more real and important than this, a place of joy for the blessed initiates and of torment for those who were not of the company of the elect. This other-worldliness and the ascetic life which went with it were very different from normal Greek beliefs and religious practice and had an effect of the greatest importance on later Greek philosophy and religion. As we shall see, Plato himself and later Platonists were deeply influenced by the Orphic-Pythagorean tradition.

5. The Pythagorean Brotherhood, which was founded in one of the regions most deeply and lastingly affected by Orphism, South Italy, took over from the Orphics a good many details of organization and way of life. But very much more important is their whole-hearted adoption of the Orphic doctrine that the soul is divine and immortal, that it has fallen and is imprisoned in the body, and that it is doomed to continual reincarnation until it can purify itself, escape, and return to the divine world. The Pythagoreans, however, held distinctive views on the manner of the soul's purification and return and the nature of its divinity, and it is these views which entitle them to be called philosophers. But before discussing these distinctively Pythagorean views it is necessary to say that it is extremely difficult to determine what the teaching of Pythagoras himself or the earliest Pythagoreans was. The Pythagoreans had an unbounded veneration for their founder, to whom they were liable to attribute all doctrines that later became current in the school, and also a passion for pious forgeries, which members of the school in later generations published under the name of famous early Pythagoreans. (This of course was in the Hellenistic and Roman world a common method of showing respect for tradition and adding authority to one's own opinions.) Consequently it is very difficult to determine whether a particular doctrine belongs to the first generation of the school, to the Pythagoreans contemporary with Plato, or to the Neo-Pythagorean revival which began in the first century B.C. It seems, however, fairly probable that the teaching of Pythagoras himself was something to the following effect. That which makes the soul divine is the intellect, the power to know eternal unchanging truth. This truth is the element of form, order, proportion, limit and harmony in the universe, as represented above all by musical harmony, the fixed proportions of the scale, and by the order of the heavenly bodies, the two for Pythagoras being closely related. By contemplating this the soul is purified and returns to its godlike state. This formal order is conceived mathematically. "Things are numbers" is a fundamental Pythagorean doctrine, interpreted in many different ways at different times and by different members of the school, but always meaning that the

essential reality of things can in some way be completely expressed in numerical terms: from this primitive doctrine a long and complicated line of development leads to modern mathematical physics. Early Pythagorean cosmology may have consisted in an account of how a dark indefinite vapour (the Milesian primal stuff) was drawn into the universe continually by a process like breathing and order and geometrical shape imposed on it. For the Pythagoreans form, order, limit or definite shape, light, and rest are all aspects of the good: indefiniteness, darkness, disorder, motion and change are bad. Form, the male principle, is good: matter, the female principle, is evil. This opposition, this emphasis on unchanging form and order as the good, the only valuable reality in the universe corresponds exactly to the belief in the soul as divine and the body as its prison and pollution. The two together make up the great contribution of the Pythagoreans to philosophy, a contribution which from their day to ours has been richly productive of both good and evil consequences.

The contribution of the Milesians to the philosophical tradition of Europe is at first sight less easy to determine. Their primitive cosmologies seem immeasurably remote from anything which we know as philosophy. Yet by putting forward their stories about the universe as they did, simply as reasonable explanations of the phenomena, they laid the foundations of both science and philosophy as separate intellectual disciplines, distinct from theology on the one hand and empirical techniques on the other. And in their doctrine of the evolution of all things from the one primal stuff they posed for the first time, however crudely, the problem of the One and the Many, which is perhaps the central and most important theme of all traditional philosophy.

II
The Later Pre-Socratics

1. THE fifth century B.C. opens with the Great Opposites of Pre-Socratic philosophy, Heraclitus and Parmenides. They are both figures of great importance because of their effect on the subsequent development of philosophy, and the opposition between them goes very deep, extending beyond the content of their philosophies to their ways of thinking, their philosophical inheritance and the manner in which they choose to express themselves. Fortunately we possess enough quotations and extracts from their writings to form a fair idea of the general character of their philosophies.

Heraclitus was an Ionian from the great city of Ephesus, and was probably in the prime of life round about the turn of the century (500 B.C.). The background of his very distinctive and vividly personal thought is formed by the primitive Milesian cosmology described in the last chapter. He is distinguished by his absolute contempt not only for popular ideas but for the opinions of all other philosophers, and above all for what he calls "polymathy," a term which seems to cover both Pythagorean mathematics and astronomy and the collection and detailed study of ancient traditions about the origin of the universe. He relies absolutely upon his own intuition. "I searched myself" is the phrase in which he describes how he attained to knowledge of the truth. It is one of the most striking of the hundred and thirty short fragments which remain to us from the prose work "On the Universe" in which he expounded his thought. They are pungent, concise sayings, strangely and forcibly expressed, impossible for anyone who has once become familiar with them to forget (and lending themselves easily to use as texts from which to develop speculations going far beyond anything which is likely to have been in Heraclitus's own philosophy). From them can be put together a most original and impressive picture of the universe. Its first feature, and that which was afterwards taken to be the distinguishing mark of Heracliteanism is the passionate and eager acceptance of change as the law of all being. "You cannot step twice into the same river" (a sentiment on which a later Heraclitean attempted to improve by asserting that you could not step into the same river even once!) All things, for Heraclitus are in perpetual flux and change; nowhere in the universe is there to be found eternal rest, unchanging stability. And not only is there perpetual change, but also perpetual conflict. "War is the father of all things." The clash of opposites is the very condition of life. Evil and good, hot and cold, wet and dry and the rest are each other's necessary complements and the endless strife between them is the sum of existence. The only harmony possible is a harmony of conflict and contrast, "a counter-pulling harmony like that of a bow or a lyre"; produced, that is, by opposite tensions, as in a tightly-strained, well-tuned string. In all this Heraclitus is setting himself in conscious and emphatic opposition to the Pythagorean search for the eternal and unchanging, for escape from the cycle of change, and unceasing rest in the divine world (which Heraclitus makes it clear he would regard as unmitigatedly boring); and also to the corresponding Pythagorean "taking sides" between the Opposites, exalting good over evil, light over dark, male over female, and so on. For Heraclitus the two members of every pair are indivisible and equally natural and necessary; one without the other is impossible.

2. This world of change and conflict pictured by Heraclitus is not however a mere chaos. It is governed by an immanent principle of order and measure. Heraclitus speaks of its work sometimes in mythological terms. "Justice" and her ministers the Furies keep the Opposites or the heavenly bodies within their due bounds. But his name for the ruling principle is the Logos. This is a word of very varied meaning in ordinary Greek speech (the article on it in the new Liddell and Scott's Dictionary occupies the best part of three double-column pages). Among its principal meanings are reckoning, proportion or relation, explanation, argument, reason (in many senses), story, language (grammatical) sentence. It makes its first appearance in philosophy with Heraclitus, and he first begins to give it that peculiar and very profound meaning which later made it so valuable for expressing the Christian revelation. The Logos of Heraclitus is the universal "proportion of the mixture," the law or principle of measure and just order which effects the harmony of opposing tensions. But the Logos is law because it is God, a living all-ruling intelligence which seems to be in some way identified with the Ever-Living Fire which is the stuff of the universe, as Heraclitus's great phrase "The Thunderbolt steers all things" suggests, if "thunderbolt" here really means the Fire. This Fire is not

identical with the visible, elemental fire we know, and is "ever-living," not immortal, for it is in turn transformed into all things and all things into it. This transformation of all things into each other according to the living divine law which somehow per-sists when the Logos-Fire itself is transformed is a cyclic, ever-recurring process, the "way up and down." The Logos is the principle of life and intelligence to men, but they have the choice of shutting themselves up in their private worlds of ignorance and stupidity (as most men do) or of opening themselves to the universal Logos and the unbounded depth of its wisdom (as Heraclitus himself did).

The Logos is thus for Heraclitus a universal principle which is the cause of order, proportion, balance, harmony and rationality in the continual flow of being and is at the same time vividly alive. It is this union of life and rationality in the single concept of the Logos which is one of Heraclitus's great contribu-tions to our traditional inheritance of thought. The other is his extraordinarily vivid intuition of the nature of the world in which we live: a world in which all things are subject to the law of perpetual change, and die continually into each other's life, and in which the only possible harmony is a delicate and precarious tension of opposing stresses; but a world which is no mere chaos but one and governed by a living law. It is a view of the world of time and change which has been accepted by later and greater thinkers who looked beyond it to a transcendent and eternal world of the spirit; and there are surely few in our own days who would be stupid enough to deny the essential truth of Heraclitus's vision.

3. With Parmenides we find ourselves in an entirely different intellectual atmosphere. Geographically he belongs to the Italians, being a distinguished citizen of Elea in South Italy. Like a good many other Greek philosophers he took a prominent part in the affairs of his native state, and was appointed to draw up a code of laws for it. It is perhaps worth remarking that the professional and professorial philosopher, detached from the normal life of the state and society and entirely absorbed in the work of teaching or research within his philosophical college or community, does not appear in Greece before Alexander the Great, and we have to wait till the Roman Imperial period for the most perfect examples of the type to be found in the ancient world. Parmenides was in his prime about 475 and was thus a

younger contemporary of Heraclitus. He expressed his philosophical convictions in a lengthy work written in rather inferior verse, in the epic hexameters which were the most ancient medium of any sort of literary expression in Greece. Of the two parts of this poem, the "Way of Truth" and the "Way of Opinion" some long continuous fragments are preserved. The prologue has all the trappings of an Orphic book of revelation. The poet is conducted to the Gates of the Sun, guarded by Justice, and within them receives from a goddess a revelation of the truth. But the influence of the Orphic-Pythagorean "Italian" tradition on Parmenides does not go very much further. There is no trace in him of Pythagorean religion and "care for the soul" and his whole conception of the nature of reality is utterly different. The ancient Greek historians of philosophy regarded the system of Parmenides as derived from that of Xenophanes of Colophon, a wandering religious teacher rather than a philosopher, of the second half of the sixth century, who attacked the traditional mythology and preached a sort of pan-animism; God for him is one, acting as a whole, immovable, governing all things by the power of his thought, and (as far as we can tell from the fragments of Xenophanes which survive) an immanent all-pervading world-soul. But there is no real evidence that Parmenides was influenced by Xenophanes, and his own thought was very different. The one point which the two have in common is their conviction that all reality is one, but the two men conceive its unity in quite dissimilar and incompatible ways. The most striking fact about Parmenides's way of thinking is that he is the first Greek philosopher who reasons. Earlier thinkers, as far as we know, had made no attempt to base their picture of the universe upon logical reasoning, or to defend it by rational argument. The logic of Parmenides, however primitive it may seem, is the starting-point from which Platonic dialectic, Aristotelian logic and the whole Western tradition of philosophical reasoning have developed. His basic proposition is "That which is *is*, and it is impossible for it not to be." This is the "Way of Truth." Absolute non-existence is absolutely unthinkable, and thought cannot follow the Way of Not-Being. The conclusion born of sense-experience and accepted by all earlier philosophers that things in some sense "are and are not," that change takes place, new entities appear and older states of being pass away, is rejected as a delusion. For Parmenides "is" has only one sense, the most absolute. "That which is" means the whole of actually existing reality and nothing else. All those distinctions between the different meanings of "is" which seem to us the merest common sense were worked out by Plato in solving the problem which Parmenides set later philosophers, and by Aristotle after him.

4. All earlier philosophers had assumed that nothing could come out of nothing and that the world is derived from a single everlasting principle. In that sense reality for them was one. Parmenides makes the same assumption, but since for him "is" means "exists fully, actually and completely: is all it can be," his primal One remains for ever unchanged and immovable. It cannot diminish or increase or divide. Nothing can come out of it. The elaborate cosmologies of the old myths and the first philosophers are impossibilities, delusions, disproved by reason. Parmenides demonstrates to his own satisfaction by a regular process of logical proof that his One Reality does not come into being or perish or move or change, that it is homogeneous and cannot be divided, and is continuous and equal in every part ; and finally that it is limited and has the form of a sphere occupying the whole of space. There is no void. In fact it is a geometrical solid, with qualities neither material nor spiritual, but simply mathematical and logical. And this for him is the one and only reality whose existence can be proved and believed in rationally. His preference for unity, rest and limit, which has thus by a remorseless process of logical reasoning carried him to the opposite pole from Heraclitus and to a denial of the existence or even logical possibility of the world revealed to us by our senses, is Pythagorean in origin, but his system destroys Pythagorean cosmology as completely as Ionian, and also Pythagorean religion. Parmenides calls his One "divine" (probably meaning no more than eternal and unchanging) but seems to have attached no religious significance to it.

After all this it is rather startling to find the whole of the second part of Parmenides's poem taken up by a long and elaborate traditional cosmogony. Parmenides makes it perfectly clear at the beginning of this second part that he is no longer giving an account of the truth which can be demonstrated by reason but only of "what seems to mortals." But his account of this universe of appearance has several original features and there is nothing in it to suggest that he is not putting forward his own views. The most probable explanation of what he is doing, and that which

fits best with his own words is that while he is certain that
reasoning can only lead to knowledge of the one and only reality,
the Sphere, yet some account, and the best possible, must be given
of this strange universal mirage, the world of appearance revealed
by our senses. There is a gulf between the one reality and the
manifold, changing appearances, and Parmenides is clear-sighted
enough to see that, so far as his reasoning goes it is unbridgeable.
5. Parmenides presented the problem of the One and the Many
in its sharpest and clearest form to succeeding generations of
philosophers; and in doing so he destroyed the very foundations of
the older physical philosophy, in which a living and changeable
One evolves naturally into the many beings of the world we
know. The dilemma of Parmenides was really a logical one, and
it was not adequately solved until Plato showed in the dialogue
"Parmenides" and in the "Sophist" that the logical reasoning of
his formidable predecessor was not as conclusive as it seemed.
The immediate successors of Parmenides however tried to deal
with the problem he had set them in a physical and cosmological
way. They accepted the doctrine of Parmenides up to a point.
There is no longer any real change, growth or development of a
living stuff in their systems. Instead there are various combina-
tions of a number of bodies of which each one is unchangeable
and everlasting and is in fact endowed with most of the properties
of the One of Parmenides. These elementary bodies are moved
and arranged by a separate moving cause or causes. This
separation of the moving and arranging cause from the bodies
which it moves and arranges is an event of the utmost importance
in the development of Greek philosophy. It points directly forward to the theology of Plato, with the Great Soul or Demiurge
forming and governing the material world.

The two greatest of the Pluralists, as this group of immediately
post-Parmenidean thinkers is sometimes called, are Empedocles
of Agrigentum and Anaxagoras of Clazomenæ both in their
prime in the early decades of the second half of the fifth century.
Beside them stand a very little-known or knowable but probably
influential group of Pythagoreans of the younger generation who
taught a sort of "mathematical atomism," a doctrine according
to which all reality is ultimately constructed of indivisible mathematical units, and who seem to have put forward an elaborate
cosmology in which earth, sun, and the other heavenly bodies
revolve about a central fire (this cosmology may however belong

to the next century). It was probably against these Pythagoreans and their theory of discontinuous quantity that the chief disciple and successor of Parmenides, Zeno of Elea, who also belongs to the middle of the fifth century, directed his paradoxes "Achilles and the Tortoise," the "Arrow," the "Runner," the "Race-course," which can even now puzzle anyone who is not a very advanced mathematician and which were designed to pro⸩ that the consequences arising from the assumption of motion (a⸩ the Pythagoreans understood it) were more absurd than those arising from the assumption of Parmenides that motion was an irrational delusion of the senses.

6. Empedocles of Acragas is a magnificent figure in the full Orphic tradition of South Italy and Sicily. He was at once philosopher, statesman and poet, and the long fragments which survive of the two poems in which he expounded his cosmology and his doctrine of the soul and its destiny are real poetry, very different from the uninspired verses of Parmenides. He was the sort of person round whom legends collect, and his fame and the influence of his philosophy survived for many generations after him. His system is an extremely complex one. The passive element is represented by the four "roots" or elementary bodies Fire, Air, Earth and Water, the standard four elements of later Greek philosophy. There are two moving causes, the principle of unification, Love or Aphrodite, and the principle of division, Strife or Ares, and the cosmic process is an ever-recurring cycle in which each prevails in turn. It starts with the "Sphere," in which the four elements are perfectly mixed under the complete domination of Love. This "Sphairos" of Empedocles is a conception closely related to the Orphic World-Egg, and the idea of a perfect mixture or balance of opposing elements as being a state of health or perfection is one of great importance in Greek medicine and ethics, and perhaps more deep and lasting in its influence than has generally been realised. The next stage in the cycle is when Strife gradually gains ground, until a state of perfect separation of the elements is reached. Then Love gains ground again, until the cycle returns at last to its starting-point, the perfect mixture of elements in the "Sphere." Only in the intermediate stages, when there is neither complete separation nor complete fusion of the elements can individual entities and the universe as we know it exist.

With this cosmology Empedocles combined the full traditional

Orphic doctrine of the soul, its divine origin, its fall, its successive reincarnations, and its final return to the company of the gods. How he related the doctrine to his cosmology the surviving fragments of the two poems do not allow us to determine, but that he did bring the two into some relation satisfactory to himself there seems no reason whatever to doubt. Many of the details of Empedocles's biology and astronomy are interesting and odd, and influenced later philosophers and poets, but there is no space for them here.

7. Balancing Empedocles in the other half of the Greek world is the dry clear-headed Ionian Anaxagoras of Clazomenae, the friend of Pericles and the dominant figure in the intellectual life of Periclean Athens. In him the common-sense attitude and religious indifference of the Milesians re-appear, but, since he lived after Parmenides had revolutionised Greek thinking his system, expounded according to the Ionian tradition in prose, was of the new pluralist type. His doctrine about the unchanging elementary bodies which his moving cause stirs up into a cosmos is an interesting and heroic attempt to solve the problem of change and the infinite diversity of things more satisfactorily than was done by Empedocles's theory of the Four Elements. Unfortunately the evidence of the fragments of his work which survive and of the allusions of Aristotle to his doctrine is by no means easy to interpret, and there are vigorous controversies among modern scholars about what Anaxagoras's meaning really was. Possibly the general outline of his thought was something like this : all natural substances, flesh, bone, and other animal-organic substances, vegetable substances, and also the Milesian Opposites or "weather-substances," hot and cold, etc., and the Opposites concerned in nutrition, sweet, bitter, etc., are elementary, that is, can never be ultimately resolved into more ultimate elements like the Four Roots of Empedocles. The parts are always like the whole, however far you divide them. How then are changes, such transformations as that of food in digestion to be explained? Here modern interpreters disagree violently. All that is certain is that he held that "things are not cut off from each other with an axe:" the traditional Opposites, hot and cold, etc., are never found in isolation; and there is in some sense "a portion of everything in everything," whether this phrase is to be taken of the presence in things of traces, indefinitely small portions of everything else (so that a thing is what it is simply

through the enormous predominance of one kind of element in its composite make-up); or whether some more subtle solution must be found.

Anaxagoras's moving cause is even more interesting than his elementary bodies. He calls it, and he is the first Greek philosopher to do so, *Nous*, Mind or Intelligence. It is unlikely that he, any more than any other Pre-Socratic, thought of it as immaterial; it is rather composed of the finest and subtlest sort of matter. It is "unmixed," always distinct from the mass of elementary bodies which it moves, though it pervades the whole mass. It is essentially mobile (probably) and is certainly the source of ordered motion to all else. This ordered motion is conceived of as a gradual process of separating out and distinction from an original mixture, by which the universe of individual things as we know it (and perhaps many other universes) comes into being. To start with the elements, most of which are present in such small parts as to be indistinguishable, are mixed in a chaos. Then Intelligence starts a "vortex," a whirling motion in chaos which begins the process of ordered separation, eventually resulting in the universe we know; in this, incidentally, the "four elements," fire, air, earth and water are not thought of as simple but as composite and containing a portion of every elementary substance, some of which, e.g., the hot and the bright in fire, are large enough to be perceived. There is no reason however to suppose that Anaxagoras used Intelligence merely as a stick to stir up chaos with. It is the moving and directing force in the whole process of ordered formation of the universe. Socrates's complaint against Anaxagoras in the "Phaedo" of Plato is not that he made Intelligence a mere mechanical initiating force but that he made no attempt to explain the purpose for which it acted and how it ordered all things for the best. The Anaxagorean Archelaus of Athens in the latter part of the century was however probably a good deal more mechanistic and materialistic in his view of the cosmic process.

Anaxagoras explained sensation by saying that we experience heat, cold, light and other sensible qualities by the presence in us of their opposites. Sensation goes by contraries. The hot in us is cooled, the cold in us heated by the contact with the cold or hot external object. Empedocles on the other hand held that "we know like by like," fire by the presence in us of fire, air by air, and so on. This debate as to whether we know by likenesses or by contraries persisted into the classical period of Greek philosophy and stimulated Aristotle in developing his distinctive doctrine of sense-perception.

8.   Other fifth-century followers of the Ionian tradition are less important, though Diogenes of Apollonia, with his divine intelligent world-arranging air, is interesting and had some influence. The Atomists however, the most original of the Pluralist schools, must be dealt with in some detail, not so much because of their importance in the development of Greek philosophy, which was not great, but because of the attention which has been paid to them in modern times. They combine oddly a crude materialism with distrust of the evidence of our senses. Their frame of mind is not particularly scientific; and the only later thinker who accepts the Atomist doctrines is the very dogmatic and thoroughly unscientifically-minded Epicurus.

The first of the Atomists, Leucippus of Miletus (first half of the fifth century) is a rather shadowy figure whose teaching we cannot distinguish clearly from that of his successor Democritus, a vigorous and cheerful person who was born about 460 and founded his school at Abdera about 420. His system gets over the difficulties raised by Parmenides by simply ignoring them. Logical perplexities mean nothing to him, though his system shows the influence of his time and is pluralist in type, but much more rigorously material and mechanical than that of either Empedocles or Anaxagoras. His elementary bodies are the Atoms, small lumps of stuff which may be logically analysable into parts—that does not interest him—but are physically indivisible; they are *atomoi*, you cannot cut them. They are of all sorts of different shapes and sizes; hard substances like metals being made of hooked atoms which cling closely together, fine and subtle substances like air, fire, or the soul of very small smooth round atoms, very mobile, like the motes in a sunbeam. These atoms are in perpetual movement. There is no cause for their movement and no directing force. It is simply assumed to account for the existing state of affairs. And, so that they may have somewhere to move about in, the existence of empty space is assumed also, regardless of the canon of Parmenides that the void absolute non-being, is absolutely unthinkable. These are the only basic realities, atoms and void, and the various universes, of which there may be many, and all individual things in them, are simply produced by chance comings-together of atoms in their endless movement in the void. This applies to the human soul and the gods as well as everything else.

With this crudely materialist physics goes a distrust of the senses, which can only give a "bastard sort of information about reality" and an exclusive reliance on reason to find out the truth of things. This is necessary to the system (for after all things do not *look* like chance collections of atoms) but derives from Parmenides rather than from Ionia. It was combined rather curiously in Democritus with a taste for the detailed observation of phenomena (his position of course was quite different from that of the modern scientist, whose delicate and elaborate instruments and technique of experiment and observation enable him to obtain evidence perceptible to the senses of the properties and the underlying structure of things which are concealed from casual observation). The ethical system of Democritus is the first example of a type which was to become very common later in which peace of mind, an untroubled calm derived from rational knowledge of the nature of things, is put forward as the goal to be attained by man. The fact that he was interested in ethics at all and had a morality to teach shows clearly that we are now on the threshold of a new epoch in Greek philosophy. We are passing from the world of thought of the Pre-Socratics, with their almost exclusively cosmological or cosmological-religious preoccupations to that of Socrates and his contemporaries (Democritus was about ten years younger than Socrates) with their profound concern about the good life and the proper end of man.

9. A note may be added on the philosophical attitude of the great Greek doctors of medicine of the fifth century. Their practice and thought are revealed to us in a collection of forty-one treatises which passed in the ancient world for the work of the most famous of Greek doctors, Hippocrates of Cos (born about 450). These show that medicine in the Greece of the fifth century had reached a far higher level than any other science, and some of them also show something which we have not yet discovered in the Pre-Socratic world, a genuinely scientific attitude of mind. Their authors are not interested in the contemporary speculations about the nature of the physical world, with their very scant foundation of observation and experiment. They concentrate on accurate diagnosis, precise observation of the available facts, and treatment which has been proved sound by experience.

Other writers of the group however are deeply influenced by fifth century physical speculation and hold that an understanding of the nature of the universe is necessary to an understanding of the bodily constitution of man : and it must be remembered that their theories about the universe, unlike their theories about man, could not be controlled by experiment and precise observation with the techniques then available, so that the genuinely scientific quality of their work was bound to diminish in proportion as they were influenced by the physical speculations of the philosophers.

We have now come to the end of our survey of Pre-Socratic philosophy and are about to enter the very different world of thought in which Socrates untiringly pursued his enquiry about what man is for and the nature of the good life. We may sum up by pointing out the most important of those elements which passed into Plato's thought from that of his predecessors and which through him have influenced the later development of the central tradition of European philosophy. (The use made of Pre-Socratic thought by Stoics and Epicureans will be noted in its appropriate place). From the Milesians Plato derives much of his conception of the matter of the physical universe. From the Pythagoreans comes the essence of Plato's doctrine of the nature and destiny of the soul, his insistence on eternal form and order as the supremely important reality and proper object of the intellect, and the emphasis in his thought on mathematics and astronomy. From Heraclitus he gets his vision of the transitoriness of all sensible things and the flux of the material world. Parmenides and the Eleatics leave him a clear though inadequate vision of eternal being, the beginnings of logical reasoning, and a logical problem to solve. From the Pluralists he takes the separation of matter and moving cause, and from Anaxagoras in particular the idea that the moving cause is Mind, though the Cosmic Intelligence of Plato is, as we shall see, a Power very different, far more greatly and profoundly conceived than the *Nous* of Anaxagoras. But all these conceptions inherited from his predecessors are transformed, immensely developed and re-ordered in the light of the teaching and personality of Socrates. It was Socrates who was incomparably the greatest influence on Plato, and it was Socrates who changed the whole nature and direction of European philosophy.

III
The Sophists and Socrates

1. THE period in which the last of the philosophers mentioned in the previous chapter lived was one of unprecedented intellectual upheaval in Greece. The great Persian Wars had ended for all practical purposes with the battle of Platæa in 479. There followed the "Great Fifty Years", the period when Athens was the greatest power in Greece and when Greece, and Athens in particular, reached the height of its material prosperity and the fullest magnificence of its artistic achievement. But it was also a period when the traditional foundations of Greek society were disintegrating rapidly. It is worth emphasizing that Greek religion and morality at this time, outside the small Orphic sects, were exclusively based on ancestral custom and tradition. The Greeks had no inspired scriptures and consequently no Church or authorised body of theologians to interpret them. Nor at this time had they any great systems of philosophical theology and ethics. The worship of the gods, the stories told about them, the rules of public and private morality, all depended upon inherited tradition, varying somewhat from city to city, and of course entirely different from the religious and moral traditions of the non-Greek peoples with whom the Greeks were increasingly coming into contact. Tradition unsupported by reason or revelation can be tremendously strong in its hold upon the average man, and it is probable that the average Greek in the period we are considering and for long after continued to hold to his traditional beliefs. But it is also immensely vulnerable to intellectual criticism and to any change or unsettlement of the traditional social structure. And in fifth century Greece, and especially at Athens, its political, economic and intellectual centre, the foundations of the traditional religious and moral order were being increasingly found insufficiently substantial. The dislocation of the Persian wars and the great new material expansion were important causes of the flight from tradition, but it was perhaps mainly the result of the coming to a head of tendencies which had been developing in the politically and intellectually restless Greek world since the beginning of the sixth century or earlier. The tragic end of the great age in the long savage struggle of the Peloponnesian War, which filled the last third of the century, and the demoralization which it

produced, is a witness to the inadequacy of the traditional foundations to stand the strain placed on them.

Ionian philosophy played its part in this negative process of the disruption of ancient tradition without putting anything positive in its place, but the part which it played was, generally speaking, a rather oblique and indirect one. There had been a certain amount of direct and vigorous criticism of the traditional myths and (more important if anyone had taken much notice of it) of the traditional cult-practices, notably from Xenophanes and Heraclitus. But the philosophers did not normally set themselves in a direct opposition to the old traditions. They merely ignored them, and produced pictures of the world into which the gods simply would not fit and in which the all-embracing nexus of natural and more and more mechanically conceived causes left no room for the simple apparatus of divine sanctions and divine guidance, of thunderbolts and omens, which had safeguarded the traditional morality. Furthermore, the physical philosophers did not even agree among themselves. Their world-pictures were obviously and flagrantly incompatible with each other, and when finally there came the devastating criticism of the Eleatics, above all Zeno, it seemed to reduce the whole business of searching for truth about the nature of things by reason once and for all to absurdity. We have seen already how some of the Hippocratic doctors dealt with the situation. They turned away both from tradition and from physical speculation and concentrated on the practice of their art according to the data furnished by immediate observation. In a somewhat analogous way the more cultured citizens of the Greek states, feeling increasingly unsure of the traditional foundations of their life and with an increasing conviction that the physical speculation which had occupied the cultivated intellects of the generation before was futile, turned in the second half of the fifth century to a whole-hearted concentration on their proper art and business in life. It must be remembered that for the citizen, and especially the well-to-do citizen of a Greek city-state his citizen's duties were his most important, supremely absorbing, and sometimes pretty well full-time occupation. The art then on which he concentrated was that of success in public life. It was an art which required teachers, and the teachers were duly forthcoming.

2.   These teachers were the so-called "Sophists", a name which,

before Plato wrote certain of his dialogues, had not the bad sense which we incline to attach to it. The best way to describe them is perhaps to say that they were travelling professors of this all-important art of success in public life. They were international figures, originating from various parts of the Greek world: Protagoras from Abdera, Gorgias from Leontini, Prodicus from Ceos, and Hippias from Elis, to name the four most important. They travelled from city to city, imparting their instruction for very substantial fees to the young men of the wealthier citizen families, and they naturally tended to gravitate to Athens. The central subject of their courses was rhetoric, the art of persuasion by eloquent speech, and they claimed to be able to teach their pupils to speak persuasively to any "brief", to argue both sides of any case. With rhetoric went the subordinate verbal arts, grammar and the study of the meanings of words (in which last Prodicus was particularly interested) and a general emphasis on all the elegant arts and accomplishments of life. An all-round virtuosity and a supreme skill in the art of persuasion were their ideals for themselves and their pupils.

Of course these Sophists were in no sense philosophers. They never professed to be anything of the sort, and had no use for philosophy in the sense in which it was understood at the time, namely, physical and cosmological speculation. Their attitude to life might be described as a humanist agnosticism. Protagoras, whom Plato took more seriously as a thinker than the others, expressed it very well in a couple of sentences which have been preserved: "Man is the measure of all things, of the reality of those which are, and the unreality of those which are not"; "As to the gods, I cannot know whether they exist or not; too many obstacles are in the way, the obscurity of the subject and the shortness of life". A successful civilized human life is the central concern; and there are no absolute standards of unchanging reality, religion or morality with which the individual mind must conform. There was a discussion, already widespread in fifth century Greece before the Sophists appeared, as to whether religion and morality were Natural, part of the inborn essential order of things or simply an affair of Custom and Tradition. The relativist humanism of the Sophists led them of course to accept the second alternative. Religion and morality were for them simply a matter of man-made custom. This did not however by any means imply, for the great Sophists of the first generation, that a man should not observe the customary morality of the city-state society in which he lived. As even the unfriendly evidence of Plato shows us, the great Sophists, like Protagoras and Gorgias, were figures as morally respectable as any Victorian agnostic, and they were genuinely shocked at the cynical immoralism, the doctrine that morality is only the right of the stronger, which developed among some of the clever and ambitious young men whom they had taught. Yet the influence of these Sophists undoubtedly helped on the process of disintegration, for they destroyed the sanctities of tradition in the minds of their pupils and put nothing adequate in their place. And so the age moved on, from the magnificent utterances of Aeschylus, the greatest religious poet of Greece, and Sophocles's hymns, full of light and glory, to the eternal moral law, to that feeling which pervades some of the plays of Euripides that all the Powers of the universe are evil or irresponsible and there is nothing in earth or heaven which man can trust, and finally to the utter cynical nihilism of Critias, most brilliant of young intellectuals and most cruel of tyrants.

3. The Sophists then did not help the situation very much. In fact they made things worse, though without any evil intention. And those who clung to the old traditions were intellectually powerless, though increasingly sore, angry, and exasperated with these nasty subversive "highbrows". Their mentality is displayed in some of the comedies of Aristophanes, notably the "Clouds", for traditionalists of this sort made up the greater part of his audience. The great religious prosecutions, too, which drove Alcibiades from Athens and helped to lose her the Peloponnesian War, when suspicion of sacrilege united with political suspicions produced a real wave of popular hysteria, showed the reaction of the traditionalists conscious of and puzzled and angered by the new movements to the new type of sophist-educated young aristocrat politician. Meanwhile however there was one man, and as far as we know one only who, in the midst of all the confusion and disintegration, was trying to find a better solution to the problem of the good life for man than superficial humanism or cynical immoralism or bad-tempered irrational clinging to ancestral custom. This was Socrates. When he drank the hemlock in 399 he was over seventy years old, born somewhere about 470, nine years after the battle of Plataea, and had lived through the whole period of fermenting intellectual activity and final

disintegration and demoralization. He had lived from the age of physical and cosmological speculation through the age of the humanism of the Sophists to that most unpleasant period when certain of the young men whom the Sophists had educated (some of them his own friends) put into practice their logical deductions from their masters' teaching. And as he grew older he had put all his great power more and more single-mindedly into the finding and propagation of his solution.

There is no one else in the whole history of European philosophy who has changed the direction of thought so completely simply by what he was; for Socrates's thought springs directly and inevitably in a very special way from the whole character and make-up of the man. It is therefore as a man that I want to try and present him, and not as The Socratic Problem, even at the cost of being excessively dogmatic. But it is impossible to speak either about his teaching or his character without first saying something about the evidence on which our hypotheses about either must be based. Socrates himself wrote nothing, and all our contact with him must necessarily be through what survives of what his contemporaries, friends and disciples wrote about him. The impression which he made upon them was so great that the volume of these writings was very considerable, and the form they took was curious, that of the Socratic Conversation. This was a dialogue, either wholly imaginary or based on memories of a real occasion, in which Socrates appeared as the chief character, carrying on his well-known activity of cross-questioning people, convicting them of ignorance in the most important matters, and forcing them to think for themselves and look to the good of their souls. By far the most important works of this kind which we possess are those dialogues of Plato (the great majority) belonging to his early and middle period in which Socrates is the principal speaker. There are however also writings of this sort surviving by Xenophon, and the greater part of his "Memoirs of Socrates" takes the form of reported conversations. We know too the names and have some fragments of the Socratic Conversations written by another member of the group of Socrates's friends, Aeschines of Sphettus. Then we have a fearful and wonderful caricature in the "Clouds" of Aristophanes in which the name of Socrates is given to a composite figure who seems to represent the "highbrow" of the late fifth century as seen by the average Athenian, and who combines impossibly the characteristic traits of an Ionian cosmologist, an Orphic sectary, and a Sophist of the worst type (the effect is rather as if a character called T. S. Eliot were to appear on the London stage wearing a Dominican habit with a beard and a red tie and expressing opinions drawn from Marx, Maritain and the Theosophists with cheerful indiscriminateness). We have also a few fragments of contemporary gossip and information of doubtful and varying value preserved by later Greek scholars, and some brief remarks of Aristotle which are of the greatest importance in determining what Socrates's teaching really was.

4. Of this evidence incomparably the most important part consists of the Socratic writings of Plato and Xenophon. And by far our best and deepest insight into the character and way of life of Socrates in his later years comes from the dialogues of Plato, his intimate friend and disciple. Xenophon, the soldier of fortune and country squire, a competent writer of historical prose with a relatively commonplace mind, was only slightly acquainted with Socrates and wrote down his recollections of him many years later, in defence of his memory, probably with the help of other already existing Socratic writings. Nobody now would prefer Xenophon's portrait of Socrates to Plato's where the two disagree, though Xenophon is often useful to corroborate and on some points of fact to supplement Plato. But it is from Plato that we really learn to know the old man—old, for Plato only knew him towards the end of his life and we can for the most part only guess at the long earlier development of intellect and character which made him what he was. He was an ugly little old man, with a face like a satyr or a Silenus and strangely staring eyes. He possessed an amazing physical toughness and vitality, and was completely indifferent to the needs of the body, though he did not practice a deliberate asceticism and could drink any literary man in Athens under the table if the occasion required it. His physical and moral courage were complete, and Plato's description of him retreating in battle is unforgettable, "stalking along like a pelican" very much at his own pace, and looking so formidable that no-one dared to interfere with him. His moral courage and absolute straightforwardness and integrity, the way in which he invariably said and did what appeared to him right and true without any regard for the consequences to himself, were particularly well manifested in his reluctant contacts with the political life of the city. When the democracy demanded his co-operation

in the illegal preliminaries of a hysterical treason trial, or the oligarchy of the Thirty Tyrants required him to assist in one of their murders in legal form, he flatly refused, though in each case the refusal might well have cost him his life. Closely related to this moral integrity was his amazing power of intellectual concentration, which he displayed strikingly on one occasion while serving in the Athenian army at Potidaea, when he stood without moving for a day and a night thinking out a problem, apparently quite indifferent to his surroundings or the needs of the body.

Towards the end of his life he put the whole of this tremendous and concentrated moral and intellectual power into the fulfilment of what he accepted as a divine mission. We have the story of this on the best authority, and there is no reason to doubt its truth. The Delphic Oracle, consulted by an admirer of Socrates, declared him to be the wisest man in Greece. Socrates, his modesty shocked by this pronouncement, proceeded, as a duty laid upon him by divine authority, to examine all those available who had a reputation for wisdom in order to find out what the oracle could have meant; and eventually came to the famous conclusion that he was really wiser than them all, because he at least knew that he knew nothing and they were ignorant even of their ignorance. The story, taken seriously as it should be, indicates Socrates's deep and direct piety more effectively than the famous "supernatural sign", which does not indicate any belief on Socrates's part that he was in special communication with the divine world, and amounted to no more, in spite of the mystifications of later writers, than a sort of uncanny anticipation of bad luck.

Of the trial and death of Socrates I shall say nothing which will absolve my readers of the duty of reading Plato's "Apology", "Crito" and "Phaedo", which, especially the last, are the greatest things in Hellenic prose literature and of which there are many admirable translations. It is however worth remarking two things. First, the charges brought against Socrates, of introducing new divinities and corrupting young men, were so demonstrably absurd that they were obviously only cover for other charges which could not be openly stated. Behind the official accusation lay the old Athenian hostility to the intellectuals, whom the ordinary man regarded as in some way responsible for the recent disasters and distresses of the city; then there was the resentment of prominent political personalities whose emptiness had been effectively shown up by Socrates's methods of enquiry and who therefore regarded him as a subversive influence. More deadly was the remembrance of Socrates's friendship with Alcibiades and Critias, with the traitor who had done more than any other man to bring about the defeat of Athens and with the leader of the unspeakable tyranny of the Thirty. In some confused way the citizens, or a group of them, thought Socrates responsible for the misdeeds of these men. More important, however, than to understand the charges rightly is to realise that Socrates's death was in a very special sense the fruit and crown of his moral integrity. If he had not insisted on saying exactly what he believed to be true about himself and had been prepared more or less to plead guilty, and to go into exile on his own proposition, the death sentence would never have been passed. Probably neither prosecutors nor judges wanted it to be. And if he had not insisted on continuing that precise obedience to the laws of the city which he had practised all his life long, he could easily have escaped between his trial and his execution.

As far as Socrates's character is concerned we have been able to follow Plato's account very closely. When however we come to his teaching we encounter the real difficulty of our evidence. This is to determine how far Plato, in those dialogues in which Socrates is the principal speaker, developed and expanded the thought of his master far beyond any point which Socrates himself had ever reached, so as to produce what is really an original metaphysic of his own. The literary custom of the time and the conventions of the "Socratic Conversation" in particular would, I believe, have permitted him to do so. Aristotle, who after all was in close personal touch with Plato for many years, says quite plainly that he did. And I believe that it is possible, by applying Aristotle's evidence to Plato's dialogues, to reconstruct a coherent and probable version of Socrates's teaching, deriving naturally from his character, and with it accounting fairly well for the immense veneration in which he was held and the great influence he exercised. It is in outline the version accepted by most Platonic scholars, though there are very weighty opinions on the other side, in favour of making Socrates responsible for much more of Plato's thought. But the nature of the dispute must not be misunderstood. Nobody, I think, maintains that there is a clean break or an absolute contradiction between Socrates and

Plato on any point. The question is where one leaves off and the other begins in a continuous process of development.

5. This, then is the version which I propose to give of Socrates's teaching. First and foremost, he held, man's business is to take care of his soul, to make it as good as possible; and Socrates was perhaps the first man in Europe who had a clear and coherent conception of the soul as we understand it, of the soul, that is, as the intellectual and moral personality, the responsible agent in knowing and acting rightly or wrongly. Before his time "psyche" (the Greek word which we translate "soul") had meant to the average Greek "life-breath", a vaporous substance which was necessary for physical life but was not the seat of consciousness and source of action and could only survive death as a poor strengthless, senseless, feebly squeaking shade. The "psyche" without the body was the shadowiest sort of ghost. For Heraclitus the "psyche" had been much more important, for it was part of the ever-living divine Fire, the Logos, and for the Orphics and Pythagoreans it was a god imprisoned in the body. But even they do not seem to have thought of the soul as the moral and intellectual personality, that which makes the man a real person, and perhaps the distinction which they drew between the divine life proper to it and the human life into which it had fallen was too sharp to enable them to do so. After Socrates the conception of the soul as personality and of the care of the soul as the most important thing in life becomes pretty well universal among thinking Greeks. It is one of the most important and decisive changes in the whole history of human thought, and it did more than any other development in Greek philosophy to prepare the way for Christianity.

Socrates's reasons for making the care of the soul the supreme human activity are also important. The first is implied in the new conception of soul itself. It is the soul which makes the man and the goodness or badness of the soul which makes him a good or bad (and therefore a happy or unhappy) specimen of humanity. But there is also Socrates's religion to be taken into account. The deep Socratic piety which Plato inherited centres on the faith that the world is ruled by good intelligent divine powers who order everything for the best. Of the nature of these powers Socrates did not probably have very much to say, and he worshipped them according to the tradition of his city; though he is not likely to have approved of the traditional mythology any

more than Plato himself did. What is important to notice here
is that Socrates's piety, as any piety according to reason must,
makes his whole view of the world teleological. Everything is
ordered for the best, and there is an appropriate and natural good
which is the end of all movement and endeavour. In the case of
man, (and it is only in human life that Socrates is interested. He
leaves the cosmic application of his principle for Plato) his natural
good, the end to which he must as a matter of religious duty
attain, is the health, the true well-being of his soul. The unsur-
passable and vital importance of this teleological religious outlook
for the further development of Greek and all European thought
is obvious at once, and will become still more obvious as we go
on with the story.

6. How then is this health and goodness of the soul to be
attained? Socrates says that it is attained when the soul really
knows goodness and consequently acts rightly. He holds, rather
startlingly, that virtue *is* knowledge of the good; right action
follows inevitably from right knowledge; and therefore all wickedness is involuntary and due to ignorance. This doctrine that
virtue is knowledge is not really as silly as it sounds. It is perfectly true that Greek philosophers generally had a very imperfect
understanding of the part played in the human make-up by the
will; and that Socrates and Plato particularly deserve the common-
sense criticism of Aristotle on this point. But we must remember
that, first of all Socrates did not mean by "knowledge" simply
abstract knowledge of a proposition. He meant full and immediate realization, sight or intuition, an opening or turning of
the "eye of the soul" to a direct and therefore compelling vision
of the good. It is important to realize and remember that this full
realization and direct and compelling sight of the object is what
Plato and Platonists as well as Socrates meant by "knowledge"
in its highest and most proper sense. Further, no man does evil
simply because he knows it to be evil and bad for him. He acts
always, however perversely, in pursuit of some imagined good,
something which he has persuaded himself is the most important
good for him at the moment. Therefore perhaps in a sense it can
be said that his vice is ignorance. But it remains true that Socrates
was insufficiently attentive to that "war in our members", that
unhappy state of man who so often knows the good and does the
evil, which St. Paul and St. Augustine and the whole Christian
tradition have realized so vividly. He was, in later life at least

and perhaps always, one of those fortunate people who always seem to find it easy to act rightly, to live up to their own ethical code, and whose advice on moral matters always for that very reason seems naive and unhelpful to those who are more vividly conscious of that inner conflict which must be present to some degree in all of us. It is of great significance, as we shall see, for the future development of Greek thought about human behaviour that Socrates, with his straightforward and simple moral rectitude, his ease in well-doing, was the established ideal of human conduct, the type of the virtuous man, for almost every philosophical school which came after him.

From Socrates's doctrine that virtue is knowledge, rightly understood, follows his other doctrine that all virtue is one and also his peculiar method of discussion. All virtue is one because, if virtue is knowledge in the Socratic sense, a man does not really know it unless he knows it as a whole, unless he has a permanent single realized vision of human goodness as such which will serve to guide him in all the circumstances of life, will show him when, if he is to act like a good man, acts of bravery are required, when self-restraint and respect for his neighbour's rights, and so on. And a man must see this vision for himself. If virtue is knowledge then in a sense it can be taught, but it is not an external technique which can be taught in the manner of the Sophists. All that the teacher can do is to persuade his pupil so to turn himself that the vision strikes the "eye of the soul", to exercise his mind so as to draw out of it the truth which is being sought. This Socrates did by first showing his partner in discussion (he never taught formally but always through chance conversations whenever the opportunity offered) the hopeless perplexity, the "aporia" or position with no way out, in which his ordinary muddle-headed notion about this or that virtue would land him if its implications were worked out. Then he would stimulate him gently to discover the right solution, which often, in those early dialogues of Plato which most faithfully portray Socrates in action, is not expressly stated but only implied. This is, the "midwife's art" of Socrates (his mother had been famous for her skill in midwifery and he often jokes about having inherited it); and it is the foundation and origin of all rational constructive philosophical discussion since his time.

Of the status in reality of the goodness which the soul must see and realize in order to be itself good, Socrates, on the view of his teaching which I am here presenting, had little to say. It is necessary to his whole doctrine that it should be objective, not a creation of the mind, and unchanging and universal, not varying from individual to individual and time to time. In this insistence that the definition of goodness is universally and always true the universal concept emerges clearly for the first time in the history of European philosophy, a development of the very greatest importance. But it was Plato, not Socrates who tried to determine exactly what sort of reality this goodness was. Again, we cannot be certain what Socrates believed about the destiny of the soul and the future life. That he believed in the immortality of the soul I am almost certain. But in his speech in his defence at his trial (the "Apology" reported, probably accurately, by Plato) he speaks as an agnostic on this point; and though the language suggests that he may be making a concession to the general opinion of his judges rather than expressing his own convictions, the passage must leave a certain amount of doubt about his own belief. All we can be certain of about the teaching of Socrates, is that for the first time probably in the history of European thought he saw the soul as the intellectual and moral personality and that he held and with all his might propagated that doctrine of the care of the soul as a religious duty, making it good through realized knowledge of goodness, which sprang directly from his character, from his moral integrity, his intense power of intellectual concentration which gave "knowledge" this particular meaning for him, and from his piety which looked always for the good end for which the gods must have set man in the world.

IV

Plato (1). Life and Writings. The Forms and the Soul

1. With Plato, Socrates's greatest disciple, the great central tradition of European metaphysics really begins. He is in a special way the philosopher of beginnings, the source and originator. There was never a less systematic philosopher, and it is often difficult to find out what his final solution of any of the great metaphysical problems which he raises is; and when we find it, or think we have found it, it is seldom one which we can accept as finally satisfactory, even if we profess ourselves to be Platonists. But he does raise, directly and consciously or implicitly and unconsciously, all the great metaphysical problems; and again and again his solutions, even if we do not accept them, point the way which we must follow if we are to arrive at the truth. And his writings have always the Socratic quality, the power of rousing our desire for the truth, the power of making us examine ourselves to find out what is worth looking for and how we are to seek it, which makes those who desire to attain truth through rational thought return to him again and again in every generation. I do not of course wish to suggest that for Plato in the pursuit of truth "to travel hopefully was better than to arrive." He had no trace of the modern agnosticism and despair of certainty about universal moral and philosophical truths. He had the spirit of Socrates in him and was therefore ceaselessly examining his own doctrines and developing and modifying his thought. But he aspired to attain to certain knowledge of the truth, and, especially towards the end of his life, he believed that he had attained to final truth in certain important matters. It is only relatively to us that his philosophy is a philosophy of beginnings, incomplete and everlastingly suggestive rather than providing finally satisfactory solutions.

This is intended to be a history of philosophy, not of philosophers, and I do not mean to say more about the lives of the philosophers than is essential for the understanding of their teaching. Certain facts of Plato's life are very relevant to an understanding of his moral and political teaching and will be considered when we come to discuss it. For the present all we need say is that he was born in 427, and as a young man was a close and devoted friend of Socrates till his death in 399; that he travelled extensively in Egypt, Cyrene, and, most important, in Sicily and South Italy, where he came into contact with the Pythagoreans, in 390 to 388; that on his return he founded the first of the great philosophical schools of Athens, the Academy, and devoted the rest of his life to his work there, except for two more journeys to Sicily, in 366 and 361 (of which there will be more to say when we come to consider his political teaching and activity). He died in 348, active in teaching and writing to the last. The constitution of the Academy, the greatest of the philosophical schools of Greece, deserves some attention. It was legally a religious association for the worship of the Muses, and celebrated their feast yearly. As such it was a recognized corporate body which could own property, and the small estate of Academia, from which it took its name, near Colonus on the outskirts of Athens, remained in its possession till the school was closed by order of the Emperor Justinian in A.D. 529. Here it erected the sanctuary of the Muses and the buildings necessary for its corporate life and work. It was more like a research institute than a school or university in our sense. It granted no degrees, though it gave courses of lectures which as the generations passed became more and more formal and systematic; and many of its members devoted their whole lives to scientific and philosophical research within the school; though Plato's original intention was that it should also provide a training for men who were to be active beneficially in political life, and he would have been very far from altogether approving the later type of professional philosopher, completely withdrawn from the world.

2. Plato's writings have, as far as we know, all been preserved, though very little record of his oral teaching given in the Academy has survived. There is, however, no reason to suppose that it differed in essentials from that of the Dialogues, though it may well have cleared up some points which they leave obscure. These Dialogues of Plato are in no sense systematic and ordered expositions of a complete philosophy neatly divided into sections. The earlier ones are true "Socratic Conversations," most vivid and lifelike presentations of Socrates at his work of making men examine themselves by his characteristic method of discussion. Then come dialogues in which Plato puts forward more and more of his own philosophy through the mouth of Socrates, but still

in the informal manner of a true conversation and with the dramatic setting and the characters of those taking part in the discussion clearly and delightfully indicated: for Plato was not only a great philosopher but the greatest of all writers of Greek prose, and his Socratic dialogues are a continuing joy to read. In these dialogues there appears a new element which is of very great importance. This is the Myth. The Platonic Myth may be defined as a symbolical narrative in which Plato expounds some doctrine in the truth of which he firmly believes but which he holds can only be expressed by symbols and not by the ordinary methods of reasoned argument. Most of the myths are concerned with the nature and destiny of the soul and its life after the separation from the body which we call death. But in several of the myths there are also pictures of the cosmos and the greatest of them all is the account of the formation of the universe in the "Timaeus"; though there too, Soul has a central position.

The character of the later Dialogues gradually changes. They cease gradually to be real conversations and become continuous expositions of particular philosophical doctrines (though by no means treatises forming part of the ordered presentation of a philosophical system). Dramatic setting and characterization disappear. Socrates is no longer the chief speaker. His place is taken by a mysterious "Visitor from Elea," by Timaeus the Pythagorean, or, in the last of the Dialogues, the "Laws" by Plato himself, thinly disguised. The other persons of the dialogue are shadowy figures whose only function is to say "Yes," "No" or "Why indeed?" at the proper places. In the "Timaeus" and the "Laws" very little attempt is made to keep to the conversational form at all, and most of them consists of continuous exposition. This change of form corresponds, as we shall see, to a development in Plato's thought.

It may be useful to append a list of the Dialogues grouped according to the period at which they were written. Modern Platonic scholars are generally agreed on the order of the groups (though not of individual dialogues within the groups) for reasons derived both from the accurate observation of stylistic peculiarities and the development of Plato's thought (we know the "Laws" to be his last work on good external evidence, and have one or two other probable fixed points).

I. Early Socratic dialogues. *Protagoras, Ion, Apology, Crito,*

Euthyphro, Charmides, Laches, Republic Book I, Hippias I and II.

II. Socratic dialogues in which Plato expounds his own philosophy. Middle Group. *Gorgias, Meno, Menexenus, Euthydemus, Phaedo, Symposium, Phaedrus, Republic Books II to X, Cratylus.*

III. Later Dialogues. First Group. *Parmenides, Theaetetus, Sophist, Statesman.* (These four form a connected series, expounding and applying Plato's fully developed method of dialectic; the *Sophist* is the first of the dialogues of the distinctively "late" literary type.) Second Group. *Timaeus, Critias* (an unfinished sequel to the *Timaeus*), *Philebus, Laws, Epinomis* ("Appendix to the *Laws*," possibly by a disciple of Plato).

There are also half a dozen dialogues generally regarded as spurious, and thirteen *Letters*, of which most are now considered genuine, and of which one in particular, the *Seventh*, contains most valuable information about Plato's activities in Sicily.

3. To present the doctrines contained in these writings of Plato systematically is almost inevitably to do violence to his thought. Some degree of systematization is unavoidable, however, in so summary a treatment. I propose to concentrate my description of Plato's teaching on what were to him the only fully real beings, the Ideas or Forms and Soul, to deal first with that basic doctrine about the Forms and the human soul at which he arrived comparatively early and which he maintained consistently to the end of his life, and then to go on to deal with the later developments of the doctrine of Forms and with the subject which occupied him more and more in his later years, the cosmic function of Soul, his teaching about which may legitimately be called his theology. His moral and political teaching I shall treat separately, for convenience and not because it can really be separated from the rest of his thought. It must be realized throughout that this précis of Plato's thought utterly fails to do justice to its richness, its endless suggestiveness, and its frequent inconsistency.

Plato started to develop his own characteristic doctrine at the point where (in the opinion of most modern scholars) Socrates left off. Socrates had taught that there was such a thing as moral goodness, that it was the same for all, and that only by really knowing it could we become good men. He had not attempted to define what sort of a thing this goodness was. Plato's first task then, in developing his master's thought was to determine the real nature of goodness and of the soul which by knowing goodness becomes good. In doing this he was helped by his contact with the Pythagoreans and his knowledge of their doctrine. This Pythagorean teaching was, it may be remembered, first that "things are numbers," that there is an eternal reality transcending our senses which is expressible only in numerical terms, which is number, geometrical pattern and harmony (i.e., the relation of numbers to each other); and second, that the soul is a fallen god imprisoned in the body, divine, immortal, and pre-existent, which can realize its divinity and return after death to its proper place by contemplating eternal numerical truth. This Pythagorean teaching and the moral doctrine of Socrates are the two roots of Platonism.

The doctrine at which Plato arrived by combining these two elements, and from which he never departed, may be expressed shortly as follows : There exists a world of eternal realities, "Forms" or "Ideas," entirely separate from the world our senses perceive, and knowable only by the pure intellect. The common name for these realities, the "Ideas", is a remarkably misleading one, for in English "idea" means a thought existing in a mind, and Plato's eternal Forms (as I shall call them henceforth) are certainly nothing of the sort. They are realities existing "themselves by themselves", independently of the minds which know them or the things which "participate" in them (see below), though they are contained in and caused by a supreme Reality, the Good, which is a Form and more than a Form. They are the only objects of true knowledge, the unchanging realities which our mind perceives when it arrives at a true universal definition. When we consider, for example, "justice as it is in itself" or "equality as it is in itself," passing from individual cases of just behaviour or pàirs of apparently equal objects to the universal reality which lies behind them, we are thinking about the Form of Justice and the Form of Equality. And because for Plato the world perceived by our senses is a perpetual Heraclitean flow of ever-changing appearances of which no real knowledge is possible, this thinking about the universal Forms is the only kind of thinking which attains truth.

This would seem to imply that there is a Form corresponding to every "universal" or general idea which we can think of, a

Form of Mud, a Form of Toe-nail, and a Form of Bed, and an infinite number more, as well as Forms like that of Justice or Equality. Plato in the *Parmenides* (130 A-E) indicates himself that this is the right conclusion; and in the Seventh Letter (342D) he gives a very comprehensive list of Forms which does seem to represent his real thought about the extent of their world; it includes mathematical universals (circle, line etc:), shapes, colours, moral universals (good, just etc:), forms of manufactured and natural bodies, the four elements, all living things, the characters or qualities in souls, and all actions and affections. This wide extension of the World of Forms, though required by the logic of his thought, takes him a very long way from his starting-point, the moral Forms corresponding to Socrates's universal definitions and the mathematical Forms suggested by the Pythagorean Numbers, and raises difficulties from the point of view of the function of the Forms as universal standards or norms and as objectively existing perfections. The world of Forms is seen and portrayed by Plato in the period of the early and middle dialogues with sensuous vividness as a world of radiant perfection, all beauty and glory (the original meaning of the word *eidos*, "external appearance," would help him unconsciously to this way of thinking about them): and he makes Socrates admit, in the Parmenides passage quoted above, to a reluctance to allow anything vulgar or mean in that perfect world, though he makes it clear that he thinks this reluctance unphilosophical. And he would seem logically compelled to admit even Forms corresponding to negative universal terms, denoting absence of good—sickness, ugliness, evil, etc:. He does in fact mention such Forms several times in the Dialogues. But their existence is very difficult to reconcile with the function of the Forms as universal standards or ideals, with his doctrine that all Forms derive their being from the Good, and his conviction, expressed in a famous passage of the *Theaetetus* (176A-177A) that evil belongs wholly to the lower world and has no place in the realm of real being. We do not know how Plato solved these difficulties, and it is possible that he never solved them at all, though they were certainly vigorously discussed in the Academy. It is certain, however, that he never wavered in his conviction that the moral Forms provide the eternal and objective standards by which men must order their private, and still more their public lives, and that he also regarded the

World of Forms as true reality and, with soul, the whole of true reality, the ground of all genuine knowledge about everything.

Plato came to lay more and more stress on the idea that the Forms do make up a world, an organic and harmonious structure with which the movement of our thought must correspond if we are to think truly. Of Plato's views on the method of thinking we ought to employ to arrive at the truth I shall say more when discussing the later developments of his doctrine But already in the "Republic" he shows how the mind may ascend through the hierarchy of Forms till it reaches the highest and most universal Form of all, the Form of the Good, which is the "sun of the intelligible world," the cause of the other Forms and of our knowledge of them, the first principle and final explanation of reality; he also says, without explanation that it is "beyond being." The whole passage is strangely isolated and difficult to interpret. Plato never develops his thought about the Form of the Good in any other of his written works, though we know that he delivered in the Academy a Lecture on the Good, towards the end of his life, of which all that has survived is the statement "Good is One." Plato seems always to have spoken of this highest reality with the greatest reverence and reserve. The later Platonists built much on these isolated hints, but we should not attribute all their conclusions to Plato. It does however seem fairly clear from the passage in the "Republic" (508E) and a few suggestions elsewhere that the Good is something very like what we mean by God.

As cause both of the Forms and our knowledge of them it transcends the great distinction which Plato makes in the spiritual world between Forms and Soul, object of knowledge and knower; and so, though it is the highest of Forms, it is something more than a Form like the others which it includes. It is the single transcendent reality of absolute perfection which is the ultimate cause and explanation of the universe. The Good, however, is not the God who rules and orders the visible universe. This God, as we shall see, is for Plato a Soul not a form.

What is the relation of the Forms to the particular things which we perceive by our senses? Plato never really makes it very clear. He is quite definite that it is the Forms which make individual things what they are—in so far as they can be said to be at all. It is, he says, by "participation" in the Form of Circle that things are circular, and so on. But what exactly he means by "participation" he never explains. We shall see, however, one way in which he tried to bridge the gap between the Forms and the sense-world when we come to consider his theology.

4. With the doctrine of Forms, the universal unchanging objects of true knowledge, Plato's doctrine of the soul is inseparably connected. There must be Forms for the soul to know if it is to .attain its proper goodness, and the soul must be of a certain kind in order to know the Forms. The soul, for Plato as for Socrates is the intellectual and moral personality, the most important part of man; and for Plato it is not only the most important, but is by far more real than the body, an exact reversal of earlier Greek beliefs. But Plato's doctrine, as I said before, has a double origin, and the soul for him is not only the personality, according to Socrates, but the divine soul of the Pythagoreans. Plato follows Pythagorean tradition on some points very closely. The soul for him is truly divine in the Greek sense; it is a being immortal in its own right and not by gift of any higher divinity, and therefore it has existed always, before its indwelling in any body, and will continue to exist after it has won final release from its chain of incarnations. Immortality is part of its nature. It is altogether a creature of the higher world in which are only Forms and Soul, and has nothing really in common with the world of the senses in which it finds itself, and any "this-worldliness" or accommodation to earthly existence on its part is a sin to be punished in the periods of purification in the other world which intervene between its successive incarnations. It has duties to perform in this world, but must never behave as if it belonged here. Plato takes the doctrine of rewards and punishments in the next world extremely seriously, and expounds it in a series of magnificent myths, or symbolical narrations, in which great stress is laid on the punishment of the wicked.*

The Pythagorean doctrine of the pre-existence of the soul is of the greatest importance to Plato, for it provides the foundation of his theory of knowledge. Both the Forms and the soul, we have seen, belong for Plato to a divine, transcendent world, utterly remote and alien from the shadow-show, the flow of appearances, which is the world which we perceive with our senses. (Plato, incidentally, does not hold to the Orphic-Pythagorean doctrine of a "fall" of the soul, and never explains clearly why it has to be embodied; the best solution he gives is that in the "Timaeus"; but the question of the reason for the soul's being in the body at all was much discussed by later Platonists and gave them considerable trouble.) It is therefore quite impossible for Plato to believe that the soul acquires any sort of knowledge of the Forms through its bodily senses. There is nothing in this world of transient individual appearances which can tell us of the existence of that other of unchanging universal truths. Yet the soul appears to learn truths when it is in the body, and to learn them with the help of the senses. How does it do it? Plato's solution is the famous doctrine of Anamnesis or Recollection.

This is simply that the soul has known the Forms in its divine existence before incarnation in a body, and is "reminded" of them by perceiving through the senses those particular things in this world which "participate" in them. So it comes, apparently but only apparently through sense-knowledge, to know universal truths and their properties and relationships which have nothing to do with the world of the senses. The part played by the body and the senses in true knowledge is thus entirely subordinate and incidental. Knowledge of reality is an encounter of the Forms and the soul taking place in that world transcending the material to which they both belong. The Christian Platonists abandoned the doctrine of Recollection because (except for Origen) they rejected the doctrine of the soul's pre-existence and successive incarnations. But it remains a distinguishing mark of the great Christian Platonist thinkers that they will none of them accept the doctrine of the Christian Aristotelians that the soul attains to such measure of eternal truth as is possible for it through the medium of sense-perception. Instead, to take the place of Plato's Recollection, they produce a doctrine of how God illumines the mind to enable it to know eternal truth, which is originated by St. Augustine and developed to a wonderful subtlety and profundity by St. Bonaventure. No Christian Platonist or Augustinian will accept the Thomist statement that there is nothing in the human mind which did not come to it through the senses (a statement which St. Thomas himself makes with many safeguards and which is easily misunderstood in isolation).

5. So far we have been dealing only with what for Plato was incomparably the most important part of the soul, that is, the reason, the part which knows. But the soul according to Plato is a complex and composite structure of three parts. First there is the reason, the rightful ruler of the whole, which in a properly

ordered soul sees the truth and directs the activities of the whole
man according to what it sees. Its abode (for highly inadequate
and fanciful reasons) is located in the head. Then there comes
that part in which the higher emotions have their seat, love of
fame, for instance, or just anger. This abides in the breast.
Finally there is that part to which belong all the lower, carnal
lusts and desires, the "savage, many-headed monster" whose
abode is in the belly and its adjacent regions. The "spirited"
or "soldierly" part, as we may call it, is tractable and obedient
to the dictates of reason and is its faithful support and collaborator
in the microcosm, the inner commonwealth of Man. The animal
part to which belong the carnal and worldly lusts and desires
is intractable and rebellious, and can only be brought under
the control of the reason after a hard struggle. It is also inwardly
disorderly, without any unity in itself, restless and chaotic. A
superb picture of the tripartite soul in action is given in the
image of the Charioteer and his Two Horses in the "Phaedrus,"
where the Driver (Reason) aided by his good and tractable horse
(the higher emotions) fights a mighty battle to subdue the
undisciplined fury of the bad horse (carnal lust), which yet for
all its unruliness remains a necessary member of the team and
part of the whole.

This division of the soul into three parts may seem to break
up man to such a degree as to leave human personality very
little unity and consequently very little reality. There is, however,
besides the single control of reason in the well-ordered soul (or
"fully-integrated personality" in modern jargon) another single
and therefore in a sense unifying force which Plato recognizes.
This is Eros, Desire. Plato's conception of it is in some ways
strikingly like the "libido" of Jung (which has been much
misunderstood because of its unfortunate name). Eros in Plato
is the motive force behind all human thought and action, the
drive of longing after a good unattained which impels the soul
on without rest till it is satisfied. There is nothing in the nature
of Desire in itself to specify the good at which it aims. Its force
can be used by any of the three parts of the soul which gains power
in the man. It can be squandered on the base ends of the lower
lusts, or directed by the higher "spirited" part to such ends as
the acquiring of honour. And it can drive the philosopher on
from the desire of mortal beauty till at last he reaches the "great
sea of beauty", the absolute and unchanging beauty of the World

of Forms. Then it will be serving reason and attaining its true end. Plato thus provides his tripartite soul with a single rightful ruler, the reason, and a single driving force, Eros or Desire; and he would have said that man was not truly one or truly man unless reason ruled in him, illumined by the eternal truths of the Forms, and his desire was directed to its proper end, the attainment of that transcendent world. With this we should agree, with certain important differences; and Plato comes closer to the Christian perception of the war within us than Socrates seems to have done. Yet later philosophers have generally considered the tripartite psychology too sharp and crude a dividing-up of man, and I think we must agree with their criticism, though as an imaginative and symbolic representation of our present state it remains of the greatest value.

*Note on Plato's Later Doctrine of Soul and Body

But in his later years, as we shall see, Plato came to stress much more strongly the idea of the soul's function in the visible world and to see it as a link between the Forms and body; and he also emphasised the distinction, very important in all later pagan Greek thought, between the two parts of the visible world, the pure unchanging world of the heavenly bodies and the lower world of earth and the surrounding atmosphere, the region of change and corruption, of birth and death. So he came to think of the soul as having a true bodily home in the heavenly world, and of its ultimate destiny not as complete disembodiment, but attachment to a pure and everlasting heavenly body. What is wrong with our present state is not so much, in this later stage of Plato's thought, that we are embodied as that we are, for good reasons connected with the order of the universe, in the wrong sort of body, an earthly, animal one: and Plato and all later pagan, and some Christian, Platonists always regard our earthly body with its characteristics of sex and death as unworthy of man's true nature.

V

Plato (2). The Structure of the World of Forms and how to Think truly. The Making of the Visible World. Theology

1. As Plato grew older he came more and more to think of reality in terms of a series of ordered worlds, "kosmoi", the world of the Forms, the visible heaven or world of the everlasting heavenly bodies, the most perfect possible image of its archetype in the world of Forms, the ideal, perfectly-ordered State, the image of the visible heaven among men, and finally the human soul, a microcosm, an image in miniature, of both heaven and the state, and moreover related to the ordering principle of the visible heaven or material universe. This conception is already indicated in several places in the dialogues of the middle period, and especially in the "Republic"; but it is not until the later dialogues that Plato begins to work it out fully.

We have already seen how in the "Republic" there is a hierarchy of Forms through which the mind ascends to the ultimate and universal Form, the Good. We must now pay a little attention to the reverse process, which completes the attainment of truth by the mind. The ascent consisted of a series of leaps of intuition from one hypothesis to another until at last the first principle of knowledge as well as being, "the beginning which is not a hypothesis", the Idea of the Good, is reached. Then we can, so to speak, turn round and come down, passing in order and without a break from more universal to less universal Forms, perceiving the dependence and relationship of the Forms among themselves, and so seeing what were formerly to us true hypotheses no longer as hypotheses but as truths depending upon and contained in more universal truths. The process of getting to know the world of Forms and its structure and the relationship of the Forms to one another is what Plato calls Dialectic. It must be carefully distinguished from the logic of Aristotle, which is a study of the forms which propositions may take, of the constituent parts of propositional forms (subject, predicate etc.) and of the relations between these forms of propositions considered in the abstract without reference to the content of any particular proposition. Logic operates with symbols; it considers, e.g., the propositional form "All A is B" where A and B can stand for any number of different things, and the truth or falsehood of any particular proposition in that form depends on what they do stand for. Plato's dialectic, on the other hand is not concerned with anything so abstract as the types of forms under which propositions can be classified. It is not concerned with propositions at all (though of course it expresses itself in propositions, and it is often quite possible and legitimate to put a Platonic argument into syllogistic form and criticize it from the standpoint of Aristotle's logic). But what Plato is trying to do with his dialectical method is to study the complex structure of a world of concrete spiritual realities, the world of Forms, and by so studying its structure to arrive at the exact definition of the Form he wants (e.g., the Form of "geometrical figure" or "statesman") and its relationship to other Forms. This he does by the method of Collection and Division. By Collection the mind, by an upward movement of intuitional leaps like that described before, gathers together under one Form sufficiently universal to be the starting-point of the investigation in hand the number of scattered and apparently disconnected less universal Forms from which it starts. Then by dividing and sub-dividing this more universal form, by finding, so to speak, the joints in its structure, the mind arrives at a clear conception of the order and relationship of the less universal Forms included under it, one of which is the Form of which the exact definition is required.

The world of Forms revealed by this method of dialectic is a very complex structure, and Plato insists repeatedly in his later dialogues that it is the business of the philosopher to acquire as exact as possible a knowledge of it. He must know the contents and divisions of the more universal Forms (and it must be noted that for Plato, as for Christian metaphysicians after him, the more universal a term is the richer is the content of the reality to which it refers. The Good for Plato is not a remote abstraction, a sort of lowest common denominator of all real individual goodnesses. It is a reality of immense richness, containing in itself all the kinds of good there can possibly be). Also, Plato insists, he must know how the Forms combine with or partake in each other, and which will combine and which will not. The Forms of Likeness and

Unlikeness, for instance, will combine, each partaking of the other; for Likeness is "like" itself and "unlike" Unlikeness while Unlikeness is "unlike" Likeness and "like" itself. Motion and Rest will not combine for Rest is no sense in motion or Motion at rest; but they both partake of Likeness and Unlikeness, being "like" themselves and "unlike" each other.

Towards the end of his life it appears that Plato came to think of the Forms in more Pythagorean terms as being in some way constituted by number, or dependent on a set of higher realities, the Ideal Numbers, from one to ten; these were timelessly generated by a pair of ultimate principles, the One (which was probably identified with the Good), the principle of limit or definite reality, and the "Great-and-Small" or Indefinite Dyad, the unlimited or indefinite principle on which limit is imposed. This way of thinking persisted in the early Academy, and it is extremely difficult to distinguish between the thought of Plato and that of his immediate successors. We are dependent for our knowledge of this whole phase of the thought of the Academy on some very obscure criticisms by Aristotle and a few allusions elsewhere.

It may be worth noting in conclusion that these mathematically conceived Forms must be clearly distinguished from an inferior class of eternal realities, the "mathematica" which appear already in the "Republic". These are simply the many circles, triangles, etc., about which mathematicians think, e.g., in theorems about the relationship of two or more triangles to each other. These cannot be the Form of Triangle or the Form of Circle because there are more than one of each kind; but they are not the visible material triangles or circles which the geometers draw because they have no material, only purely geometrical qualities. Therefore a separate class has to be made for them among the eternal entities which are the objects of thought, not of sense-perception, below the Forms but outside and above the material world.

2. Plato in his later years not only developed his doctrine about the structure of the world of Forms and the detailed process by which we know it, but he made a great effort to answer the criticism that there is an unbridgeable gulf between that world and the world of which we become conscious through sense-perception. The intermediary between the two worlds is for him Soul. From Socrates he had inherited the intense religious conviction that the world is directed by good intelligent powers

to a good end. From the Pythagoreans he took the conception of soul as having a place in both worlds, that of Being, the divine and eternal, and that of Becoming, the material and transitory. From Anaxagoras came to him the conception of Mind or Intelligence as the cause of all motion and the coming to be of things (however inadequate Anaxagoras's use of that idea may have seemed to him). All these elements are combined in Plato's fully developed doctrine of Soul's place in the cosmos. In the "Phaedrus" (245 c5 ff) he lays the foundations by proving that Soul (Soul as such, not any particular soul or group of souls, divine or human) is immortal, ungenerated and self-moving and is the source of motion or change in all which is not soul. Aristotle later on started from this Platonic conception of a self-moving cause of all motion and change and by a further analysis arrived at his conception of an Unmoved Mover. But this conception of Soul as the source of motion does not go very much beyond Anaxagoras; and Plato in subsequent dialogues makes it very clear that Soul for him is not only the self-moving principle but the intelligent directing power which rules and orders all the material universe to good ends by bringing it into the most perfect possible conformity with the world of Forms, of part of which it is an image. This doctrine, that the world is moved, ruled, and directed towards the good by a living and intelligent principle or principles is the very substance of Plato's theology as he expounds it in his later dialogues, with the greatest clarity and emphasis in the last of all, the "Laws". Its most memorable presentation and the one which had the greatest influence on later thought is the great myth of the "Timaeus". Here it is presented in symbolic form and there are consequently many difficulties of interpretation, but I think a fairly clear and probable summary of what Plato meant by the myth can be given which will do something to explain more precisely the relationship of the moving and ruling Soul to the world of Forms and to the material world which it forms and governs.

In the "Timaeus" we are presented with the figure of a divine Craftsman who forms the soul and body of the material universe out of pre-existing material according to a pattern which he contemplates in the world of Forms. This Craftsman is a symbol of Soul performing its cosmic function; he is an intelligence contemplating the Forms and therefore moving and ordering all material things to a good end; the end is good because he has the virtue of a good craftsman. He is generous and ungrudging, giving to his model as much of the perfection possessed by its archetype in the world of Forms as the rather refractory material will take. This idea of the generosity of the Craftsman, while falling far short of the Christian conception of the love of God overflowing in Creation, is a very great improvement on the traditional Greek idea of the jealousy and grudgingness of the gods, who visited with their wrath any human achievement or good fortune which raised man above his proper station. It is against this old belief that Plato's insistence on the generosity of supreme goodness as displayed in the work of the Craftsman is directed, and it certainly prepared the Greek mind to accept the Christian doctrine when revealed to it. So we find Plato's words applied to God the Creator by the great Christian philosophers; but with a meaning which goes beyond Plato.

3. It should be clear from what I have already said that Plato's symbol of the Craftsman is something entirely different from the Christian profession of belief in God the Creator. The point, however, is one of great importance for our understanding of Plato and it will be as well to set out the points of difference more precisely. First of all, we must realise that the Craftsman is a symbol, and that there is no sufficient reason in the dialogues for supposing that Plato, any more than any other Greek philosopher, believed in One God in the exclusive and absolute Judaeo-Christian sense. In the "Timaeus" itself there are subordinate gods whom the Craftsman calls into being to help him in his work. Plato certainly regarded the soul of the world and individual human souls as "gods" in the Greek sense, beings immortal in their own right. In the "Laws" he seems indifferent whether there are one or many good directing Souls to rule the universe; all he insists on is that they should be thought of as good and intelligent. At the very end of his life, in the last book of the "Laws" and the "Epinomis" he shows himself a strong believer in that religion of the heavenly bodies which was beginning to penetrate into Greece from Chaldaea. Besides, though there was much dispute among the ancient Platonists on this point, it seems fairly clear that Plato did not intend his description of the Craftsman to be taken literally to the point of asserting a beginning of the world in time. He is giving us a cosmology in the time-honoured mythical form of a cosmogony, showing what he regards

as the essential elements in the universe by telling a symbolical story of its making.

And these essential elements are three, as in all human making; the pattern, in the world of Forms, the moving and ordering cause, intelligent Soul, and the material which is formed and ordered. There seems no clear evidence in Plato's writings which can justify us in asserting positively that he held that the first two are only aspects of the same ultimate reality. It was an inevitable next step for Platonists to take in developing Plato's thought to bring the two into a unity, and the Platonists of the Roman Empire did it, as we shall see, with consequences of immense importance for all later philosophy. But in Plato's own writings we are left with two ultimate principles, not one. There is Soul at its best, most perfect and most rational, the ultimate principle of life and ordered motion, of goodness in action. This is the Good Craftsman of the "Timæus". And there is the Good Itself, the ultimate principle of the World of Forms, the static perfection of goodness; this is the ultimate principle from which proceeds that model in the World of Forms which the Craftsman copies, the "Absolute Living Creature" or eternal pattern of the visible universe. There is good reason, as we have seen, for regarding the Good as in a real sense Plato's God, but not as the Creator of heaven and earth.

The Craftsman, then, is not represented as omnipotent. He is limited by the pattern which he has to copy and by his material. About the pattern not much more need be said. It is the complex Form of the Universe, that part of the World of Forms which contains the exemplars of everything necessary for the perfection of the visible universe, both body and soul. For Plato and for all pagan and some Christian Platonists after him the visible universe is a living being with a soul, the World-Soul, as well as a body. In the pattern, the Absolute Living Creature, then, are the Forms of the four elements, of all living creatures, and all other Forms involved in the structure of this living material universe, most perfect of visible beings.

4. The material on which the Craftsman works needs rather fuller discussion, because it is in his account of it that Plato suggests most clearly his view of the origin of the evils and imperfections of the visible universe. They cannot come from the Craftsman, who is good and makes all things as good as he can, or from the eternal perfection of the Forms. They come from

the material therefore, on which he has to work. This material Plato describes very strangely, and he makes it clear that the reason can hardly apprehend its nature at all, since it is just exactly the irrational element in the cosmos. It is an endless play of shifting and indefinite qualities, in perpetual disorderly motion, within what he calls the "Receptacle" or "Nurse of Becoming". This Receptacle or Nurse is Space, or perhaps better Place, a space which is not empty or unlimited but which is entirely filled with and agitated by this chaos of restless motions. Space itself is "neutral" entirely without quality or character, and thus able to receive all qualities or characters. We can perhaps form a not too inaccurate imaginative picture of Plato's chaos if we think of the colours shifting and passing endlessly into each other under the play of light in clear restless seawater. But in Plato's chaos there is nothing to correspond to the solid bottom of rock and sand and seaweed which gives the sea its shifting colours. His qualities are only qualities, not substantial realities. They are material but they are motions or changes, becomings, not beings.

Plato's chaos then is a confusion of disorderly motions in space. All its motions are in straight lines. Plato, following a tradition which goes back to the early Pythagoreans and their contemporary, the physician and philosopher Alcmæon of Croton, regards motion in straight lines as essentially irrational and imperfect and motion in a circle as perfect, proper to rational beings, and the best imitation possible in the material world of the spiritual movement of the rational soul. Thus the endless circular movement of the heavenly bodies is the most perfect example in the visible universe of intelligent activity. This idea is very remote from our own usual ways of thinking, but it continued to play a very important part in later Greek thought.

These perpetual movements of chaos must have a cause, and the only ultimate cause of any sort of movement, orderly or disorderly, straight or circular, rational or irrational, which Plato recognizes, is Soul. It seems then that the cause of the motions of chaos must be a disorderly or irrational soul, as other passages in the later dialogues suggest. But here we must remember that the "Timæus" is a myth, describing the eternally co-existing elements which are necessary to account for the visible universe by means of an imaginary account of its making. Therefore we should not think of the Craftsman as "rationalizing" an irrational soul which existed before in an entirely irrational condition.

What Plato means rather is that there is a permanent irrational, disorderly element in the universe, a sort of force of blind brutal chance, which he calls Necessity. (For the Greeks the idea of Necessity was opposed to the idea of Law or rational purpose; a thing happened either because someone had planned and willed it or as the result of some blind force, a purely chance concatenation of physical circumstances, which was called "Necessity". The Ionian physicists had explained that things happened because the elements of the universe had to behave in a particular way; it was a physical necessity, not determined or regulated by any law or purpose that they should do so). This disorderly element of blind casual physical necessity is according to Plato (or rather to what seems to me the most probable modern interpretation of what he says) never completely mastered by the Divine Reason. The World-Soul, like the human soul, always has this lower element in it struggling against the rule of reason and sometimes getting its own way to a limited degree. That is why there are evils and imperfections in the visible universe. It is not perfect, only the best possible, the best the Craftsman could do with his strange refractory material.

The details of the mythical construction of the soul and body of the visible universe and of the creatures in it are extremely odd and interesting, but are not of the first importance for the understanding of Plato's philosophy, and there is no room to dwell on them here at length. In the description of the making of the soul, which is described as a very complex structure of circles like the circles of the visible heaven, combining both rational and irrational elements, we can see very clearly that close association in Plato's mind between spiritual activity and motion in a circle which I have already mentioned. The body of the universe is framed by the imposition of mathematical shape, definite degree and limit, on the shifting mass of indefinite qualities in chaos, hot–cold, wet–dry, and so on. The Craftsman starts with the first plane figure, the triangle. From triangles he constructs the regular geometrical solids which form the constituent units of the four elements—fire, air, earth and water. From these all other things are constructed.

Finally we should remember that there can be for Plato only one visible universe, everlasting and all-embracing. There can be no succession of universes in time, or co-existence of different universes in space. The existing universe is a complete and exhaustive copy of an unique archetype, the Absolute Living Creature in the World of Forms. And in spite of the imperfections due to the irrational element, it is the best possible universe. Plato's emphasis on the goodness of the visible world is worth stressing in view of the equally Platonic emphasis on life as a "rehearsal for death", on complete disembodiment as the best state for the soul, on the need for man to transcend the visible and material if he is to attain his proper destiny. The visible universe must certainly be transcended by the rational soul, whose business it is to reach the transcendent World of Forms where alone it belongs. Yet the visible universe in its proper place and station is good, beautiful, glorious and necessary. That is the true Platonic doctrine, and though it is by no means the same as the Christian, yet it is far closer to Christianity than it is to the black pessimism of the Gnostics or Manichees. We should not try to make Plato into a Christian, yet neither should we confuse the Platonic attitude to the visible world with the Gnostic, as some superficial Christian writers are inclined to do.

VI

Plato (3). Moral and Political Teaching

1. THE starting point of Plato's moral teaching is that doctrine of Socrates which I have described in Chapter III; that the care of the soul is the most important business of man, that virtue is knowledge, direct sight and vivid realisation of the good, and that all virtue is one and can only be taught in a very special sense. All Plato's morality is simply a development of this teaching. The way in which he develops it is inseparably bound up with his development of Socrates's teaching about the soul into his own fully-formed psychology described in Chapter IV. The doctrine that virtue is knowledge receives new meaning from the theory of Forms and of Anamnesis. The virtuous man is the man who is obedient to his divine reason enlightened by the recollection of the Forms which it has seen in a previous disembodied existence. Virtue is exact correspondence with the moral Forms, Justice Itself, Courage Itself, and the rest, which the ruling reason in man has power to perceive. This development of Socrates's doctrine has an important consequence. It gives to Plato's morality, especially as expressed in the dialogues of the middle group, a sharp other-worldliness which belongs, like the origins of the theory of Forms and the pre-existing divine soul, to the Orphic-Pythagorean rather than to the Socratic side of Plato's inheritance. The real Socrates, as far as we can tell, would not have been very likely to say, as Plato makes Socrates say in the "Phædo," that the whole life of the philosopher is a rehearsal for death. He would not have held with the complete conviction which Plato inherited from the Italian philosophers that the earthly body was only a prison, and that a life of contemplation in a higher world was the only one proper to the human spirit.

We must not however exaggerate the influence of this other-worldliness on Plato's moral teaching. He never instituted in his school anything like the organized practice of outward asceticism, the vegetarianism and rigid insistence on ceremonial purity which we find among the Orphics and the early Pythagoreans. Even in his picture of the ideal state, though the life prescribed for the "guardians" or philosopher-rulers is unnatural enough, as we shall see, there is no suggestion that they should adopt ascetic practices of the Orphic-Pythagorean kind. The cheerful indifference of Socrates to bodily things, the inward austerity which was compatible with a normal outward life, remained Plato's ideal. It is only centuries later in the history of Platonism, among the Neo-Platonists, that we meet a revival of the Pythagorean scrupulosity about details of dress and diet. Also Plato, for all his insistence on death and escape from the earthly body as the one desirable end, and on a contemplation transcending this world as the supreme human activity, insists equally strongly on the philosopher's duty, while still in the body, to rule and guide the society in which he lives. This duty we shall discuss further when we come to consider Plato's political teaching. But first we must consider the effect on the development of Socratic ethics produced by Plato's doctrine of the three parts of the soul.

2. I spoke before of the ruling reason and of man's duty of obedience to his reason, and this is certainly an essential part of Plato's morality. At the end of his life it is the great dominating theme of all his thought, this rule of the divine reason in man, in the State, and in the universe. But as applied to man it requires that there should be in him a kingdom for reason to rule over, some non-rational but still living and conscious elements whose duty it is to obey. These the three-part psychology provides. The way in which Plato conceives the other two parts of the soul also has very important effects on his moral and political teaching, and especially on his views on education. In Plato Reason, whether in the universe, in the State, or in man, never rules by brute force but always relies to a great extent on "persuasion." The Craftsman in the "Timæus" myth has to "persuade" his refractory material, animated by its irrational soul, into the best form possible. In the "Laws" persuasion and rational and convincing explanation of the laws is one of the main duties of the legislator and the ruler, though if persuasion fails there is a very vigorous appeal to force as the ultimate sanction. Within the soul of man reason can only control the lowest part of the soul, the carnal lusts, through the help of the nobler emotions which, if properly developed, give it willing and eager support. The tripartite psychology seems to us a very stiff and unnatural scheme and it is bound up with a good deal of very extraordinary physiology. But we can now see the enormously important truth which it contains, that a true intellectual perception of the nature of right and wrong will be quite unable by itself to make

men act rightly unless it is supported by the right sort of emotions, rightly directed, aroused by the right objects, and in the fullest strength possible. The same lesson is taught by Plato when he speaks of the right training and direction of Desire in the "Phædrus" and the "Symposium." The bestial part of man can never be controlled by reason alone but by reason working through and in co-operation with the high and noble emotions.

It is for this reason that Plato insists so strongly that one of the most important functions of education, in the early stages the most important one, is the training of the emotions and of desire. If the child is ever to grow into the full life of goodness according to reason it must be trained to have the right emotional responses before it can reason at all. It must be trained to feel pleasure at beauty and love of goodness and disgust at ugliness and hatred of badness instinctively, so that when it is of an age to reason it will accept the teaching of reason gladly and reason will find its proper emotional support ready. In this training of the emotions art, poetry and music are all-important. This is the reason why Plato insists on such a strict control of the arts by the authorities of his ideal State. We may disagree with his methods, object to the sort of authorities he would put in control, and find his standards of judgment for the arts too narrow. Christians will think that the rightness of intellect and emotions at which Plato aims, their full accordance with the eternal pattern of the World of Forms, cannot be attained by purely human means. But on the main questions here at issue, of the vital importance of the higher emotions in moral life, of the need of training and directing those emotions in the young so that they are aroused by the propei objects, and of the essential function of the arts in that training, I do not see how anyone who wishes for the survival of anything like the ideal of man and human life which our tradition and the traditions of civilised men everywhere have taught us to form, can seriously disagree with Plato.

Because for Plato virtue is one, and is essentially the rule within man of reason contemplating the moral Forms, he makes no very rigid distinction between the particular virtues. The four cardinal virtues, Prudence (practical wisdom), Justice, Courage and Temperance, which Aristotle so sharply separates and distinguishes, are in Plato different ways of looking at a single life, the life of virtuous activity under the rule of reason. Thus prudence is the application of the eternal universal truths to particular cases in the field especially of government and social life; it is reason teaching us the right course of action to be taken now, in this particular set of concrete circumstances. Justice and Temperance are very closely allied, and shade into each other with no very precise boundary between them. Justice is the virtue which keeps everything in its proper place, both the parts of the soul and the citizens of the State. It is the virtue of good order, and the just man is he who keeps the parts of his soul in proper order internally and in the State maintains and fulfils all his rights, duties and responsibilities to the State as a whole and the other members according to his position in the social organism. Temperance, in a sense the most fundamental of all the virtues, is a more dynamic way of looking at the same ordering activity of reason. It is particularly the right ordering and control of the passions and desires whether within the personality or in the body politic. Both Justice and Courage depend on it, and it is intimately related to Prudence. Finally Courage is virtue in action against opposition, the fearlessness and self-devotion which gives mastery over things and makes the realization of right order possible, and which itself springs from the perfect self-mastery which is Temperance. All the virtues interplay and overlap and shade into each other because in the last analysis all virtue is one and it is impossible to have one virtue without having them all, to be truly just without being prudent, temperate and brave or to be truly brave without being prudent, temperate and just. It is impossible, I think, to read Plato's account of the virtues without perceiving that behind it lies not only Socrates's teaching but Socrates's personality. Goodness, that is, did not present itself to Plato in the form of an abstract scheme arrived at by generalisation and analysis but in the form of a person of extraordinary unity and integrity.

3. In our account of Plato's moral teaching we have already, according to the too rigid division which we are inclined now-a-days to make almost instinctively, more than once crossed the border between private and public morality, between ethics and politics in Aristotle's division. Of course for Plato there was no such division and Aristotle is only making a division for convenience of treatment and not in any way suggesting that, as we are sometimes most perniciously inclined to believe, our public and private life are governed by entirely different kinds of principles. (For Aristotle, in fact, "ethics" is a part of "politics"

which is the complete science of the good of man). Plato's political teaching is simply an extension and elaboration of his moral teaching. In common with most Greeks he held that a man could only live a full human life in and through the political community. In his life, in his writings and in the training which he gave in his school he showed the strongest sense of the philosopher's duty to society. In the "Republic" he insists that the philosopher who has passed through his long and laborious training and attained the vision of the Forms must not simply remain detached from earthly cares on that summit of contemplation but must come down and play the part which he alone can play in the life of the State because he alone knows the truth, must take on the burden of ruling for the good of his fellows and the whole social organism. In his own life it is true that Plato took no part in the politics of his native city, Athens. It was the judicial murder of Socrates by the restored democracy which finally convinced him that Athenian political society was so vitiated and perverted not only in its practice but in its principles that any participation in it was worse than useless. But his two later journeys to Sicily were undertaken in the most determined following-up of an attempt which he had begun on his first visit to establish the rule of philosophers at Syracuse, first of all through an extremely unsuccessful attempt to train the younger Dionysius, son of the great prince Dionysius I of Syracuse, as a philosopher-king and then through establishing the influence of Dion, cousin of the younger Dionysius and a very close personal friend of Plato's since his first visit in 388. The first attempt broke down largely because young Dionysius, though very eager to be presented by his teacher with sensational pieces of esoteric knowledge about the nature of the universe, was not prepared for the years of hard mathematical study which were for Plato the indispensable preliminary to the serious study of philosophy. The affair of Dion ended tragically with a series of plots and counter-plots, in which members of the Academy were involved, ending with the assassination of Dion in 353. But the ideal of establishing a perfect state ruled by philosophers remained alive in the Academy: though Plato himself came to see in his later life that we cannot hope to find the true Philosopher-King, who is above all law, in this very imperfect world, and that the best the philosopher can hope for or advise is the establishment of the rule of good laws, in itself very much a second best.

A conception which brings Plato's ethics, politics and cosmology into very close and organic connection is that of microcosm and macrocosm. The cosmic order, the eternal circling of the heavenly bodies in proper and harmonious relation to each other and to the whole is the perfect exemplar of the rule of reason in the visible universe, the "pattern in heaven" which men must follow if they are to order themselves and the State rightly. The individual human being is a little realm or cosmos and the State is a unitary society concerned with human life as a whole, moral and spiritual life much more than bodily needs, and in it the workings of human psychology can be seen and studied more easily because on a larger scale. The principles of moral order by which we must live for our soul's health are the same principles which should govern the State and which are perfectly exemplified in the divine rational order of the visible universe.

Plato's doctrine of the State may well seem to us over-simplified and likely to lead in practice to an unpleasant kind of totalitarianism; but we must remember the sort of State about which he was thinking. Both he and Aristotle are exclusively concerned in their political philosophy with the traditional Greek city-state, a single small city, the centre of a compact block of territory normally sufficient for its economic support, with a small and exclusive body of citizens, personally known to each other, devoting their main energies to the service of the State in politics and war. It is with the perfection, and the maintenance as far as possible in the most perfect conditions, of a city-state of this kind that Plato is exclusively concerned. Plato did not believe in progress any more than most other Greeks. When he describes a process of political development, as he does most brilliantly in the "Republic," it is a process of decadence, a steady passage from better to worse till the lowest depth is reached. And the only hope of a return to better things is afforded by the belief, an extremely important and persistent one in all ancient Greek thought, that all becoming is cyclic, that the succession of things goes round endlessly in circles, coming back at regular intervals to its starting-point. This belief Plato expresses very strangely in the myth in his dialogue "The Statesman," where he speaks of the universe in the Golden Age as having revolved with a movement opposite to that which it now has, and under the direction of a divine intelligence, so that everything went perfectly, whereas it now spins blindly backwards bereft of divine

guidance and producing the disorder and universal decadence
which we see; and this will continue until the god takes charge
again, reverses the motion, and turns the world back into a new
Golden Age. (The myth is not of course to be interpreted literally
any more than that in the "Timæus." Plato certainly never
believed in a withdrawal of divine guidance of the universe at any
period in its history. All we can be certain he meant to suggest
was the cyclic movement of history with its alternation of periods
of stability and happiness and others of degeneration and disorder and misery).

4. It is because of this belief in cycles and inevitable decadence
that Plato, however drastic the reforms he proposes, is so intensely
conservative in the spirit of his political thinking. He has an
immense respect for ancient traditions and myths, traces of an
earlier wisdom transmitted to us obscurely, across cataclysms
and disasters, from a primæval wiser and better world. (This
is quite compatible with his extreme disapproval of the mythology
of Homer and Hesiod. An intelligent fifth century Greek, like
Herodotus who incidentally anticipated Plato in his interest in
the immemorially ancient civilization and religious traditions of
Egypt, was fully aware that the poets and their stories about the
gods were comparatively modern). And what he is trying to do
in his political writing is not to start off a process of progressive
evolution towards an entirely new ideal of the State but to establish by his usual method of Socratic enquiry the most rational
and perfect form which can be taken by the traditional Greek
city-state which we have described and to see how, given an
exceptionally favourable concatenation of natural conditions,
such a state might possibly be established and confirmed so as
to resist the inevitable decay as long as possible. Plato is always
concerned with stability; when and if the perfect State is established its structure must be made so strong, its constitution must
be bound with such rigorous safeguards and sanctions as to
prevent the smallest change in political or social life, because all
change means decay and degeneration. In the "Laws" he insists
that even the pattern of the children's toys must be kept unchanged from one generation to another. This striving after
fixity, this attempt to establish a satisfactory form and maintain
it unchanged is characteristic of all Greek political reformers.
Whenever a new constitution is established, whether the full
democracy at Athens or the authoritarian military regime at

Sparta, it is always hedged with safeguards to ensure that it shall endure as long as possible unchanged, because the only change conceived as possible is decadence, not progress.

In this discussion of Plato's conservatism another very important element in his thought has appeared. This is the conviction, as apparent in his political thought as in his psychology or cosmology, that reason is never working in a beautiful emptiness where it is sufficient to produce a theoretically perfect construction for everything to go perfectly. Plato always pays great attention to the material which reason has to work on in this world, the irrational element of nature or necessity, never completely reducible to rational control. In politics this element appears first in the environment of the State, its climate and geographical situation (to this latter Plato attaches great importance) and still more importantly in the natural inborn characteristics of the citizens. This regard for nature, for the given material, appears in the "Republic," which is partly a symbolic exposition, a demonstration on a large scale of how reason should rule in the individual soul, and partly a picture of a pattern city-state perfectly conformed to reason and the order of the universe but never intended to be realised in practice as well as in the "Laws," that work of Plato's old age which gives a detailed account of the sort of rationally satisfactory city-state which it might be possible to realize in practice, given exceptionally favourable conditions. If we once grasp this we shall find it very much easier to understand, if not to accept, certain strange and to us repellent features of Plato's political thought. We have to remember that Plato never imagines himself to be constructing Utopias in an indefinite dream-future where everything is easy. He once planned to describe a State of the Golden Age, primitive Athens, in action, engaged in a struggle to the death with the Great Power of Atlantis, so as to show the perfect and reason-ruled city of the "Republic," with which he identifies primitive Athens, as it were alive and moving and not merely static as in the "Republic" itself. But he never accomplished this design and his two greatest works on the State are concerned with considering how from difficult and refractory human material philosophers may construct a fortress which will for a time resist the flux of inevitable decay, the law that all must pass away that comes to be. Plato's cities are beleaguered cities, doomed to fall at last by treachery from within if not by attack from without.

but designed for as long and as heroic a resistance as possible.
5. Let us then consider very shortly some of the details of Plato's
picture of the State as it should be in the light of what I have
suggested are his basic principles, the idea of the State as the
individual "writ large," the belief that all change is necessarily
for the worse once the highest point of the cycle is reached, the
regard for the given material and situation, the idea of justice
as primarily the virtue of order. They all apply simply and
obviously to the "Republic." The "guardian" class, the philosopher-rulers and the warriors, represent the ruling reason and the
nobler emotions working in close co-operation to dominate and
order the great mass of the people of the city engaged in agri-
culture, manufacture and such trade as is permitted, who
represent the carnal desires, since the driving motive of their
activity is love of gain. In order to produce human material of
the highest quality to undergo the long and laborious training
which makes a ruler, the guardians are deprived of all natural
use of marriage and subjected to fantastic breeding regulations,
the times of the rare and strictly controlled sexual intercourse of
those of fertile age being determined by mathematical calculation.
In order to eliminate that disunity of powerful families which is
the beginning of decay and to prevent the ruling class from being
tainted with acquisitive desires all private property and family
life are forbidden to the guardians. All things are held in common
and children are reared in common, with no knowledge of their
natural parents. Private property is permitted under strict
control in Plato's Republic, but only to those who have no
political power. Otherwise, it would seem to Plato, the order of
the powers of the soul would be reversed in a monstrous manner
and the acquisitive instincts would rule, contrary to justice.
Finally we should note that in order to fit in with the rigid paral-
lelism of State structure with the tripartite psychology and
with the interpretation of justice as the virtue of order which
keeps everyone in their proper place, Plato only considers human
beings in terms of function and not as whole personalities. This
is the real reason for his insistence on the equality of the sexes.
Only those qualities of mind and character which fit an individual to be a philosopher-ruler, a warrior, or a producer are
considered. (Arrangements are provided for dealing with those
exceptional people who do not fit the caste into which they are
born, for moving up anyone from the lower classes who is mani-

festly fitted to rule and moving down children of the guardian class who are manifestly unfit).

In the "Laws" the structure of the state is much less rigidly stylized to correspond obviously to the structure of the individual soul, and a great deal more attention is paid to finding a practicable way of dealing with the human material likely to be available and to the geographical environment, but the spirit is essentially the same, and if we understand the different purposes of the two great dialogues, we shall not find any fundamental disagreement between the "Laws" and the "Republic." In the "Laws" too the State is a hierarchical organism and individuals live only to perform their function in the State. Social stability, the establishment of a rational and just order which will unite the diverse elements so perfectly that change and decay will be staved off as long as possible and the best possible corporate life will endure, is the great aim. This is the reason for the careful choice of a site well removed from the sea and the deliberate isolation of the citizens from foreign contacts, which may be dangerous to their native institutions. Foreign trade and foreign travel are both strongly discouraged. This is the purpose too of the elaborate "mixed" constitution, the strict regulation and limitation of property, and the careful, all-embracing, beautifully-planned totalitarian education. Above all it is the reason for the enforcement by the State authorities under penalty of imprisonment and even death in extreme cases of the fundamental Platonic orthodoxy in religion, the belief in an all-ruling Divine Providence which cannot be bought or bribed or turned aside from its purposes by sacrifice. Unless the State is founded on the truth about the universe and the powers that rule it, it cannot survive. The city-state of the "Laws" which was perhaps intended to be realised in practice is even more obviously a fortress city, a little island of temporary stability amid the flowing tides of decay, than is the visionary and symbolic city of the "Republic." It is necessarily a *little* island, a fortress with a severely limited garrison. Strict limitation of the number of citizens is an essential requisite of the good state according to Plato. Pagan Platonism was never very much interested in what became of the mass of mankind.

We have talked a good deal about the inevitable process of decay which States, like all other things which come to be, must pass through. It may be perhaps worth while to give a short summary of the details of the process as described in the "Republic." Perhaps here Plato still has something to teach us. The process begins with the break-up of the communal way of life of the ruling class and the appearance of private property. The philosopher-rulers disappear and all power in the state passes into the hands of the warriors, who neglect the study of truth for the sake of physical culture and the practice of war. The state becomes a military aristocracy. Deprived of the rule of reason the nobler passions do not long maintain themselves against the baser. Among the proud, quarrelsome warrior-nobles the love of riches becomes stronger than the love of honour and the aristocracy degenerates into an oligarchy or plutocracy, in which wealth is the title to rule. Then the great social gulf or cleavage becomes that between rich and poor. Eventually there is a successful revolt of poor against rich, led by young members of the ruling class impoverished by their own extravagance and the usury of the dominant financiers and a democracy is established. This represents the complete emancipation of the disorderly rout of the passions from the rule of reason. "Liberty" is its watchword, and everyone does what he likes; but it is a false freedom, for as Plato always insists, the man who follows his passions without restraint of reason contemplating moral good is the worst slave of all. Finally the inevitable nemesis of liberal individualistic democracy is tyranny, the rule of the man who has utterly abandoned himself to this worst passions and above all to the unbridled lust for power, who has cut himself off from all real contact with or sense of responsibility to the rest of the human race. It is the exact antithesis of the government of the philosopher-rulers with which we began, the rule of the worst as opposed to the rule of the best, and corresponds to the state of the tyrannical man himself, in whom one monstrous and diseased passion has come to dominate all others.

6.   In the short and inadequate account I have given of Plato's political teaching it is easy to see the influence of his upbringing, environment and social prejudices. It is the political philosophy of a Greek city-state aristocrat, with his contempt for manual labour and his dislike for the extreme democracy of Athens; not that Athenian democracy was really so very extreme; we should remember that it meant government by public meetings of a small and exclusive citizen body very jealous of its privileges in a state of which the majority of the population were slaves, or resident

aliens without hope of naturalisation. "Votes for Slaves" would not have been a popular cry with even the most extreme Athenian democrats! We can see in Plato that admiration which was fashionable in his time among Athenian intellectuals for the institutions of Sparta, that strange barrack-city   here a citizen army in a state of perpetual mobilization lay always on guard to hold down a potentially hostile serf population, an army of occupation even in their homeland. He admired too the rigid caste system of Egypt, a country in which intelligent Greeks took much interest. But though Hellenic and class bias and the influence of an idealisation of particular existing societies of the time are only too obvious in his works it is a most foolish mistake to assume as some modern writers do that we can dismiss not only his political philosophy but his whole philosophy as the automatic product of his economic and social environment. The method is too easy and can be applied just as easily to the critics as to the systems they criticise, to the ultimate destruction of all hope of attaining truth by reason. A philosophy must be judged, if it is to be judged at all, by its truth or falsehood and not by the social environment of the philosopher who originated it.

At the end of this most inadequate sketch of Plato's thought there are two things to do. First, I ask any reader there may be to prove and supplement its inadequacy by reading as much of Plato's own writings as possible. All are available in English translations, and they are not difficult to read. Then I would like to write a few lines about his relation to our own thinking, to the still living tradition of western Christian philosophy, and to the strange intellectual situation in which we find ourselves to-day. In a way it is easy to do this, for what the central tradition of European thought owes to Plato is simply its own existence. He is the philosopher of beginnings, who started the serious discussion of almost every great philosophical question. And not only do those who still belong to that tradition find the study of Plato a continually vitalising experience but many modern systems of thought outside the tradition owe a great deal to the stimulation of their originators' minds by the reading of Plato. Everyone who believes in an objective and unchanging standard of morality governing public as well as private life, in the soul as immaterial and immortal and the most important part of man, in the governance of the world by Divine Reason and in the existence of eternal archetypes or patterns of all things that come to be and pass away, with which our behaviour and thought must conform, everyone who believes all this or an important part of it can claim to be in the tradition which goes back unbroken to Plato and Socrates: though the later development of the Platonic school and, much more, the transforming influence of Christianity have very much altered the content of these beliefs, yet the tradition of their development has been continuous. However much we may find ourselves in disagreement with Plato on really serious and vitally important subjects, the nature of God, the eternity of the cosmos, the uncreatedness of matter, the value to be attached to the body and to sense-experience and sense-perceptions, yet in other vital matters we are still of his school. As against the host of materialists, relativists, pragmatists, positivists, deniers of any eternal universal and objective truths or standards, who dominate so much of our thinking to-day and whose feebler predecessors were dealt with by Plato in his time, we who still hold to the older tradition are on Plato's side and he and Socrates are on ours, and we should reverence them as of the greatest among the founders and fathers of our thought.

VII

Aristotle ·(1). Life and Works. The Academy after Plato's Death. Logic. Criticism of Plato

1. FROM the group of philosophers prominent in the Academy at Plato's death there gradually emerges the tremendous figure of Aristotle. This greatest of Plato's pupils was a native of Stagira in Chalcidice on the north coast of the Aegean. He was of pure Greek blood (that is, as far as we know), but from the very edge of the Greek world, well within the sphere of influence of the rising, doubtfully Greek, power of Macedonia, and his father was Court Physician to Amyntas II of Macedonia. The Macedonian connection affected the course of Aristotle's life, but was not important for the development of his thought, though it might well have been, as we shall see. What was important was that his father was a doctor and that there was a long family medical tradition behind him; for his family belonged to the great medical clan or hereditary guild of the Asclepiadæ. It is very probable that Aristotle's passionate interest in biology and the way he makes the individual living being studied scientifically the centre of his philosophy is the result of the medical tradition which he inherited. Biology is for him the key science of his philosophy, as mathematics was for Plato; and he was a great original biologist, as Plato was not a great original mathematician.

When he was eighteen (he was born in 384 B.C.) Aristotle entered the school of Plato at Athens and remained there for twenty years till Plato's death in 348. During all that time he seems to have remained a perfectly loyal and contented member of the Academy and on the best of terms with his master Plato. There is no doubt whatever that the philosophy of Plato was the dominant influence in Aristotle's thought. However drastic his later disagreements with Platonism he always remains as it were within the same country of thought. Platonists and Aristotelians can always each understand what the other is getting at even when their battles are at the fiercest. And the greatest periods in the history of traditional European philosophy have been when the traditions of Plato and Aristotle have been in fruitful inter-action (admittedly with a good deal of often embittered incidental controversy) rather than in the sterile opposition which it has sometimes been suggested is their only possible relationship.

2. It was at Plato's death that Aristotle began gradually to separate himself from his fellow-Academics. Plato's successor in the headship of the Academy was his nephew Speusippus, philosophically a very curious personage. It may be as well at this point to say something about the thought at least of the two chief Platonists of the generation after Plato. There will hardly be another suitable opportunity of discussing what is called the Older Academy, and the ideas of Speusippus and Xenocrates are important for the understanding of later developments of Platonism. All we know about their thought comes from incidental criticisms by Aristotle and a few quotations and allusions in later writers; and it seems probable that Aristotle sometimes misunder-stood or misrepresented them, Speusippus in particular. But one or two very interesting points do seem to emerge from our frag-mentary information. Speusippus carried the "Pythagorean" tendencies of Plato's old age still further, and substituted numbers for the Forms. He also seems to have regarded reality not as a single whole but as composed of a number of apparently separate and self-contained systems, of numbers, of magnitudes, and of soul, each with its own first principles, only related by analogy, whose relationship to each other he did not more clearly explain. But it is when we come to the principles of number (and so, ultimately, in some way of all reality) that Speusippus's thought appears most original. He believed in a One beyond being and higher than being, not identical with the Good.(good only appears at a later stage of the procession), which was the ultimate principle of limit and determination, and in an ultimate principle of multiplicity and in-determination, which was not evil or the cause of evil, and perhaps was said to be beyond non-being in the same sort of way in which the One was beyond being. No later philosopher followed Speusippus exactly in his account of this second ultimate principle. But the conception of the One beyond being (a develop-ment of ideas to be found in Plato) makes Speusippus one of the most important sources of Neo-Platonism.

Xenocrates, the other most notable Platonist of the first

generation, accompanied Aristotle in his departure from the Academy when Speusippus succeeded to the headship; though the two can hardly have had very much philosophically in common except, perhaps, a dislike of some of Speusippus's ideas. The thought of Xenocrates is less original and closer to that of Plato, but it too in its way points forward to later developments. He appears to have reduced everything to numbers and magnitudes, not only the Forms, but the soul, which he defined as a "self-moving number" and the visible universe: in this he seems only to have been carrying on and exaggerating elements in Plato's later thought. His first principle is the One which he identifies with the Good and with Mind and the supreme god and male principle of generation of the universe. With it he couples the Indefinite Dyad, supreme female, passive or receptive, generative principle, mother of the gods, which contains the Form-Numbers generated by its union with the One. Then come the Olympian gods, who are the heavenly bodies conceived as living and intelligent. Xenocrates held strongly to the new astral religion, the worship of the heavenly bodies, which Plato in his last years had expounded in the "Epinomis." Below the gods come the "daemones," supernatural beings intermediate between gods and men, of whom Plato had spoken in the myth of Eros in the "Banquet" and who play a most important part in later Platonic theology. The whole system of Xenocrates, as far as we know it, with its bringing together of Soul and Forms, and above all its identification of One, Mind and Good as the single supreme principle, and with its elaborate hierarchical theology, points clearly forward to the type of thinking we find in the revived Platonism of the Roman Empire. The beginnings of Middle and Neo-Platonism, if they cannot be found in Plato himself, can certainly be traced back to the Old Academy.

3.   After their departure from the Academy and from Athens Aristotle, Xenocrates, and a few others went to the principality of an old fellow-student of theirs, Hermias. This extremely interesting and attractive personage had risen from slavery to be ruler of Atarneus and Assos in Mysia, on the coast of Asia Minor, and was the nearest thing to a philosopher-monarch that the Academy ever produced. He maintained his precarious position on the edge of the Persian Empire till at last he was betrayed to the Persians and crucified. Aristotle, who had loved

him dearly and had married Pythias, his niece and adopted daughter, wrote a very noble poem in his memory. After three years at Assos Aristotle moved to Mitylene, near by. He seems to have spent a good deal of his time on the coast of Asia Minor in the study of biology, especially marine biology. From 343-340 he was tutor to the young heir to the throne of Macedon, Alexander. This association of Aristotle and Alexander the Great has aroused much romantic interest but it produced little lasting effect on the minds of either tutor or pupil, though their relations always remained friendly. This lack of real intellectual contact was most unfortunate in the field of political philosophy, where Alexander in later life could have taught his old master a good deal, and an Aristotle of wider sympathies and a more oecumenical outlook could have helped Alexander greatly.

In 335-4 Aristotle, after a few years probably spent at Stagira, returned to Athens and founded his school, the Lyceum, in buildings which he rented (as an alien he could not buy them) in a grove outside the city sacred to Apollo Lyceius. The organization of the school was not unlike that of the Academy, but it seems to have been better provided with the apparatus of learning. Aristotle established a collection of manuscripts, the first really important library in Greece, a collection of maps, and a natural history museum. Here Aristotle settled down to an immense activity of teaching, lecturing, and co-operative scientific work which lasted till 323, the year of the death of Alexander. Then there was an outbreak of anti-Macedonian feeling at Athens, and Aristotle's close connection with Macedonia made him suspect. A fatuous charge of impiety was brought against him, and he handed over the school to Theophrastus, an Athenian citizen and his most notable pupil, and retired to Chalcis, where he died in 322. His will has been preserved, and gives a very pleasant picture of his character and his relations with his family and slaves, all of whom he secured against being sold and some of whom he set free.

4. It is quite impossible in a book of this size to give any comprehensive account of the philosophical work contained in the very large body of Aristotle's extant writings. Aristotle was not only a great philosopher, but a philosopher on the largest possible scale. He established the great divisions of philosophy which are still generally accepted, and in every one of them he did work of the greatest permanent value. In addition,

in the field of biology he made a contribution to scientific knowledge which was not superseded until the modern study of biology developed and was perhaps the greatest contribution ever made by a single man working independently. His work in Logic, Philosophy of Nature, Metaphysics, Ethics, Political Philosophy, Psychology and Epistemology, and Aesthetics, still has to be taken seriously by sensible philosophers of all schools, whether they agree with him or not. All I can hope to do, then, is to give an outline of the general principles of his thought and indicate how he applies them in a few historically important and generally studied fields. Of his biology and his literary criticism I shall be able to say nothing, and very little about his logic, which is the less unfortunate as any good text-book of Logic, whether written from a modernist or a traditionalist point of view, gives an adequate account of the logic of Aristotle.

Even to give the names of all his extant genuine writings would take too long, but it is necessary to say something about them. In his earlier life, when he was still a member of the Academy and a convinced Platonist, and during the transition period, before he founded the Lyceum, when his mind was moving away from Platonism towards his own philosophy, he wrote dialogues in the Platonic manner, which he himself published and intended for general reading, and which according to Cicero and Quintilian possessed great beauty of style (Cicero speaks of Aristotle's "golden flow of speech" which is rather startling to those who only know his extant works). These have all perished except for a few fragments, and we have only his very different later works. These later works are written in an extremely compressed style, often in what is really note form, and are frequently rough and unfinished, and contain many repetitions and digressions. They are undoubtedly closely connected with Aristotle's lectures at the Lyceum, though many of them contain material of an earlier date. Some of them may be Aristotle's own lecture-notes, but possibly the best suggestion about the origin of most of them is that they were memoranda written by him after the lectures for the benefit of pupils who had missed them and to provide a permanent and accurate record of their contents. It should be noted that the longer extant works were not written as wholes but are collections of essays on related themes sometimes put together by Aristotle himself, sometimes (as is that extraordinary hotch-potch the "Metaphysics") by his editors.

The works of Aristotle may conveniently be classified as follows:
  (I) The group of logical treatises which has been known
      at least since the sixth century A.D. as the *Organon*, that
      is, the Instrument of Thought, or Tool for Philosophers.
 (II) Treatises on the philosophy of nature, the *Physics* (the
      most comprehensive and important), *De Caelo*, *De
      Generatione et Corruptione* (On Coming-to-be and Passing
      Away. The Latin titles of Aristotle's works are generally
      used in references to them, with one or two exceptions)
      and *Meteorologica*. The *De Mundo* is spurious and late
      Stoic in its philosophy.
(III) Treatises on psychology, the great work *De Anima* and the
      group of small treatises called the *Parva Naturalia*.
 (IV) The biological works, the great *History of Animals* (some
      books of which are not genuine) and a group of im-
      portant treatises in which Aristotle expounds his bio-
      logical theories.
  (V) The group of treatises on what Aristotle calls "first
      philosophy," the science of being, put together by his
      ancient editors under the general title of *Metaphysics*.
      This probably only meant originally the treatises which
      came after the physical works in an early edition.
 (VI) The ethical treatises, of which the most important and
      best known is the *Nicomachean Ethics*. The Eudemian
      Ethics is almost certainly a genuine early work. With
      these may be placed the *Politics*, and the only survival
      of the material on which the *Politics* was based, the
      "*Constitution of Athens*." Aristotle made a collection of
      no less than 158 similar descriptions of constitutions.
(VII) Finally there are the treatises on the art of speaking
      and writing, the *Rhetoric* and the fragmentary but cease-
      lessly studied and always valuable *Poetics*.
5. Before beginning to discuss the movement of Aristotle's mind
away from Platonism and the fundamental principles of the
philosophy at which he finally arrived it will be as well to say
a word or two about Aristotle's logic. (Aristotle himself, by the
way, does not use the word "logic". His most general term for
the study of reasoning is "analytics", but this is rather less
general in its application than "logic" as we understand it.) To
understand the purpose of what may seem to us the fantastic
abstractions, the insubstantial dance of As and Bs and Cs, which

are to be found in Aristotle's logical treatises and those of later writers in the same tradition, a good starting-point is the name given to the collection of these writings, the Organon, or instrument of thought. Logic for Aristotle is not strictly speaking a science. He divides sciences into three classes, the theoretical, the practical and the productive, according to their ends or ultimate purposes, which are knowledge of truth, the conduct of the good human life, and the making of useful or beautiful things. Logic falls into none of these classes, but is a general preparation for the study of all the sciences, for it is only by the study of logic that we can learn to reason rightly and so arrive at knowledge of truth, which is necessary in all the sciences, of course, though it is only the ultimate end in the theoretical sciences. Logic is the study of the structure of rational thought, the analysis of thought considered as an instrument for attaining truth.

Ross sums up the essential character of Aristotle's logic very well as follows: "It is for him [Aristotle] a study not of words but of the thought of which words are signs; of thought not with reference to its natural history but with reference to its success or failure in attaining truth; of thought not as constituting but as apprehending the nature of things" [W. D. Ross, *Aristotle*, p. 21]. This is true not only of Aristotle but of the whole scholastic tradition of logic; and it is just this concern with thought precisely as an instrument for attaining truth which serves to distinguish it from contemporary systems of logic, which are the work of men concerned only with constructing internally valid patterns with no reference to anything outside, and generally with a complete disbelief in the existence of truth or the power of logical reasoning to attain it.

Aristotle starts his analysis of thought with a consideration of the meanings of separate words, the number of different kinds of realities to which they can refer, so arriving at his list of "Categories"—substance (the primary one which all the others presuppose), quantity, quality, relation, place, date, position, state, action, passivity. Then he goes on to analyse and consider the possible meanings of propositions, statements or complete sentences: and then he proceeds to the most important part of his analysis, the analysis of the syllogism, the rational argument by which, given certain premises, it can be shown that a further truth follows necessarily from them. Aristotle in practice confines rational proof to those cases where a relation of subject and predicate between two terms is inferred from relations of subject and predicate between them and a third term (e.g., A is true of B, B is true of C, therefore A is true of C), and it is this type of argument of which the term "syllogism" is exclusively used. It is a limitation which has given rise to much controversy. Aristotle recognizes inductive as well as deductive proof, though his account of induction is rather confused and inconclusive. And he is very clear that an argument does not really prove anything just because it is a valid syllogism, though it must be a valid syllogism in order to be a proof. To be a real scientific demonstration establishing a truth the premises must be true, and furthermore at the starting-point of a scientific demonstration they must be primary, indemonstrable, and immediately certain, like geometrical axioms. They must be more clearly seen to be true than their conclusion, "prior to and more intelligible than it" and they must state facts which are the causes of the conclusion in reality, as well as being themselves the causes of it in logic. Aristotle distinguishes very clearly between the scientific syllogism which proceeds from first principles certainly true and apprehended by intuitive reason, the dialectical syllogism whose premises are only probable, not certain, and the contentious syllogism, the merely silly debating society argument whose premises are not even probable or which does not reason correctly from them. He has a very interesting discussion in this connection of logical fallacies (the treatise called "Sophistic Elenchi").

6. In studying the movement of Aristotle's mind away from Platonism towards his own distinctive philosophy we must try above all to understand Aristotle's rejection of the Theory of Forms. This is the essential point of difference between Plato and Aristotle (though not, it must be noted, between Christian Platonists and Christian Aristotelians, who both accept the late-Platonic doctrine of Forms existing eternally in the Divine Mind). Aristotle's criticisms of Plato's doctrine must many of them seem to us cavilling and inconclusive; some of them had been anticipated by Plato himself in the "Parmenides"; and they entirely ignore one of the most important elements in Plato's later doctrine. Nevertheless they do strike at the most serious weaknesses in Platonism and, though we need not trouble about the details of the not always very impressive arguments which Aristotle

uses, we must, if we are to understand Aristotle at all, grasp their general purport and the attitude of mind behind them.

Plato had believed in a world of unchanging eternal immaterial Forms, corresponding to universal definitions "Beauty Itself," "Equality Itself," "Man Himself," and so on. This was for him the only real world, and the Forms were the only objects of true knowledge. The material world, the world of growth and decay, this changing world perceived by the senses in which we live our bodily life, is not strictly speaking real or knowable at all. Any show of reality which it may have derives from a mysterious, never explained or defined "participation" in the Forms. The intermediary between the two worlds, which in Plato's later thought does a great deal to bridge the gulf between them, is Soul. Aristotle, on the other hand, moved steadily away from this Platonic doctrine towards a dominating interest in the world of concrete individual things perceptible by the senses which our immediate experience reveals to us. He continues to agree entirely with Plato that our business as rational beings is to know objective truth and that the objects of true knowledge are immaterial and unchanging. But it seems to him that the Forms are so completely cut off, in the Platonic doctrine, from the material world that they cannot possibly be the objects of our knowledge, immersed as we are in that world. Furthermore, they are so completely cut off that they cannot be causes of the being of the things of which we have experience, any more than of our knowledge of them: and in any case the things of which we have experience are individual concrete things, and how can a separately existing universal be their cause? For Aristotle the individual things which we perceive by our senses are the primary realities. It is *in* this changeable world of individual things that we have to find somehow the unchanging objects of true knowledge which are necessary for science and philosophy. Plato, it seems to Aristotle, evades the problem instead of answering it by asserting the existence of a world of unchanging eternal universal entities, transcending our world and utterly separated from it. Even if they existed they would have nothing to do with our knowledge or our world. Aristotle by no means denies the existence of universals, general characteristics of things, or supposes them to be creations of our minds. They exist objectively, but only as characteristics of individual things, not, as Plato had taught, in a transcendent world of separate substantial beings.

Aristotle in his criticism of the doctrine of Forms reveals an attitude of mind very different from Plato's by his acceptance as the primary given reality of that world of changing individual things revealed by sense-perception which Plato had not regarded as truly real at all. Yet it may well have been the increasing respect for and concern with this visible world of here and now which Plato showed in his later years which led Aristotle to his increasing dissatisfaction with the theory of Forms. And for all the feebleness of some of his arguments Aristotle in his criticism strikes at the weak joint of Platonism, the absence of any satisfactory explanation of how the world of Forms, the world of the intellect, is related to the world of individual material things, the world of the senses. In abandoning Plato's doctrine and working out his own theory of immanent substantial forms Aristotle is trying to answer a question which the Platonist who retains the theory of Forms must answer too if his position is to be rationally tenable. In fact we find that later Platonists find it necessary to accept not only transcendent universal Forms in the Divine Mind but also Aristotle's substantial forms immanent in the material world.

There remains, however, a most serious defect in Aristotle's criticism of Plato, and that is his complete ignoring of the part played by Soul as a connecting link between the two worlds. It is true that Plato's account of the functioning of Soul in this capacity is vague and often expressed in mythical and symbolic terms, and that he never gives a satisfactorily clear description of the relationship of the individual soul to its body or the cosmic soul to the material universe. Yet it remains true that Soul in Plato does act in a manner very much resembling Aristotle's own "efficient cause," which he complains that Plato does not recognize. One reason for this, besides Plato's own vagueness, may be that the contemporary philosophers of the Academy, Xenocrates in particular, also misunderstood and neglected Plato's later doctrine of Soul as moving and forming cause of the material world, and Aristotle's main concern in the controversy is with them rather than with Plato himself (this may account for much that seems unsatisfactory in his criticism of the Theory of Forms). Another reason may be that the moving or efficient cause, the link between pattern and copy is always for Aristotle immanent in matter. Biological generation, the father begetting a child with a human form like his own, is for him the typical, pattern, case of the production of a new reality. And with this Plato's poetic metaphor of the Craftsman and theology of a transcendent Divine Providence has nothing to do. But it is nevertheless a pity that Aristotle did not enter more deeply into the later thought of his master on this point, and did not try to give Plato's doctrine of Soul as the moving, efficient, formative cause of the material universe that philosophical precision which it lacked. If he had done so he might have avoided some of the most serious defects of his own philosophy and have anticipated some most important later developments.

VIII
Aristotle (2) Basic Ideas and Philosophy of Nature

1. WE have seen that Aristotle had come to the conclusion that Plato's attempt to solve the problem of true knowledge by postulating a world of transcendent separate Forms as its objects was a mistaken one and that reality of which we can have certain knowledge must be looked for in the world in which we find ourselves, the world revealed to us by our senses. The individual concrete entities of this world, Aristotle maintains against the Platonists, are real and scientifically knowable. Aristotle is of course too reasonable and too deeply influenced by Plato to say that these are the only real beings. He admits, as we shall see, the existence of immaterial entities perceptible by the reason alone and transcending and separate from the visible universe, but only so far as they seem to him necessary to explain that universe or to explain the workings of our own minds. And, of course, he admits the existence of universals of all sorts, but not as separate substantial realities, only as immanent and inseparable characteristics of the substances which we perceive.

This acceptance of the individual beings of the sense-world as real and as the objects of true and accurate, that is scientific, knowledge, sets Aristotle a formidable problem to solve. He continues Platonist enough to be quite clear that the realities which are the objects of true knowledge must be stable, permanent and unchanging and not a mere flux of appearances. Yet the world revealed by the senses is one of unceasing change, in which things grow and decay and are perpetually transformed one into the other. It was this character of the sense-world which had made Plato look for reality elsewhere, and the questions which Aristotle had to answer when he rejected Plato's solution were first precisely what were the stable and unchanging realities which exist in this world of change, and then precisely how could one reality of this kind change into another, as the things revealed by our senses appear to do. It was, as far as we can tell, more by trying to answer these questions than by any other line of approach that Aristotle arrived at the great basic conceptions of his philosophical system, Substance, Form and Matter, Act and Potency

2. A substance for Aristotle is simply a real thing, a thing which actually exists. It is the thing as a whole, including its dimensions, qualities, relations, etc., which can only be separated from it by a process of mental abstraction but cannot actually exist apart from it. That is what Aristotle means when he says that substance is the primary category, which all the others presuppose. And it follows that a substance for Aristotle is always an individual thing, never a universal like a Platonic Form.

But then the question arises; what is it in the individual substantial realities revealed to us by our senses which makes them substantial realities, and what is it which enables them to change? It is substance which is being in the strict and proper sense, the permanent and unchanging object of our thought; and yet individual substantial realities do change. Aristotle's solution of this problem is to be found in his analysis of the concrete substantial reality into Form and Matter, and in his doctrine of Potential and Actual being. The form of a thing is that which makes it what it is. A substantial reality cannot for Aristotle just vaguely, indefinitely, or abstractly " be ". It must be something, some one thing definite and distinguishable. The form is just this definite, delimiting reality of things, the precise "thisness" or "thatness" of them which corresponds to their exact scientific definition in our minds. Aristotle is always very much concerned with this aspect of the form, as the unchanging reality with which the scientific definition of the thing must correspond if it is to be a true definition. For this reason he maintains the curious and difficult doctrine that, although individual things are the only things that exist yet the form in each individual thing is not a unique individual form but the form of the species, the narrowest class which can be scientifically defined. The forms of individuals are only numerically distinct, otherwise identical. In the case of concrete beings in the visible world which are compounded of form and matter, the matter is the principle of their individuality; though it is difficult to understand how this can be, for "matter" to Aristotle, as we shall see, is purely negative and has no proper characteristics of its own. And in the case of pure forms, immaterial substances which are form uncompounded with matter, Aristotle gives no clue to the reason or nature of their individuality. The Neo-Platonists and the Christian Platonists reject Aristotle's doctrine and unhesitatingly postulate forms, even transcendent Platonic

Forms, of individuals: and St. Thomas finds Aristotle's doctrine awkward when dealing with the angels and still more awkward when dealing with human personality, though he accepts it and makes heroic efforts to explain it in a reasonable and Christian sense.

The form of a substantial concrete material reality can for Aristotle never actually exist in separation from its matter. The two are only distinguishable by a process of mental analysis. They are not two things which are compounded mechanically or chemically to make another complete thing. The technical terms used by modern Aristotelians are particularly unfortunate here. "Form" and "Matter" suggest something like a jelly-shape or a children's seaside bucket into which some solid stuff is packed and then turned out with a definite external appearance. "The imposition of form on matter" suggests it even more definitely. Nothing of course could be further from what Aristotle means. The form is the intimate inward structure, the "thingness" of the thing; the matter is just the possibility of being that or another thing which is made actual for the time being by the reception of a particular form. If we were to speak of Pattern and Possibility instead of Form and Matter, though they would not translate accurately the Greek words Aristotle uses, they would perhaps convey a more accurate impression to modern minds— and would have more of the witch-doctor's-patter impressiveness of modern philosophical jargon. The purely-intellectual and non-physical character of the analysis which distinguishes Form and Matter, the fact that you can only separate them in your mind and not in reality, appears even more clearly in the analysis Aristotle makes when he is considering the actual process of change more closely. In this a third term appears, Privation, which means the fact of not being that which is going to be the result of change. A thing is what it is, by reason of its own substantial form; it is not some other definite thing into which it may change, by reason of its privation of the other form; it has the possibility of being what it is or another thing by reason of its matter.

Matter then is simply the element of possibility, of changeableness in things. Form is the stable, permanent, knowable, scientifically definable element in things. Matter is that element, itself undetermined but capable of successive determinations, which makes change possible. Of course the possibilities of change in a thing are limited, because the matter which received the final form which made the thing what it is was already informed in a certain way. The matter which receives the form of "table" for instance is not just "matter" but "wood", that is matter which has already received (to simplify the process) the forms of the elements involved in the constitution of wood and the form of wood itself, and this to some extent determines and limits future developments. But if we pursue our mental analysis far enough we shall get down to something which Aristotle never actually mentions by name but to which he often clearly refers, the Prima Materia or "first matter" of the scholastics, which has no form at all and is simply a bare, undefined and unlimited possibility of becoming. It never of course actually exists by itself. Matter without form can by its very definition never have any actual existence. Form on the other hand can exist without matter, as it does in the eternal substances, purely immaterial intellects, which form the highest ranks in Aristotle's hierarchy of realities.

3. From what I have just said about Matter it should already be fairly clear how Aristotle explains change. Everything in the material world actually is something and has in it the possibility of becoming other things. This is one of the most fundamental of Aristotle's doctrines, that of actual and potential being. It seems to us the merest common sense to say that a thing can be one thing actually and all sorts of other things potentially, but it took a very long development of Greek thought before Aristotle arrived at his simple-seeming doctrine, and it was not until he arrived at it that it was really possible to explain reasonably how a thing could be at the same time fully real and capable of change. It was really Plato in his later years who made it possible for Aristotle to develop his doctrine by clearing up some primitive and elementary logical difficulties about the meaning of the word "is" (there is an important discussion about this in the "Sophist"). This doctrine of Act and Potency is perhaps the most important in Aristotle's system of thought, and is capable of very wide application, e.g., in ethics and psychology. We can now see the doctrine of Matter and Form as a special application of the doctrine of Act and Potency to real but changeable beings in the material world. The form is the thing's actuality, the matter which has not yet received a particular form is that thing potentially. For Aristotle Act always precedes Potency. The cause of

a potential being coming into existence is always another being already existing in act. In this Aristotle is true both to the spirit of Plato and the dictates of common sense. A possibility of being a man which as yet is actually non-existent cannot, so to speak, lift itself into existence by the scruff of its own as yet only potential neck. There must be a father, in whom the form of man is already actualized, to beget and so start off the process of coming-to-be. The actual of course need not always precede the potential in time. But wherever a potentiality is coming to be actual there is always an actual being existing in full actuality from the beginning of the process which can be recognized as its cause. So behind the world of changing and moving things which we perceive by ours senses there exist eternally one or more pure actualities, with no potentiality in them at all, substantial forms without matter which will never pass away because they have never come to be.

We are here on the threshold of Aristotle's theology; but before we go on to discuss it we must spend a little more time on his philosophy of nature, keeping close to the fundamental theme of changeable reality.

The first topic that suggests itself is Aristotle's analysis of the different kinds of change and movement. The most important distinction which he makes is that between change involving the dissolution of one substantial thing and the coming-into-being of another, which he prefers not to call change at all but rather destruction and generation, and all other kinds of change (including local motion). This distinction is parallel to the distinction of Substance and Accidents, which is not really quite as important, I think, in Aristotelian philosophy as later theological controversies may suggest; it is in fact sometimes rather difficult to decide whether a particular quality or characteristic is part of the essential make-up of a thing, an indispensable element in its definition, an inseparable property or "proprium" of substance, or whether it is an accidental property, which can change, appear or disappear without affecting the substance. Yet a broad commonsense distinction can and must be made between properties essential to a substance and qualities which can vary and be there or not there without affecting the essential nature of the thing they qualify. Platinum-blondeness is fortunately not an essential part of the definition of "woman".

Aristotle, then, makes clear the distinction between substantial transformation (destruction–generation) and change, which does not involve transformation of substance. It should be noted that for Aristotle destruction and generation are an inseparable pair. If one thing comes to be, it is out of the matter of something which has passed away. The sum of nature remains constant and the life of the sublunary world is made up of endless cycles of coming to be and passing away determined ultimately by the movement of the sun in the ecliptic. The other kinds of change which Aristotle recognizes may be roughly summed up as those of quality, quantity, and position. Change of quantity is a specialized kind of motion in space, expansion over a larger space or contraction into a smaller one. Local motion, change of position, like all change is the actualization of a potentiality, the potentiality of being somewhere else. Therefore, like all other actualizations of potentiality it requires a cause already in act. A thing cannot move itself, like Plato's Soul, or be assumed to be in eternal uncaused motion like Democritus's atoms. This is a principle of very great importance in Aristotle's philosophy of nature and theology.

4.   Like Plato, Aristotle is never satisfied to know simply how a thing happens, he wants to know why as well, and is convinced that things in general happen for some purpose. But he is more interested than Plato in the "how" as well as in the "why" of things. And he classifies the "how and why" of things under four heads. These are the famous "Four Causes", the four reasons which explain the fact that a particular thing has come to be, and is this definite thing and not another. They are : (i) the material cause, the matter out of which the thing is made; (ii) the efficient cause, the actually existing being necessary to initiate and some-times to carry through the process of coming into being of a material thing; (iii) the formal cause, the form of the thing which as already explained gives it its definite being, makes it this thing and not another; (iv) the final cause, the end or purpose for which the thing comes into being. Of all of them the "efficient cause", the mover or initiator of the process of change, and perhaps the "final cause", the reason for the thing's existence, are the only ones which correspond at all to what we mean by a cause, and for this reason the translation "four *causes*" is rather misleading. They are rather the four Reasons Why the thing exists and is what it is.

The formal and final causes are generally identified by Aris-totle. This means that the end or purpose for which a thing exists is to realize its form as perfectly as possible, to be as good a specimen of man, horse, tree, table, etc., as conditions will permit. In the case of natural (as distinct from manufactured) objects, too, the efficient cause is in a sense identical with the formal and final. For the principle that generates a plant or animal is normally another individual of the same species— spontaneous generation (*see* p. 98) is a curious exception to this rule—and the form in individuals of the same species, though numerically distinct, is in all other ways identical.

The final cause is in a way the most important and interesting of all for Aristotle, for like Plato he is a thorough-going teleologist and believes that everything exists for an end, and a good end, a principle which he applies vigorously throughout his biology, trying to show the purpose of every organ and distinctive feature of the animals which he studies. For Aristotle, however, unlike Plato, the purposefulness of things is immanent, inside them, though ultimately directed, as we shall see, towards a transcendent end. It is a natural impulse which drives everything to try to realize its form as perfectly as possible, thus imitating the divine perfection, and to take its place in the universal order. But he simply takes this natural inward impulse towards perfection and order for granted, and never seems to see that it must involve a directing intelligence, as well as a final perfection to aim at. In the same way he never tries to explain why the universe is an ordered universe at all. He has rejected Plato's conception of a ruling and ordering Mind as too mythical and has nothing to put in its place except the thoroughly unsatisfactory conception of an unconscious natural drive or tendency towards perfection and order. In this he sinks below the intellectual level of Plato and approaches that of the English nineteenth century. Another weakness of Aristotle's teleology is that he takes over from Plato the conception of "brute fact" or material necessity, the thwarting or limitation of the ordered purpose of the universe by the obstinate and at times refractory material on which it has to work. It is in this way that he explains, for instance, monstrous births. But if matter is according to his own philosophy a purely passive potentiality of becoming and form belongs entirely to the realm of purpose, how can even formed matter show this sort of blind brute refractoriness? The idea of material necessity seems to be in his system a sort of undigested remnant of Platonic cosmology. Aristotle is not a complete determinist, though according to the logic of his system it would seem that he ought to be. He is however very anxious to make room for human free will, and therefore insists that future events are not completely determined, that there is a real undetermined possibility of either of two future alternatives happening, and that there is quite a large class of happenings which are not bound by the strict necessity of cyclic succession (which governs, for example, generation or the movements of the heavenly bodies) and which therefore happen not necessarily but only normally, and are not absolutely certain and fixed. It is within this class of not absolutely determined events that human actions fall.

5. So far everything which we have discussed except the actual doctrine of Substance falls according to Aristotle within the bounds of that division of philosophy called Physics or philosophy of nature. In order to understand more precisely where Aristotle draws the boundary between this and First Philosophy or Theology (Metaphysics) it will be helpful to give a short sketch of the universe as Aristotle conceived it. It is a tidy and compact sort of universe, even more tidy and compact than Plato's, eternal and all-embracing, with nothing outside it, spherical in shape and with no void, no entirely unoccupied space, within or without. It is a hierarchically ordered universe in which every change and movement (with the restrictions noted above) has its cause and purpose, subordinated in its turn to a higher cause and purpose until we come to the highest of all. It is of course like almost all Greek pictures of the universe geocentric, with the spherical earth in the middle, immediately surrounded by the sublunary atmosphere, beyond which comes the largest and most important part of the cosmos, the system of the divine spheres of the heavenly bodies. Aristotle's universe is a stiffened and elaborated version of Plato's visible universe, very much affected as regards the spheres of the stars by the latest astronomical theories and calculations worked out by Eudoxus and Aristotle's own friend Callippus.

The central region inside the sphere of the moon, which includes the earth, is the region of change and decay, of the coming-to-be and passing-away of individual substances. That which is eternal and unchanging in it is the persistence of the species, of which there are a fixed and limited number. All things in it are made of the four elements, the first forms received by primal matter, earth, water, fire and air, which have each their natural motion in a straight line, the first two downwards to the centre, the second two upward to the circumference. It is the eccentric movement of the sun in the ecliptic which prevents them from ever separating out completely into their natural places and so making the existence of individual substances impossible. This oblique motion of the sun, which brings it in regular succession nearer to and further from the earth, is the ultimate efficient cause of all coming-to-be and passing-away of individual substances by the increase and decrease of heat which it causes, for heat to Aristotle is the most essential factor in generation. The sun then is the highest cause in the ordered hierarchy of causes operating to produce the endless succession of generation and destruction of individuals which makes up the life of the sublunary world. But it is very far from being the highest cause in the universe. The cause of its motion is the tremendous machinery of the celestial spheres.

To give anything like a complete account of this would be impossible within the scope of this book, but something must be said about it if we are to understand the picture of the universe which was in most men's minds from the time of Aristotle until well after the time of Copernicus. For Aristotle, as for Plato, the sphere is the most perfect of figures and the rotation of a sphere the most perfect of motions, since it is self-contained and not directed to a goal outside itself like motion in a straight line. For him, therefore, as well as for Plato, the universe is a sphere in which the heavenly bodies rotate. The system of the celestial spheres, however, does not derive from Plato directly but from the observations of the great contemporary astronomers Eudoxus and Callippus. These, by a most brilliant piece of mathematical ingenuity, had succeeded in expressing the observed and apparently irregular motions of the sun, moon and planets as compound motions made up of the regular rotations of series of concentric spheres, rotating at different speeds and in different directions, each with its poles fixed in the surface of the larger one immediately outside it. On the basis of these calculations Aristotle built up a most elaborate mechanical explanation of the observed movements of all the heavenly bodies, which supposes them to be carried round by a nest of concentric spheres in contact, moving in different directions and at varying speeds. These spheres are material, made of a mysterious, translucent, bright, incorruptible substance, capable of no change (in our sense) or growth, but only of rotatory motion, the Aether, Quintessence or Fifth Element. They have to be in contact because there is no void in Aristotle's universe and also in order that they may impart motion to each other, for Aristotle holds that motion can be transmitted only by contact between the mover and that which is moved. In order to give a satisfactory mechanical explanation of the observed movements in accordance with these ideas, Aristotle finds it necessary to suppose the existence of fifty-five æthereal spheres. The smallest and innermost is the last sphere of the system of the moon, which encloses our atmosphere. The largest and outermost, whose motion supplies the main driving-force to the whole of the rest of the cosmic machine, is the sphere of the fixed stars, the Primum Mobile of mediæval astronomy. All the inner spheres are required to explain the apparently irregular motions of planets, sun and moon (Plato had already protested indignantly that it was an insult to those divine and celestial beings, the planets, to suppose that their movements were really as disorderly as they looked and as their name of *planets*, "wanderers", implied).

We have then in Aristotle's universe an inner world of change and succession of individual things, of coming-to-be and passing-away in an endless circular process allowing for individual variations within a fixed framework of causality; the causes are arranged in hierarchical order, culminating in the eternal movement of the sun in the ecliptic which co-operates with all other causes of generation and destruction ("Man begets man, but so does the sun"). Through this motion of the sun the relatively small inner world of generation and destruction is linked to the far vaster region of the Spheres beyond the moon, which are eternal and indestructible, and in which there is no coming-to-be and passing-away but only perpetual motion in a circle. Both regions, outer and inner, fall within the scope of Philosophy of Nature; Aristotle defines Nature as a principle of movement or change within things themselves, and all things which are actuated by such an immanent (though not self-caused) principle of movement or change are to be studied by Philosophy of Nature or Physics. It is only when we ask: is there some more ultimate principle of movement or change? What is it that makes the spheres go round? that we pass on to Theology or First Philosophy.

IX

Aristotle (3). Theology and Psychology

1. The subject of First Philosophy, Theology, or as we call it Metaphysics, is reality or being as such. The primary kind of reality, that on which all others depend and which shows most fully the nature of being is, of course, Substance. It is therefore Substance which Metaphysics studies, and in acquiring a proper and complete knowledge of Substance it necessarily acquires a knowledge also of those less perfect forms of reality which cannot exist except in dependence upon Substance. It therefore is the business of Metaphysics to give an account of the distinction between Substance and Accidents, Form and Matter, Actuality and Potency, and to explain the precise meaning of these terms. Furthermore there are different grades of Substance. Besides the separate substantial individual beings which are subject to change, with which we have been mainly concerned in the last chapter and which are studied by Philosophy of Nature, there are, Aristotle says, separate substances which are free from change, pure actualities with no potency in them at all. These are the highest class of substantial being, the most completely real things that exist. It is therefore on them that Metaphysics concentrates, because by studying being at its most perfect and complete it obtains the fullest possible knowledge of being as such. It is therefore First Philosophy because it studies the primary forms of being and Theology because these primary beings are divine.

2. How does Aristotle demonstrate that unmoved and unchanging substantial reality exists? Like all pagan Greek philosophers of the central tradition he believes most firmly in the everlastingness of the universe. He has no conception of eternity (in the Christian sense) and therefore holds that time must be everlasting, as otherwise there would be a time before time was and a time after it ceased, which is contradictory and absurd. But if time, then change, for time is only the "number" or measure of change. Now the only kind of absolutely continuous change, the only kind therefore which can be everlasting, is circular motion (motion being change of place). Therefore the circular motion of the spheres must be everlasting, without beginning or

end. But motion is the actualization of a potency, and requires something already actual to produce it; and the something actual which produces the ultimate circular motion must be itself pure actuality, eternal, without movement or change, that is without potency, or we shall require a further actuality to actuate it and so on; we shall go back in an infinite regress, and there will be no real causation at all because there will be no First Cause. So the first everlasting circular motion must be produced by the ever-lasting actuation of its potency by an Unmoved Mover, an eternal substance, purely actual, with no possibility of change or motion. This Unmoved Mover must be purely immaterial, since matter is potency. It must be capable of causing motion (which Plato's Forms, Aristotle says, were not); and it must ceaselessly exercise this power. It is a very important principle of Aristotle's philosophy that there are two stages of actuality, the first in which a thing possesses all its powers in full development but is not necessarily exercising them (like a man when he is asleep), and the second when it not only possesses the powers but is exercising them to the full (like the same man awake and going about his business). The Unmoved Mover must be necessarily and ever-lastingly in act in this second and fuller sense if it is to be the necessary cause of a continuous everlasting motion.

It is clear that this eternal, fully actual, everlastingly active, unchanging, immaterial object can only be one kind of thing, a Mind. Mind fulfils all the conditions and is in any case the only kind of immaterial substance left in Aristotle's system after the rejection of the Platonic Forms. But it must be a self-sufficient Mind, for if it needed any external object to be the object of its thought, it would have in it an element of incompleteness, of potentiality. Its thought must be intuitive, immanent, directed entirely to an object within itself. In fact, as it is pure Mind entirely active in a ceaseless single activity of thought, the only object which it can have is its own thinking. Its thought, then, is an eternal "thinking upon thinking". It would seem to be Aristotle's final conclusion that the Divine Mind has no knowledge of anything outside itself.

How, then, does this remote and self-contained being act as the universal first cause of motion? Not by any action on its part, for this would detract from its perfect self-sufficiency. There is, therefore, according to Aristotle, only one way in which it can cause motion, and that is by being an object of love or desire:

The first heaven, the sphere of the fixed stars, which seems to be thought of as itself alive and intelligent, desires the absolute perfection of the Unmoved Mover and by reason of its desire imitates that perfection as best it can by moving everlastingly with the most perfect of all motions, that in a circle. And in so far as all movements and changes in the universe depend on this first movement, they are all ultimately caused by the desire inspired by the pure and perfect actuality of the Unmoved Mover, the Divine Mind or God; and it can be said in a sense that the striving towards the most perfect possible actuality, the most complete realization of form, which is for Aristotle the principle of all activity and actualization everywhere in the universe, is the expression of this desire for the perfection of God; though we should beware of misinterpreting this statement of Aristotle's doctrine in terms of later Christian thought.

But can all the movements of the spheres be thought of as simply depending upon, and being caused by the simple east-to-west rotation of the first and outermost, the sphere of the fixed stars? If so, then one Unmoved Mover will be sufficient, and the universe will appear at once as Aristotle wanted to present it, as a single integrated system of causation. Aristotle's consideration of the astronomical facts as he understood them, however, finally led him to the conclusion that the movements of the spheres required to explain the distinctive motions of the sun, moon and planets could not be regarded as being derived from the motion of the first heaven because some of these spheres were rotating in different directions. Therefore, he was driven to postulate fifty-five Unmoved Movers instead of only one, to cause those motions of the inner spheres which could not be regarded as being transmitted to them by the first heaven. We have no clue at all as to how Aristotle regarded these other Unmoved Movers (the "Intelligences" of the Middle Ages) as being related to the First Mover. The chapter of Book L of the Metaphysics in which he speaks of them (Metaphysics 1073a 26–61) was written very late in his life, and perhaps he never completed his theory. I think, however, that it is on the whole most likely that he meant to maintain his view of the universe as a single ordered hierarchy of causes culminating in the First Mover, which is a most essential part of his thought. We must therefore assume that he would have brought these other Unmoved Movers, or "Intelligences" into some sort of subordinate relation to the First, which would have remained the supreme ruling principle of the whole and the highest perfection of being. The introduction of the multiplicity of Unmoved Movers and the disorder into which (left as it is) it throws the whole of Aristotle's system, shows vividly the rigorous honesty of his thought and the care which he takes to keep close to the observed facts and the best available scientific explanation of them. It also shows clearly how very closely Aristotle's theology is bound up with his views about the nature of the material universe, and especially with his astronomy.

3. Even without taking into account the multiplicity of Unmoved Movers, Aristotle's conception of God must seem to us highly unsatisfactory and inadequate. This Eternal Mind enclosed in a sterile self-sufficiency, everlastingly contemplating its own thinking, neither knowing nor willing the universe and only affecting it through the ceaseless rotation which desire for its unattainable perfection inspires in the First Heaven, is not at all like anything we mean by the word "God". It is simply the logical culmination of the hierarchy of substances and the ultimate explanation of motion and change. But it is not a person or power exercising providence, ordering all things by its will. Still less is it a Creator or the inexpressible Absolute. Aristotle's thought is not really God-centred, but Cosmos-centred. It is the everlasting universe which is for him the Whole, the sum of being, the ultimate Reality. The First Mover or God is a part of that whole, not Absolute Being but the Supreme Being.

It is here that the great difference lies between the metaphysics of Aristotle and the natural theology of St. Thomas. It is important, I think, to make it clear, for it is impossible to understand either philosophy rightly if we think of Aristotle entirely in terms of Thomism or make St. Thomas into a mere Aristotelian. Aristotle's "cosmocentric" outlook, which makes God a part of the everlasting universal order is as characteristically Greek as St. Thomas's doctrine of the Analogy of Being, the foundation of his whole philosophy, is characteristically Christian In the light of the Christian doctrine of Creation, and with much help from that late Platonic philosophy which claimed to have reconciled Plato and Aristotle and which was transmitted to the Christian thinkers of the West chiefly through St. Augustine, St. Thomas used the great basic Aristotelian idea of Act and Potency to demonstrate the existence of a God who is not merely the most perfect of substances and fully self-sufficient but is

Absolute Being, infinite in all His perfections, knowing all things in His single and simple act of complete self-knowledge which necessarily comprehends knowledge of all His effects, on Whose free will all things depend absolutely for their being, so that the cosmos only exists at all by reason of His continual, most intimate, actuating presence. All this is very far indeed from the original philosophy of Aristotle. Traditional Thomists (though not all Catholic philosophers) maintain that the existence of God as understood by St. Thomas can be demonstrated by essentially Aristotelian arguments from Aristotle's fundamental conceptions. But in order to do so, or even to want to do so, a complete change of viewpoint is necessary. It will be part of the business of this history to show how this change came about.

4. Besides the First Unmoved Mover and the "Intelligences" Aristotle recognizes at least one other immaterial thinking substance capable of existing separately. This is the "separable reason", the highest power in the human soul. Aristotle's psychology is in a way parallel to his cosmology. It shows man, the microcosm, as an ordered unity at the summit of whose structure stands a transcendent intellectual principle; the microcosm, the universe, is as we have seen conceived in the same way. The relation between the "separable reason" and the rest of the human soul is however different and closer than that of the First Mover to the universe. It will be as well before discussing it to consider Aristotle's doctrine of the soul in the order in which he considers it in his great treatise "De Anima", starting at the bottom and not at the top, with the lowest forms of life and not with the human reason. There is perhaps no part of Aristotle's philosophy which is more valuable or has had a greater effect on later thought than his psychology, and it is founded on some particularly interesting and important applications of the great foundation-principle of Act and Potency.

What Aristotle means by soul is the form, the principle of life and being, in living things. It is thus intimately united with the body. Aristotle definitely rejects Plato's conception of the soul as a separate being designed for disembodied existence but compelled to take a series of lodgings, always more or less unsuitable, in a succession of different bodies with none of which it has any real, essential bond of unity. His definition of soul is "the first actuality of a natural body potentially having life; that is, organic". (De Anima 412a 27.) The soul is the actuality which realizes the potentiality of a body capable of having life; it is the formative principle which makes a living body a living body. It is the first actuality (for the distinction of first and second actuality, *see* p. 88), because a living body obviously remains actually living when it is asleep or inert, not exercising its functions to the full. Aristotle expresses the closeness of the relation of soul and body rather strangely by saying "If the eye was an animal, its sight would be its soul" (412b). It is the power of sight which makes the eye a real and actual eye; without it, in Aristotle's view the body, the material structure, of the eye would not really be an eye at all, any more than the carved or painted imitation eye of a statue. In the same way it is the soul which makes the potential living body the actual living body. A human or animal corpse, though it may keep the human or animal appearance for a time, is not really a man or an animal at all but only dead matter without the life-giving form which actualized its potentialities and made it thereby truly man or animal. This doctrine of the soul as form of the body and the way in which Aristotle explains it makes very clear the absence of all materialism in his conception of form. The form of a material body is itself necessarily immaterial.

A natural body which is potentially living must be organic; that is, it must have the necessary "organa" or instrumental parts for the performance of its life-functions. Aristotle's minimum definition of life, life reduced to its simplest terms, is the ability to take nourishment and to increase and decrease by the living thing's own power, not as the result of mechanical action from outside. This minimum life, the power of absorbing nourishment and growing, is found in plants. Plants therefore have the simplest sort of soul or life-principle. The next stage in the hierarchy of living beings is formed by those living things which possess as well as the powers of growth and nutrition that of sensation and the consequent powers of desire and of moving in order to satisfy their desires. These form the class of animals, as distinguished from plants on the one hand and human beings on the other. These last form the highest rank in the hierarchy of living beings or ensouled bodies because they possess reason. The three great powers of the soul-in-the-body, the living being, which correspond to these three classes of plants, animals, and men, are the powers of nutrition (on which growth depends) of sensation (on which desire and movement depend) and of thought (which in a rational being should govern and direct the use of the other powers). We should note that each of the two higher classes possesses all the powers of the class below it. An animal is all that a plant is, and more: a man is all that an animal is, and more. We should also note that in every case we are dealing with a unity. It is not the soul by itself or the body by itself, or a separate and distinct lower or higher soul, which has any of these powers. It is the ensouled living body, the concrete substantial entity of which the body is the matter and the soul the form; and matter and form here as elsewhere cannot exist separately. They are two aspects of one thing, only separable in thought. There can therefore for Aristotle be no disembodied immortality, no life for the soul after the death of the living creature of which it is the form and actuality (though he makes an exception, as we shall see, for the highest part of the human soul, the "separable reason").

5. In Aristotle's account of sensation we see the same principle of Act and Potency at work which we have already observed in his account of the relations of soul and body. There was an old debate, it will be remembered, among the Pre-Socratics (cf. Ch. II, p. 25) about whether we know "like by like" or "unlike by unlike". Aristotle holds that both sides, in a sense, were right. The sense-organ, eye or ear or whichever it may be, is actually unlike the object of perception, but it is potentially like it and becomes actually like it by acting as matter to its form, receiving the form of the perceived object into itself and having its potentiality of perceiving actualized by it. The object perceived by a particular sense-organ is of course not another concrete substance as a whole but the particular sort of accidental form which it is the business of that organ to perceive, colour for the eye, sound for the ear, etc. Thus the eye perceives the colour "white" by receiving the form "white" which actualizes a particular potentiality in it and makes it white for the moment of perception. The organ acts as matter to the perceived form. Of course each organ has only a limited range of potentialities which can be actualized in this way, and any sense-object falling outside the range either passes unperceived or destroys the organ. Too soft a sound passes unheard; too loud a sound destroys the organ of hearing. It should be noticed, in view of later controversies, that for Aristotle sense-qualities in their actual reality belong to the sentient

subject. The object which causes the sensation only has the sense-quality potentially.

Aristotle's account of the workings of the particular sense, organs is full and complicated and involves a great deal of curious and often impossible physics and physiology. There is unfortunately no space for it here. An important and valuable point is that he regards touch as the basic and most primitive sense, which is diffused over the whole body and not confined to a particular organ; the other senses may be regarded as highly specialized forms of the sense of touch. But the important thing to grasp and realize fully about Aristotle's doctrine of sensation is its basic principle. This is that the concrete living substance, the body-soul unity, only comes into conscious contact with the world of other substances, or even with the sense-data by which it knows them, through the actualization of certain potentialities in itself, through acting as matter to forms coming into it from outside. The organ perceives by becoming what it perceives and, as we shall see, the mind knows by becoming what it knows.

6.   But we cannot jump straight from the perception by particular sense-organs of accidental forms to knowledge and judgment and the formation of concepts by the mind. There are in Aristotle's psychology two very important intervening stages. (Of course Aristotle realizes as clearly as his modern readers that the whole of his lengthy exposition is the necessarily complex analysing-out of the elements in a process of perceiving-and-knowing which seems to us as we continually do it almost instantaneous and quite simple—till we begin to try and think how it is done). The first falls entirely still within the region of sense-perception. It is the activity of the "common" or universal sense. This is simply the faculty of sense-perception acting in an unspecialized way, and not another sense over and above the five (touch, sight, hearing, smell and taste). There are certain kinds of perception which cannot be attributed to any one of the five senses separately or exclusively, but which are present in every act of sense-perception and, Aristotle thinks, undoubtedly belong to the realm of sensation. These are, first the perception of the "common sensibles". Every object we perceive is perceived as having size, shape, duration, either rest or movement, and either unity or number; yet we do not perceive these by any of the special senses. Then there is the perception of the "incidental sensibles". We see something white, and perceive that it is an object having some other quality which

we have perceived before through another sense (e.g., sweetness, in the case of a lump of sugar) or that it is a substance we know, e.g., a friend. It seems obvious to us that memory and association come in here, but Aristotle does not say so. It is by the "common sense" too that we perceive, are sensible of having a sensation; and, finally, that we discriminate between the objects of two senses, which neither sense acting alone, nor yet both acting separately, can do.

The link between sense-perception and intellect is provided by the "image-making" faculty. This sometimes seems to take over many of the functions of the "common sense", and the boundary between them is not very clear. Its particular work, however, is thought of in a more active way than that of sensation, and forms the next stage in that "movement of the soul through the body" which starts with sense-perception. What it does is to form images or mind-pictures (what Aristotle and the Scholastics called "phantasmata") of the appearances revealed to us by the senses. They are reproductions of the picture presented by the whole complex occurrence of sensation, by the action of both common and specialized senses; but images differ from sensations in being entirely in the mind, in lasting after the sensed object has passed out of the ken of the sense-organs and sensation has therefore ceased, and in being less vivid and less trustworthy as guides to objective fact. Error for Aristotle can begin as soon as we get beyond particular sensations. These are infallible, in the sense that we can be quite certain that we are having a particular sensation while we are actually having it. But we can be wrong about the common sensibles (e.g., perceiving a thing as moving when it is at rest) or the incidental sensibles (perceiving the white thing as sweet when it is not), and in the process of making images of the things sensed there are most varied possibilities of error (which for Aristotle as for Plato is always wrong combination of existing elements, never thinking the absolutely non-existent, which is impossible).

Images are not of course thoughts or concepts, but they are the raw material of thought, which is impossible without them. They are the content of memory, a memory-image being distinguished by being apprehended as an image of something past. Aristotle gives an account of recollection (the deliberate re-actualizing of a memory-image which has become merely potential, that is, been forgotten) by means of chains of association which is interesting and true to experience. Images are also what we perceive in dreams.

7. Thought, the highest activity of the most complete type of en-souled being, is reception of intelligible form as sensation is of sensible form. It is the actualization of a potency. The mind becomes what it thinks. That is, when we think of a thing what happens is that the form of the thing entirely abstracted from its matter (and we must always remember the absolute immateriality of the form of a material substance in abstraction) enters our minds and actualizes the potency of thinking that thing, so that the form becomes actually present and existent in our minds. Our thought, therefore, would seem to have no positive character of its own, but to be a mere passive potency waiting to be actualized by any forms which enter it through the complex process of perception just described. This is not, however, Aristotle's complete account of our thinking. To understand fully how he really believes that our minds work we must consider the objects of our thought a little more carefully. They are concepts, and a concept is essentially something abstract. It is an intelligible form thought by itself, in separation from its matter; this division of form from matter can, as we know, never come about in the external world. It is a purely mental analysis, a division or separation made by and in the mind. This is what is meant by "abstraction". On the foundation of the concepts which are formed by this analytic act of abstraction, all our thinking is built up. We can think of single concepts in isolation ("man", "fat", "moving"); or we can build them up into judgments, statements involving a combination of concepts ("this fat man is moving") and we can link judgments together into syllogistic arguments according to the rules of logic, and so arrive at new truth—or error. As in the case of sensation, as soon as the combination of simple elements begins, that is with the judgment, there is a possibility of combining them wrongly and so falling into error. It is clear that the basic process of forming concepts involves some sort of very definite activity on the part of the mind, and not merely a passive receptivity of form. The image-making faculty presents the thinking mind not with ready-made concepts but with mind-pictures, reproductions (sometimes a little blurred and vague) of the individual concrete substances and their accidents perceived by the faculty of sense. In these the mind has to find the intelligible form in order that this form may

actualize its potentialities of thought. We must, therefore, Aristotle says, if we are to think at all, have within us an active principle as well as the passive reason. The passive reason is all things potentially. It has no definite character of its own to start with (other than that of being a mind, of course) or it would not be able to reproduce accurately the forms which enter it. It is "pure and unmixed". But if the passive reason is pure potentiality, then on the principle that Act always precedes Potency some actually existing and active power is required to illuminate and actualize the forms potentially existing in the mind. The external sense-perceptions are not sufficient cause because they do not give intelligible forms but only the raw material of sensations producing mind-pictures in which the forms can be found.

Aristotle's description of this power, the Separable (or as later writers call it the Active) Reason, is short and remarkably obscure. Like Plato's Idea of the Good, its activity in causing knowledge is compared to that of light. It makes the forms actual by illuminating them, as light makes colours actual. It is always in act, without potency, and so unchanging, everlasting and able to exist apart from the body. In fact, it is one of that class of separate substances, all of which are intellects, the other members being the First Mover and the "Intelligences", which make up the highest order of beings in Aristotle's universe. There is no reason to suppose that he identified it with his God (the First Mover), as the greatest of his Greek commentators, Alexander of Aphrodisias, and many others have supposed. Nor does Aristotle tell us whether there is only one Separable Reason common to all men or one for each individual. In any case, its survival of the body does not and cannot involve a real personal immortality. For, as Aristotle reminds us, the passive reason does not survive the death of the body, and without it there can be no thinking about anything, no continuance of our personal intellectual life.

8. A very important part of Aristotle's psychology, though it does not play a prominent part in the "De Anima", is his doctrine of the material vehicle through which soul operates on and communicates with body. This is what Aristotle calls "*pneuma*". The essential characteristic of this substance is generative and life-giving heat. It is described as "hot air", but it is not simply ordinary air heated, for it is, or at least contains something, analogous to "*æther*", the Fifth Element of the heavenly regions.

Pneuma is the active material principle which under the influence of the movement of desire in the soul produces bodily movement by bringing about the necessary qualitative changes in the parts of the body affected. It is present in the sense-organs and the channels and veins connecting them with the heart and is the material vehicle through which sense-perceptions reach the soul (the heart being the seat of sense-consciousness). *Pneuma* is also present in the seed, and is the indispensable active material principle of generation (the passive principle being moisture). In fact it is by the presence of *pneuma*, e.g., in sea-water, with its "soul-heat" which gives it power to generate soul at least up to the sensitive level, that Aristotle explains the spontaneous generation of Testacea and other lower forms of living being, in which he believes. Besides *pneuma* there is another substance in the sublunary world analogous to *æther*. This is the substance in transparent media (Air, water, etc.) which makes them transparent and whose actuality is light, the indispensable means of vision; so that this substance too plays its part as an intermediary between body and soul in a most important form of sense-perception. We have then in Aristotle's universe a special group of material substances, *Aether*, *Pneuma* and the principle of transparency and light, all hot or bright, all active, and not subject to qualitative change, whose function is to act as vehicles and intermediaries through which the immaterial communicates with and acts on all other material things. Thus the Unmoved Mover (or Movers) acts on everything else through setting in motion the heavens made of *æther* and soul acts on and communicates with body through *pneuma*. This idea is of great historical importance. It derives from Pre-Socratic thought and is the immediate source of the Stoic doctrine of *pneuma* which we shall discuss later and one of the ultimate sources of the ideas of fire or light as the active, formative material principle which are to be found in Plotinus and persist into mediæval philosophy.

X
Aristotle (4). *Ethics and Politics*

1. OF the practical sciences which regulate conduct the chief, according to Aristotle, to which all the others are subordinate is Politics, the science which governs the complete human life of men living together in a self-sufficient community, a City or State. Of this science Ethics, which deals with individual character and behaviour, is in theory only a subordinate part. Aristotle treats it, however, on a large scale and with considerable independence. In fact at the end of his most important ethical treatise, the Nicomachean Ethics, he seems to suggest that the perfection of individual character is the end to which community life and lawmaking are the means (Eth. Nic. 1179 a. 33 ff.); though of course there as elsewhere he holds that the good life for the individual can only be realized in and through the community. For us at any rate the ethical teaching of Aristotle is more important than the political. It has been more widely and continuously studied down to our own time, as something valuable in itself, than the Politics, which I think is mostly read nowadays as a document of historical interest. The reason for this lies in the twofold nature of Aristotle's ethical and political teaching. We have sometimes the most penetrating discussion of universal principles which it is still necessary to take very seriously in any discussion on ethics: and sometimes the exposition of a prosperous Greek citizen's philosophy of living at its most narrow-minded and complacent, dominated and limited by the prejudices of his class, civilization and period. It is this latter element which leads Bréhier to describe Aristotle's morality, unkindly but not altogether untruly, as "the morality of a middle-class lady in comfortable circumstances who is determined to make the best use of her social advantages". Both elements are present throughout Aristotle's ethical and political writings. But in the Politics the narrow-minded Greek citizen's outlook affects Aristotle's thought much more than in the ethical treatises, and the work is therefore of less universal and permanent value in spite of the wisdom and importance of many things in it. I shall then in this necessarily brief and inadequate survey concentrate most attention on Aristotle's teaching about individual morality as expressed in the most mature, widely read and influential of his ethical treatises, the Nicomachean Ethics. I am very conscious

of having throughout my study of Aristotle neglected the most
interesting and important topic of the development of his thought;
but it is his mature thought which has influenced later (especially
scholastic) thinkers, and I have therefore thought it best to
concentrate on presenting it as well as I can.

Aristotle is clearly aware that the subject-matter of ethics
differs from that of the other sciences. Ethics is not an exact
science like mathematics; the subject-matter will not permit the
complete accuracy which other sciences attain through rigorous
demonstration from easily apprehended first principles. Sometimes Aristotle explains that this is because ethics is concerned
with things which are not absolutely necessary and determined,
but are only "for the most part so" and "capable of being otherwise". In other places he points out that ethics reasons not from
but to first principles. We start not from universal moral laws
but from the generally held and rather confused ideas of moral
goodness which are implicit in the behaviour of decent people
who have been well brought up. Aristotle is just as insistent as
Plato on the importance of what we call "character training"
as an indispensable preliminary to that philosophical study of
ethics which will issue in a true virtue founded on reason. But
unlike Plato he attaches a good deal more importance to the
admittedly not very clear ideas of morality held by the average
decent Greek. From these he starts his enquiry and progresses
towards those universal principles, clear and intelligible in themselves but not immediately obvious, which are the real foundations
of the science of ethics.

2.   Aristotle's ethics, like the rest of his philosophy is teleological,
concerned with end or purpose. His primary object is to find
out what man, as man, is for, what is the particular work or
function for which he is intended by nature. This way of looking
at the purpose of man in terms of work or function is very Socratic.
Socrates liked craftsmen because they had a purpose in their
work and knew what they were doing. The carpenter understood
his function as carpenter: but no man, it seemed to Socrates,
understood his function as man. It was this which concerned
him so gravely and set him off on that course of inquiry into the
nature and principles of the good life which Plato continued
in one way and later on Aristotle in quite a different one. Like
Socrates, Aristotle is very fond, throughout his philosophical
writings, and nowhere more than in the ethical treatises, of

making comparisons with the crafts and the work of craftsmen to illustrate or confirm the points he wants to make.

Aristotle assumes that there is only one final end of man, one ultimate end or good at which he should naturally aim. This seems a reasonable enough assumption to traditionalist thinkers, but Aristotle never proves it satisfactorily and never succeeds completely in relating the whole of moral life to the end which he proposes (the highest human activity, theoria or intellectual contemplation). In his treatment of the individual virtues he repeatedly seems to be regarding the goodness of the virtuous act as an end sufficient in itself, and not to be making particular virtuous activities means to an end beyond themselves, as his belief in the single end of man really demands. He assumes the idea of a single end without question because he always thinks in terms of unified wholes or systems. Man's moral life should form an ordered whole directed to a single end just as the universe forms an ordered system directed to a single end; and the ordering of moral life corresponds, as we shall see, to the pattern of the ordered unity of the human soul. It seems likely that his failure to show satisfactorily the unity of the moral life is due to a certain narrowness and inadequacy in his account of its final end, which I shall discuss later.

In his endeavour to determine the final end of human activity Aristotle starts, as he holds is right in ethical discussions, from the general opinion. Now all men aim, he says, at "eudæmonia", a word which may perhaps best be translated "wellbeing" (it is wider than our modern use of "happiness" which generally signifies a state of feeling, whereas "eudæmonia" is a state of complete general satisfactoriness; the "eudæmon" not only feels happy, but all is really well with him). It remains then to define in what well-being consists. The popular identifications of it with pleasure, honour, or wealth are soon seen to be inadequate. In accordance with the Socratic principle of work or function and Aristotle's own doctrine of first and second actuality, it appears that it must be an activity, not just a state or habit, and the activity proper and peculiar to man, the activity, that is, of his highest part or faculty, that which he does not share with animals and plants. It is then an activity of the soul and of its highest or rational part. It is "an activity of the soul in accordance with reason". It is the full actualization in activity of the rational nature of man. This activity must furthermore be in accordance with virtue, and if there is more than one virtue, with the best and most perfect of them. This is an obvious statement in Greek, because the word "arete" which we translate "virtue" means simply being good at something. The "arete" of a craftsman, as such, is to be a good craftsman. The "arete" of a liar is to be a really efficient and successful liar (like Homer's Odysseus). Aristotle, however, defines the "arete" of the soul a good deal more precisely and makes it mean something much closer to what we mean by "virtue". Before proceeding to this definition, Aristotle points out that this activity of the soul according to virtue must be manifested in a complete life, not only in short periods, if it is really to be well-being, and that his definition of well-being retains all the truth which there was in the inadequate definitions of the common man and of earlier thinkers (a claim which Aristotle often makes and which gives him particular satisfaction, as he is far too sensible to think of himself as the one wise man in a world of fools). Thus the activity of the soul (the rational soul) in accordance with virtue, though it is not virtue (as some said well-being was) springs necessarily from virtue. It is necessarily accompanied by the best and most lasting and certain sort of pleasure; and it normally needs external goods for its exercise. A man, Aristotle says, who is to exercise the activity of the soul in accordance with virtue fully needs a moderate amount of wealth, good birth, health, good personal appearance and a satisfactory family life (here we can see very clearly the "bourgeoise" element in his ethics of which Bréhier speaks). Yet he is careful to add that goodness "shines through" great misfortunes and the loss of all these external goods, if misfortunes and loss are well and nobly endured.

3.   Aristotle's definition of virtue is as follows "Virtue is a state (or disposition, *hexis*, the Scholastic *habitus*) relating to choice, being in a mean relatively to us, which is determined by a rule, and as a man of good sense would determine it" (Eth. Nic. 1106 a 14). This requires a good deal of explanation. First of all, "virtue is a state"; not an emotion or a potentiality but a settled disposition of character, acquired gradually by persistence in the practice of morally good actions. We learn virtue, as we learn arts or crafts by practice, by doing the things which are appropriate to the kind of person we want to become. "A state relating to choice"; because it is with moral choice, with choosing morally good courses of action and rejecting bad ones, that virtue is essentiallyconcerned. "Being in a mean relatively to us";

here we encounter that Doctrine of the Mean which is perhaps the best known and often least well understood part of Aristotle's ethics. It is important to notice the phrase "relatively to us." Aristotle distinguishes carefully between the mean "of the thing", the exact mathematical middle point, and the mean "relatively to us," which is simply the right amount or degree for us. This distinction saves his doctrine from being nothing more than an unintelligent importation of quantitative ideas into morality or a glorification of mediocrity, a "Nothing excessive" or "It's safest in the middle". All Aristotle's doctrine of the mean as he explains it need signify is that there is a due and right proportion which should be observed in all our actions. The behaviour of the virtuous man on all occasions will be just right and suitable, neither exceeding nor falling short of what the occasion requires. And this doctrine of the relative mean, as Aristotle states it, would seem to leave room for the possibility that there may be occasions when it is right and proportionate to "go the limit", to take an extreme course of action. It cannot, however, be denied that the quantitative idea of the mean and the feeling that mediocrity, or at least moderation, is best and safest (a very deep-rooted Greek popular doctrine) do affect Aristotle's thought very considerably, and often very much for the worse. In his account of the particular virtues it leads him to represent each virtue as a mean between two vices, one of excess and one of defect, an impossibly artificial classification which forces him to invent vices or to describe as vices what are really psychological states, not moral faults, such as unresponsiveness to the pleasures of sense (though the classification works very well where a quantitative element really does enter in, as where the spending of money is concerned).

The final element in the definition "determined by a rule, and as a man of good sense would determine it" shows what is for Aristotle the final court of appeal in moral matters, the judgment of the *phronimos*, the man of good sense and trained judgment, who possesses the intellectual virtue of practical wisdom, and may be taken as the embodiment of decent educated Greek public opinion at its best. Aristotle, who rejects Plato's universal moral Forms, can find no higher or more absolute moral standard than this; and it may seem to us inadequate enough. Yet if we are Christians we may remember that we too find our ultimate **standard of conduct in a Person, not a system of moral** universals, though our Divine-Human Person (with the Saints who accompany Him and mirror His excellences) is on a very different level for us from Aristotle's "man of good sense." Still, the principle remains, that the standard and touchstone of human goodness can only in the last resort be a human character.

4. There is no space here for a detailed description of Aristotle's discussions of particular virtues and vices. This matters less because it is here above all that the limitations of his morality are most apparent. I have just spoken of the difficulties into which his doctrine of the mean leads him. A particularly good example of Aristotle speaking, not as the universal moral teacher but as the complacent Greek citizen of good social position, may be found in the account of the character who represents his moral ideal and possesses the crown of all virtues, the Great-Souled Man (or Superior Person). He is described in Eth. Nic. 1123a. 34-1125a. 35. and, though he has many good qualities, is chiefly distinguished (for readers influenced by the Christian tradition) by the intolerable degree of pompous self-satisfaction to which he attains. It would be difficult to find even a Roman Stoic or a Platonist of the Empire to equal Aristotle's ideal in spiritual pride and sense of his own value and importance.

There are, however, one or two points in Aristotle's classification and discussion of particular virtues which are worth noting. First of all, the distinction between moral and intellectual virtues. This follows naturally from his definition of well-being as "an activity of the soul according to reason" understood in the light of his own psychology. There is, he says a part or faculty of the soul which plans and reasons and lays down rules for moral action. This is the reason, and its perfections are the intellectual virtues, science, art, practical wisdom (which is the ruling principle of the moral virtues), intuitive reason, and theoretical wisdom (the highest of all, to which all the others are ordained), Then there is another part which, in the good man, follows the plan and obeys the rules of reason. This is the faculty of desire, and it finds its perfection in the moral virtues, Justice, Courage. Temperance and the rest.

A second important point to notice is that Aristotle's method in discussing the particular virtues is the exact opposite of Plato's. Plato regarded all virtue as essentially one and in his account of the particular virtues interpreted them so widely that they almost blend and fuse with each other. Aristotle narrows down the definition of each virtue as much as possible so as to separate them from each other as sharply and clearly as he can. His treatment is, however, not at all systematic. The order of the virtues is just as they occur to his mind and the scale of their treatment varies very much. Justice has a whole book of the Nicomachean Ethics to itself (Book V) and Friendship, which is for Aristotle of the greatest importance, has two (VIII and IX). Other virtues are dealt with much more summarily. The treatment of Justice is interesting and valuable, and has greatly influenced later thought. It is legal justice which is in question rather than "justice" in the wide Platonic sense, and Aristotle distinguishes three kinds, Distributive (which gives each man his proper share of any good available for distribution; we might call it social justice), Remedial (the justice of the law-courts which rights wrongs), and Commercial or Commutative (which governs transactions of exchange).

5. Aristotle, like Plato, has no clear and distinct conception of the will. In his doctrine of deliberate choice, however, he comes very near to it. Deliberate choice is for him as we have seen the essential element in moral activity. He distinguishes it clearly from mere appetite, which has nothing rational or moral about it, and from rational wish, which can be directed to impossibilities; we can wish for the impossible, but we cannot choose it. Choice, he says, must be of things within our own power, and it must follow on a process of deliberate thought. It is an act in which desire and reason are combined, "desireful reasoning or reasoning desire", "desire based on deliberation". This comes very near to later conceptions of the act of will. Aristotle, however, rather unnecessarily narrows the scope of his conception of choice by saying that it is only concerned with means not ends. Ends are rather the object of wish, and, Aristotle seems to think at least while he is discussing choice, are immediately obvious, so that we do not have to deliberate about them (though of course he himself elsewhere in the Ethics, when he is discussing the proper end of human life, is engaged in this very process of deliberating about ends).

Aristotle insists that moral activity, which is not only voluntary, but based on deliberate choice, is free, that virtue and vice are within our own power. He objects, therefore, strongly to Socrates's saying that "no man is willingly bad". He is not, however, very clear or consistent in his account of precisely **how or why we** are free to act well or badly. And when he comes to discuss the case of immoral acts committed by a weak-willed man (the akrates, whom translators in their jargon call the "incontinent" man) he eventually arrives, and admits that he arrives, at a position not so very far removed from what Socrates probably really meant. His line of argument is this. If you are an akolastos, a profligate, all you are concerned about is the satisfaction of your desires. Your mind works like this "Everything which is sweet must be tasted. This is sweet. Therefore this must be tasted." No other consideration is present to your mind. But if you are only weak-willed, you will also have in the back of your mind quite another chain of practical reasoning running like this: "It is wrong to taste certain kinds of things. This is a thing of that kind therefore . . ." But you never arrive at the "therefore" and its consequent right choice and action because the violence of your desire for the thing blinds your knowledge at least of the minor premiss ("this is a thing of the wrong kind") for the moment, and makes it merely potential, not actual, so that you only "know" it in the sense in which a man who is blind drunk may be said to know philosophical poetry by heart. Your knowledge is not conscious or practically useful. Therefore you follow out the "syllogism of desire" ("All that is sweet should be tasted, etc.") to its practical conclusion; and you certainly have not, at the time of your wrong action, that vivid and actual realization of what is right and good which Socrates meant by the "knowledge" which he identified with virtue. This analysis is in itself subtle and valuable. though it by no means covers all cases of weak-willed immorality, and leaves no room for a real moral struggle; but the reality of moral conflict is something which Aristotle often elsewhere admits.

6. In this account of weak-willed immorality pleasure has appeared as the seduction which may produce a desire so violent that it temporarily blinds our perception of right and wrong. Aristotle, however, by no means regards pleasure as necessarily evil. It is an inseparable concomitant of all activity, a thing complete and desirable in itself but which is never found apart from the activity which it in a sense perfects and makes more attractive and satisfactory. There must, therefore, be a hierarchy of pleasures, base and degraded pleasures being those which go with base and degraded activities, and the highest being those which perfect the highest activities and those most truly proper

to man. The highest pleasure of all will be that which accompanies the highest human activity, that of intellectual contemplation. In this according to Aristotle is to be found the summit of human well-being: and we may conclude this survey of his ethical teaching by trying to find out more precisely what he meant by it.

We have seen that well-being must consist in an activity fully exercised, not in a state or habitual disposition. If the being in a particular state without any exercise of activity was enough, then the life of a vegetable or a man who slept all through his life might be the human ideal, a suggestion which Aristotle dismisses contemptuously without further discussion. And the activity in which human well-being consists must be one proper and peculiar to man, therefore rational, and if there are several kinds of rational activity or activity of the mind, as Aristotle has shown that there are, it must be the highest. This is what Aristotle calls theoria, contemplation. In this the intellect, the highest part of man, finds its perfection in the direct knowledge of its proper objects, which are the realities revealed to us by metaphysics, mathematics, and philosophy of nature. This activity, Aristotle says, is most perfect because it is most continuous, can be kept up longest without weariness, and is most self-sufficient, needing nothing in the way of external goods for its exercise (though the Wise Man—the contemplator—will need external goods, in a very moderate degree, in so far as he remains a man, a composite being to whom other activities are necessary). Contemplation brings with it the purest and most exquisite pleasures. In fact, it is a life like that of the gods rather than that of men. But Aristotle remains enough of a Platonist to hold with the utmost strength to the belief that our reason is really something divine, and is capable of living the divine life and contemplating divine things. "We must not" he says, with an extraordinary force and passion "as people advise, think humanly, being human, nor as mortals, being mortal, but as far as may be we must put on the life of the Immortals and do all that we can to live according to what is best in us" (Eth. Nic. 1177a. 12-1178a.8). We can see the same pattern in Aristotle's ethics as in his pictures of the universe and of the soul. In each part of his philosophy there is the closely co-ordinated organic structure of natural, biological, common-sense, this-worldly activity; the perceptible, natural, material universe and man, the composite, his soul inseparably united to his body, very much at home in it. Then suddenly

in each case we find that the structure has towered out of the
commonplace, common-sense, this-worldly atmosphere, and that
its crown and culmination lies in the world of spiritual being,
with the separate substances, the pure Forms or Actualities
which are divine and transcendent Intelligences, with the
Separable Reason, and with the divine life of Contemplation.
It is this unique combination of the Platonic faith in transcendent
spiritual being with a practical scientific medical biologist's
outlook on the world which is, I would suggest, the distinguishing
mark of Aristotelianism and which gives it its peculiar philosophical flavour. It is a synthesis of enormous possibilities, and
also one which holds great dangers, because it depends on the
preservation of such a delicately accurate balance of truths and
values (which Aristotle and later Aristotelians often fail to
maintain).

The whole of moral life is supposed to be ordered to the life
of contemplation as its end, either because the acquisition of the
moral virtues is essential if a man is to be capable of intellectual
contemplation, for he must be free from bad desires and the
disordering and disturbing vices and imperfections of his lower
nature; or because the Wise Man is not a disembodied intellect
but remains a man, a composite being living in the society of
his fellows and therefore continually in need of the moral virtues
for the proper conduct of his life. The reason, I think, why
Aristotle is not more consistent or convincing in his presentation
of contemplation as the end to which the moral virtues are
subordinated is that his conception of contemplation is too
narrowly intellectualist. It is a highly specialized activity of the
philosophical mind which does not seem quite adequate to absorb
and concentrate man's whole being and energy; and it has no
sufficiently universal and all-absorbing object. Here Christian
Aristotelianism, which transforms the whole concept of contemplation by making it the supernatural union of the soul with
God in the Beatific Vision, can supply what is lacking in the
Ethics, and in fact transmutes and puts new life into the whole
system while keeping the essentials of Aristotle's structure.
Aristotle himself in the earlier and more Platonic "Eudemian
Ethics" gives a more adequate object of contemplation and
comes a stage nearer the Christian doctrine than he does in the
tenth book of the Nicomachean which I have been quoting:
for in the last few lines of the Eudemian Ethics he makes the end

of human life not merely contemplation, but the contemplation and service of God; everything that leads towards this is good, everything that hinders it is bad. We must remember the difference between Aristotle's conception of God and the Christian, but even so the statement is impressive, and more satisfying than anything to be found in the later and maturer treatise.

7. Aristotle's political thought moves, as we have already said, entirely within the limits of the political world of the Greek city-states. The basis for his political theories was provided by his great collection of detailed surveys of the constitutions of 158 states, a magnificent example of the methods of work of the Peripatetic school. Aristotle and those whom he trained in philosophy always believed that theories should rest upon as wide as possible a foundation of observed facts. Unfortunately only the first of these surveys of constitutions (the "Constitution of Athens," of which a papyrus manuscript was discovered in Egypt in 1890) has survived, but it is enough to show how valuable the complete collection must have been to students of politics. But perhaps this concentration on, and satisfaction with, the actual state of affairs in that world of the city-states of Hellas which was passing away in Aristotle's own lifetime, a concentration and satisfaction which are necessarily involved in the making of so detailed a survey, may have helped to narrow Aristotle's political outlook.

Since he is thinking throughout in terms of the classical Greek city-state, Aristotle's view of the State is, like Plato's, if not totalitarian, at any rate unitary. As we have seen, Politics is for him the supreme science regulating the good human life, and the State is the supreme community in and through which man attains to physical, moral and intellectual perfection. The man who so transcends humanity by his virtue and wisdom as to be a god or god-like (this possibility is mentioned, but never discussed in both Ethics and Politics) can dispense with the State. But a man who neither rises above mankind into divinity or sinks below it into bestiality needs city-state life for his full development. "It is clear that man is a social animal more than the bee or any other gregarious creature" (Pol. 1253.a.7). The State is by Aristotle's definition a self-sufficient community containing everything necessary for its citizens to live the good life; and the common realization of the good life for all its citizens is the end and object of the State. It is not, Aristotle says, just living together in the same territory or having common defences or rights of trade and intermarriage with each other which makes men citizens of the same State, but this common working for and sharing in the highest good for man.

Aristotle, however, recognizes that even the closely unified and concentrated Greek city-state is and must be a community of communities. He recognizes the necessity of family life and consequently of private property, and criticises Plato rather sharply for his proposals in the "Republic" to abolish property and the family (apparently he does not realize that these proposals were only intended to apply to the small minority who form Plato's ruling class). In Aristotle's account of the family, or rather household, it is a little startling to our ideas to find that the relationship to which he devotes most attention is that of master and slave. His views on this relationship are remarkably humane for his period; and though his doctrine that some Asiatic races are "natural slaves" is horrifying to our ideas of human equality it really limits the scope of slavery severely; for it is in Aristotle's view utterly unjustifiable to enslave anyone who is not a "natural slave"; capture in war does not give, as was generally assumed, the right of enslavement, and Greek may not enslave Greek; and if it could be proved that there were no "natural slaves," no people incapable of a full, free and responsible human life, the justification for slavery would disappear, as it would also in Aristotle's view if we could find any other way of getting servile and mechanical work done than by employing slaves to do it.

Though Aristotle recognizes the right of private ownership of property, he holds that its use should be subjected to social control, and is the originator of the formula "private property, common use" which is generally used by Scholastic and modern Catholic writers on the subject. His views on economics have, I think, more good sense in them than is generally realized. His basic reason for objecting to usury and to all but the most rudimentary forms of commerce (he even goes so far as to disapprove of a monetary economy altogether and to prefer trade by barter) is his realization that commerce and, still more, the making of money by loans at interest, tend to the indefinite and unlimited accumulation of material wealth; whereas the man whose object is to live well will realize that there is a definite limit to his real material needs and that he must observe great

restraint and moderation in his acquisitiveness. We can hardly
quarrel with the principle, though we may consider Aristotle's
application of it too rigid. His beliefs that the indefinite expansion
of wealth (especially monetary wealth) is an evil, and that an
over-developed commerce is undesirable as leading to it, have
been ·accepted by all the great traditional Christian thinkers.
Socratic detachment, Aristotelian moderation, and Cynic asceticism (which I shall discuss later) are the only three attitudes to
material wealth which seem to be permissible within the bounds
of the great common moral and religious traditions of Europe and
the Mediterranean lands.

8.   Citizenship for Aristotle is a full-time occupation. His citizens
must be free to devote their lives to the service of the State,
as soldiers when young, then as members of the legislative
Assembly in which they all take part, and as members of the
juries in the law-courts, and finally when they are advanced
in years and incapable of more active service, as holders of the
State priesthoods. Consequently he holds that full membership
of the State must be confined to the leisured classes. Agricultural
labourers and artisans are to be excluded from citizenship because
their occupations give them no time to fulfil their citizen duties
properly and also because manual labour makes a man
"banausic," a low vulgar person deficient in the virtue necessary
for a citizen. This is perhaps Aristotle's worst surrender to the
prejudices of his class, country and period.

Citizenship then in Aristotle's ideal State, as in all historical
Greek city-states, is confined to a small minority of the population,
more strictly limited than at Athens, a little less strictly than at
Sparta. In other ways too his State follows closely the historical
Greek pattern. He never imagines the possibility of representative
government, which was unknown in the ancient world before
Hellenistic times and uncommon even then. All the citizens
must take a direct and personal share in the business of lawmaking in the Assembly. Aristotle therefore logically enough holds
that the State should be small, though large enough for self-
sufficiency. If direct government by the whole citizen body is
to work satisfactorily, he thinks all its members must know each
other personally, and the Assembly must not be too large for a
single crier to be heard by all when he makes proclamations or
gives out notices.

Aristotle's classification of constitutions is based on the familiar division, monarchy, aristocracy, and democracy. Each has a true form and a perverted form, according to whether the rulers consider the common good of the State or their own interests. Aristotle has, however, a number of different cross-classifications, by the position accorded to wealth, by the principle on which office is awarded, and by the relative power of those performing different functions in the State, which help to make his discussion of the different types of constitution less abstract and to keep it close to contemporary reality. The kind of constitution which he thinks will work best in the circumstances of his time is what he calls "polity" (politeia, the general word for "constitution" in Greek, so perhaps *the* constitution *par excellence*). This is a "mixed" constitution, combining some of the features of democracy and of oligarchy, and its great virtue in Aristotle's eyes is that it keeps power in the hands of the most stable and solid element in the community, the "middle class," land-owners with small estates and moderately well-to-do. It is interesting to notice that both the English and American democracies, at the time when they took their distinctive forms in the eighteenth century, had a strong likeness to Aristotle's "polity".

Aristotle, like Plato, attaches the greatest possible importance to education. It is by means of education, more than in any other way, that the State fulfils its proper function of making men good; for since to Aristotle, as to all the thinkers of the ancient pagan world, the City is the supreme spiritual community, fulfilling the functions of Church as well as State, its control over education must be absolute and complete. All citizens belong to the State and the State must care for each of its parts; and the existence and well-being of the State depends on the quality of the education of its citizens. It is an education which begins at birth or even before (Aristotle is interested in eugenics) and which trains the whole man, body, passions and reason. Its end is predominantly moral, to produce the perfect character of the good citizen, good both as ruler and subject, who is for him the highest type of man we can normally expect to meet.

9.   It would be absurd to try to summarize Aristotle's contribution to philosophy. Perhaps no other man has made such serious additions to so many branches of knowledge by his own single effort. In every part of philosophy his thought is still a living force. Sometimes it has penetrated so deeply into our inherited ways of thinking that Aristotelianism seems to the ordinary man

the merest common-sense and we can only think in an un-Aristotelian way by a deliberate, conscious effort. To traditional Christian philosophy he has made a double contribution, through the large Aristotelian element in that later Platonism which so deeply influenced the first Christian thinkers, and through the study and use of his philosophy by S. Thomas. His influence on Greek thought after his own time was patchy. By a curious chance his later fully original works, with which we have in this survey been entirely concerned, went out of circulation so completely soon after his death that their very existence was almost forgotten; and they only emerged again in the last century before the Christian era. His school developed into an exclusive community of research scientists, scholars, and historians who stressed the naturalistic as opposed to the Platonic element in Aristotle's thought (see pp. 107-8). Thus Aristotle's successor, the great historian of philosophy and botanist Theophrastus (who wrote the famous "Characters") criticised the doctrine of the Unmoved Mover, and Strato "the Naturalist", head of the school from 288/7 to about 270, abandoned it and made the immanent activity of Nature the only principle of the universe. This line of thought had a considerable influence on the development of Stoicism. In the same way two Peripatetics of the first generation after Aristotle, Aristoxenus and Dicaearchus, represented the soul much more materialistically than Aristotle as a harmony of the four elements, a revival and adaptation of an older Pythagorean doctrine.

XI

Hellenistic Philosophies (1). Cynics and Stoics

1. THE rise of the kings of Macedonia to supreme power in Greece and the great conquering sweep eastwards of Alexander the Great finally destroyed the old intense, narrow, concentrated life of the independent, self-contained Greek city-states. It was not a clean break. There had been many forces working for a long time to loosen that close-knit fabric of city-state life. Towards the end of the fifth century, and still more in the early part of the fourth we meet an increasing number of individuals who have broken loose from it, cosmopolitan intellectuals or soldiers of fortune on whom at least the ties of their home city sat very lightly. And the great movement of intellectual and spiritual unrest of which I spoke in my third chapter had been weakening the traditional moral and religious foundations of the old life. On the other hand, these old traditions lasted on and kept much of their force for ordinary uneducated people (the great mass of the population) for centuries after Alexander; and even politically the city-states had a great deal of vitality in them. It was not till after the Roman conquest that they sank to be mere municipalities, centres only of local government, dependent entirely in fact if not in title and legal status on the central government of the whole Mediterranean world in Rome.

Intellectually and spiritually, however, the age of Alexander does mark a decisive change in Greece, which especially affected the educated minority. In the new world of great Powers, when Greek civilization was spread thinly over the whole of the Near East and a Macedonian dynasty ruled in Turkestan, the horizons of the individual Greek were very greatly enlarged, but at the same time he lost that feeling of security which life in the old city-state world could give. He was no longer simply a member of a small intimate community in which the details of his life, his moral code, his religious practices were determined by custom and environment and the close-pressing public opinion of the compact citizen body. We may say by a metaphor that the city was still there, but its walls were down, and the security and definite form which, together with some restriction, they gave to life, had vanished.

Consequently there were a large number of people who felt isolated in the world as never before and who knew that the old foundations of belief and conduct had vanished and that they had nothing to put in their place. They did not necessarily feel that the great world in which they were isolated was a cruel, terrible and hostile one. How far they felt that it was so would depend on their personal experience; but the most worshipped of Hellenistic goddesses, Tyche, Fortune, "the element of feminine caprice in the universe", is a different and very much less alarming Power than the astrological Fate which terrorized the peoples of the later Roman Empire and in which they imaged the unreasoning cruelty of their lot. The sense of isolation, rootlessness and in-security was however strong enough to set many people looking for a rule of life which would give them a sense of inward security and stability. This the new philosophies of the Hellenistic period proceeded to supply. They differ in their recipes, but they all claim to give to their followers the same good under different names, a self-sufficient, imperturbable tranquillity proof against all the shocks and changes of Fortune, the shifting restless insecurity of human affairs.

Consequently the new philosophies are distinguished by a new sort of dogmatism. The classical philosophy of Socrates, Plato and Aristotle had been deeply concerned with the well-being of man which was to be attained by the rule of right reason in him and the knowledge of the truth. The new philosophies held that the rule of reason in man and knowledge of the truth was essential to the security which they sought. But there was a complete differ-ence of emphasis and method. For the schools of Plato and Aristotle the search for truth was a life-work, a long slow process of hard patient study and scientific thinking. The Peripatetic school kept to the old outlook and method, though they became concerned more with science and scholarship than what we should call philosophy, and, generally speaking, it is in the specialized sciences and in scholarship that we find examples of this attitude in the Hellenistic age. The great development of these specialized studies, and of all the apparatus of learning, notably of libraries, is one of the most important characteristics of the intellectual life of the period. But the new philosophies had no time for all this. They wanted an infallible plan for attaining inward security, and they wanted it at once. Consequently their systems are crude and ramshackle emergency constructions, hurriedly run up out of whatever available materials seemed most useful to provide a shelter for the soul, but defended with a passionate and unyielding dogmatism as the absolutely certain truth, because if they should prove false there would be no more hope of the security which they promise.

2. The two great schools of Hellenistic or post-Aristotelian philosophy are, of course, the Stoics and Epicureans. (The Stoics derive their name from the Painted Stoa or Colonnade at Athens where Zeno, the founder, taught, the Epicureans from their founder.) The Epicureans, whom we shall deal with in the next chapter, began a little before the Stoics, but they were a markedly isolated, independent and self-contained school, not claiming to derive the essential part of their doctrine from any predecessor, and prevented by their extreme devotion to their founder from wishing to find any sources for their philosophy behind Epicurus himself. The Stoics on the other hand derived, and admitted that they derived, a great deal of their distinctive outlook on life from that curious group of ascetics called the Cynics. And later Stoics, anxious to trace a connection between their philosophy and the teaching of Socrates whom they greatly venerated, and aided and abetted by the tidy-minded Alexandrian scholars who composed Successions of Philosophers in which every important philosopher's teaching was derived from that of a predecessor in the generation before (back to Socrates and through him to the Ionians and Thales in the "Ionian Succession"), traced the origin of the Cynics to Antisthenes, a companion of Socrates. Antisthenes is a member of the group of "minor Socratics", people intellectually inspired by Socrates who, not having the metaphysical power and all-round insight of Plato, contented themselves with exaggerating some one aspect of their master's character or methods, and who were very useful to the compilers of "Successions". The only minor Socratic who did not get a later school tacked on to him was Eucleides of Megara who, with his own group of followers, the "Megarians", was much influenced by the Eleatics and addicted to a sterile, quibbling sort of elementary logic, but who sought for "impassivity" as the end of human life in the new fashion and maintained interestingly that the good was one thing under many names, and that among the names it could be called were "intelligence", "god" or "mind". Aristippus the elder, another companion of Socrates of whom we have very little reliable information, was credited with originating the

doctrine of the insignificant sect of third-century Hedonists, who started by maintaining that human well-being consists in the sum of individual, especially physical, pleasures and ended by preaching a sort of pessimistic quietism which, as taught by one Hegesias, is said to have been a powerful incentive to suicide among his hearers. The most impressive figure among the minor Socratics was Antisthenes, who certainly stressed even to exaggeration the ascetic element in Socrates's life, but who remained Socratic rather than Cynic in his manner of asceticism and was interested in logic and literature, two studies which the Cynics regarded with the utmost contempt. The real founder of Cynicism was the extraordinary eccentric and extreme ascetic Diogenes of Sinope, the Diogenes who, as we all know, lived for a time in a tub, and round whom many other stories collected. He died in 323, and belonged to the period of Aristotle, not that of the companions of Socrates.

Cynicism was not really a philosophy but a way of life, and as a way of life it persisted right down into the Christian period. It is generally found in later times as a sort of extreme wing of Stoicism. But it had contacts with Christianity, and in the fourth century A.D. we find Christian Cynics and a great deal of approval for the Cynic way of life expressed by the Eastern Fathers of the Church, notably S. Gregory Nazianzen and S. Basil. Its chief doctrine was that virtue, or the life according to nature was the only thing that mattered, and that all else was Tuphos, a magnificent term of contempt which combines the meanings of "mist" or "fog" and "wind (internal)" with all their metaphorical implications, and may be weakly translated "illusion". By the life "according to nature" the Cynics meant a life in which all necessaries were cut down to the barest minimum, the life of a wandering beggar, going barefoot and wearing a single rough garment, which with the staff and the beggar's wallet became their symbol; their food was lentils and their drink cold water. Such a life made a man utterly proof against the changes and chances of Fortune. It was in complete poverty and detachment from all worldly ties that the Cynics sought imperturbable tranquillity. It is easy to see how it differed from the detachment of Socrates, who used things as they came and would feast or fast indifferently as circumstances demanded. Cynic asceticism was deliberate and self-conscious. They laid great stress on training (ascesis) and toil as necessary for the good life. Nevertheless some Cynics reacted towards the

Socratic way of life, and we even find curious rapprochements between the teaching of moderate Cynics and the Hedonists, who held that a man should be master of his pleasures, and so fundamentally detached and not dependent on them.

With Cynic asceticism went a vigorous attack on all forms of convention, all the normal standards of ordinary people, carried on with a strong sense of vocation. The true Cynic felt that he had a mission to wander through the world as a "doctor of souls" or "inspector sent by the gods", putting false standards out of currency by his ferocious criticism, dispelling men's illusions, and teaching them the way of truth and virtue. In doing this the Cynics adopted the utmost freedom of speech and, both as advertisement and as a practical example, a deliberate immodesty of behaviour, a flouting of all the normal standards of decency, from which they got their name of Cynics, "dog-men". (The dog for the Greeks was the type of shamelessness, and a short meditation on the things dogs do in public will show the direction which Cynic flouting of convention took. Diogenes in particular carried this to extremes.) They developed a remarkable style of serio-comic popular preaching and writing, which has had a great influence on later literature. They were cosmopolitans, regarding the universe as their city, a commonwealth of gods and wise men (the foolish masses of mankind were outsiders in this cosmopolis with no real citizen rights), and extreme individualists. And because of their individualism there is great variation in teaching and way of life between different people at various times who called themselves Cynics. A considerable degree of asceticism and the sense of vocation to a wandering life of popular moral preaching are perhaps the most generally found and essential characteristics of those whom the ancient world regarded as worthy of the name. There were, of course, innumerable charlatans who imitated the Cynic way of life for their own disreputable purposes.

3. The principal master of Zeno, the founder of Stoicism, was the most attractive of the Cynics, Crates, a cheerful hunchback enormously popular at Athens, where he went about from house to house reconciling family quarrels and giving good sound practical moral advice. In this he was performing an important and unique function. If the ordinary unphilosophical Athenian had not been able to get good advice and guidance in everyday affairs from Crates he would have got it from no-one else, for the

members of the great learned schools, the Academy and Lyceum, would never have condescended to any such activity and the priests of paganism were, of course, sacrificing officials to whom no-one could think of going for teaching or advice. Popular preaching and teaching was, as I have said, the characteristic Cynic activity, and there were always Stoics, too, who engaged in it. But as compared with his Cynic master Zeno was a good deal more of a professional philosopher. When he came to Athens in 214 B.C., from his native town of Citium in Cyprus, he attached himself to Crates, and the influence of Crates on his mind was a lasting one. But he also was taught and influenced by Stilpo the Megarian and Xenocrates and Polemo the successive heads of the Academy after Speusippus, and his philosophy is in some ways a compromise between the teaching of the Cynics, which like that of the Hedonists was simply a rule of life, despising learning and with no views on the nature of the universe, and that of the older learned schools. Stoicism was first and foremost a rule of life, but one founded on what purported to be a rational and complete doctrine about the universe, and man's knowledge of it. And the immediate successors of Zeno, Cleanthes and above all Chrysippus the "second founder" of the school, developed Stoicism a good deal further away from Cynicism.

It is interesting to note that the leading Stoics of the first century of the school all came from the very edges of the Greek cultural area. Zeno (336–264) came from half-Semitic (Phœnician) Cyprus, and may have been himself of Semitic race. Cleanthes (head of the school 264–232) from Assos on the North-West Asia Minor coast, Chrysippus (head of the school 232–204) from Tarsus in Cilicia, as did three of his disciples. Zeno had a disciple from Citium, Persæus, and other prominent Stoics of the early period came from Carthage, Babylon, Seleucia in Mesopotamia and Greek cities in North Asia Minor. But I think that the Oriental element introduced into Greek philosophy by the early Stoics has been exaggerated by some recent writers. There is hardly an element in early Stoic doctrine which cannot be traced back to an earlier Greek origin. The most we can say is that their contacts with the Eastern, especially the Semitic world may have made the Stoics inclined to emphasize, as they certainly did emphasize and develop, some doctrines which were probably of Chaldæan-Semitic origin but which had appeared in Greek philosophy as early as Plato, the emphatic assertion of **Divine**

Providence and the view of the cosmos as a single ordered whole ruled by the heavenly bodies, which were living and intelligent, visible gods most worthy of our worship.

The early Stoics were voluminous writers, with generally speaking a highly unattractive style. Their contribution to the development of philosophical jargon was considerable. Perhaps partly for this reason their works have perished. Even of the seven hundred and five treatises of Chrysippus only scanty fragments remain, and of Zeno still less. The only complete Stoic writings which we have belong to a much later age, the period of the Roman Empire. We therefore have to reconstruct the doctrines of the early Stoics from scattered quotations and the accounts given by later writers, Cicero, Diogenes Laertius, Sextus Empiricus, Galen, Plutarch (a very hostile witness) and others later still, down far into the Christian Empire, and from those passages of the writings of the later Stoics which we feel fairly sure from other evidence contain doctrines going back to the early period. Any account must therefore be to some extent uncertain and speculative, but the main outlines of early Stoic teaching are fairly clear. The summary which I shall give is based mainly upon the doctrines of the great "scholastic" of Stoicism, Chrysippus, who remodelled and extensively developed the teaching of Zeno. It was the Stoicism of Chrysippus that so greatly influenced the later history of philosophy, though Chrysippus himself was not much read owing to the extraordinary difficulty of his style.

4.   The Stoics divided philosophy into three parts: Logic (including theory of knowledge), Physics (which necessarily for them, as we shall see, included Theology and Psychology) and Ethics. The Stoics made logic a real part of philosophy, unlike Aristotle's which was a "tool of thought", a preliminary art, and their logic covered a much wider field than his. It included the whole art and science of the expression of thought, and was subdivided into Rhetoric and Dialectic. Dialectic included grammar, formal logic, and, for some Stoics at least, theory of knowledge (others treated this in more modern fashion as a separate part of philosophy). The Stoics made some important advances in the scientific study of grammar and their method became the foundation of the teaching of grammar in Greek schools. In formal logic they went on from the point reached by Aristotle's immediate successors, and made a number of changes and developments which influenced mediæval logic and still interest modern

logicians. But by far the most important part of Stoic Logic, indispensable for an understanding of their philosophy, is their theory of knowledge.

In order to understand the Stoic theory of knowledge it is necessary to realize that the Stoics were and always remained thorough-going materialists. For them only bodies could act and be causes. Only bodies had a real substantial existence. God and the soul were therefore bodies. The immaterial things whose existence in some sense they recognized were not really "things", substantial beings at all but either the "whereabouts" of bodies, place, space, and void, or the things we can say ("lekta") about bodies and the judgments we make about them. Their theory of knowledge is therefore a description of how one body, the soul (a subtle fiery breath, part of the all-pervading Divine principle), is affected by other bodies, the things which we know. The sense-organs are the normal channels of knowledge, though not the only ones; but even knowledge which does not come through the sense-organs is produced in the same material way, by an affecting of the soul by the bodies known. In sense-perception the object perceived makes an impression on the soul. (Cleanthes said crudely "an impression like that of a seal on wax", Chrysippus more discreetly just "a modification".) The soul gives its "assent" to this impression, rightly or wrongly, and if it does so rightly attains "comprehension" of the body perceived, a firm, certain and immediate mental grasp of it. In order that the assent should be given rightly it was necessary that the impression or image should be the accurate representation of a real object, which the Stoics called a "gripping representation", one that took hold on the mind and compelled its assent. When pressed for further information about this "gripping representation" and how it could be distinguished from other representations, images or impressions, they had no answer to give. Zeno had said, and Cleanthes and Chrysippus repeated, that it was "an image impressed from an existing thing and in conformity with it and of the sort that would not come from a non-existing thing"; and there they left it. It was for them something self-evident and obvious, and was the principal criterion or test of truth. Some Stoics proposed other criteria, but they all referred to the same thing, the direct contact and immediate apprehension by the mind of the objects presented to it.

But "comprehensions" by themselves, though they were the

first stage of certainty, were not knowledge. This came when they had been tested by reason and shown to be stable and unshakable by it, probably by a process of comparison and combination with other "comprehensions" so as to show the rational order and connection of the objects comprehended. This systematic and absolutely certain knowledge, the final concentrated grip of the mind on facts, was the exclusive property of the Sage or Wise Man.

General notions of course for the Stoics exist only in our minds. There can be no possible place in their system for objectively existing universals like Plato's Forms. Stoic general notions are formed from particular "comprehensions". Some, the most important, those of virtue, the good, the divine government of the world, are formed spontaneously and, said the Stoics, are fully present in our minds by the age of fourteen. (The soul at birth is a blank, a tabula rasa, and gradually acquires its store of impressions and of general notions formed from them.) Other general notions are produced deliberately by teaching. In the whole of this Stoic theory of knowledge we can see the tendency, very characteristic of their system and shown especially in the doctrines of the "gripping representation" and the spontaneously developed general notions, to make things much too easy, to adopt a fallaciously simple explanation showing how everything is for the best in a perfectly rational universe, and to defend it with uncompromising dogmatism.

5. A good transition from Stoic Logic to Stoic Physics is made by their doctrine of the Categories. They simplified Aristotle's system by reducing these from ten to four, substrate or material substance, essential or formative quality or "whatness", state ("how-being", covering all non-essential qualities or accidents) and relation ("how-being in relation to something"). Qualities, since they affected and modified things were themselves bodies. They were in fact parts of the material active, informing principle of the universe. This the Stoics described in a manner at first sight reminiscent of Heraclitus as a "constructive fire" or a "fiery intelligent breath". It permeates and is transfused through the passive matter which it organizes "like honey in a honeycomb" or "a drop of wine in water". The Stoics were compelled by their theory to hold the remarkable doctrine, much derided by their opponents, that two bodies could occupy the same place, that body could pass through body.

The origin of this peculiar Stoic physical doctrine can, I think, be found in the philosophy of the fourth century. The idea that the principle of life is a "pneuma", a hot breath-like substance, was very generally accepted. It is found in the teaching of the medical schools as exemplified by the fourth-century physician Diokles of Karystos. But its most important expression is to be found in the philosophy of Aristotle. Aristotle's "pneuma" is closely related to "æther", the mysterious hot bright substance of the heavenly spheres. It is the vehicle of the immaterial soul and the instrument through which it acts on the body. Wherever, in Aristotle's system, there is life, sensation, or movement passing between the immaterial and the material, we find "æther" or "pneuma" or an analogous substance acting as intermediary. This is almost certainly the origin of the Stoic doctrine of "pneuma", but the Stoics, being materialists, invested their "pneuma" with all the characteristics of immaterial soul, making it into something more like the early pre-Socratic "living stuff," and applied the idea to the universe as a whole because they regarded the universe as a whole as a living being. This doctrine had already appeared in Plato's "Timæus", but in Stoicism it has a different atmosphere and emphasis, for the living and organic universe is the ultimate reality and does not depend on a transcendent world of higher spiritual reality as it does in Plato. In other ways Stoic Physics can be regarded as a sort of crude materialization of some other Aristotelian ideas. There is a sharp distinction between the "active" and "passive" principles, which correspond to Aristotle's Form and Matter; but for the Stoics they are both bodies, materially distinct though the one is perfectly diffused through the other, not as in Aristotle two principles, neither of them bodies and separable only in thought. The Stoic active principle, the forming and vitalizing fire, is a materialization of Aristotle's Soul as form of the body, the principle at once of life and definite reality, the cause of existence as a particular living being. But the Stoic "constructive fire" is a universal, cosmic principle. It is not simply the principle of form and life to individual things. It is the forming, ordering and ruling principle of the whole universe. It is God, Divine Providence. This is like a materialized version of Plato's doctrine of Divine Providence and the rule of soul, and it also owes something to Aristotle's conception of an immanent Nature, a life-force working to a good end. The Stoics called their active principle Nature as well as God. But their attitude to their immanent God is much closer to Plato than to Aristotle, and they go beyond even Plato in their passionate devotion and joyful resignation to Divine Providence, which may well derive from Syria rather than Greece.

The forming principles of individual things are parts of the universal principle in the most literal sense, pieces of God, but not separated or çut off from the whole. When they were considering the growth and development of individual living things the Stoics spoke of "seminal logoi", seeds of the Divine Fire implanted in them at their origin which caused their growth and development to the fulness of their form. Considering the universe more generally they said that the Divine Fire permeates all things, holding them together and giving them their definite form by a sort of "tension". The formative qualities are "tensions" of the fiery breath. In harmony with their continual attempt to keep close to bodily reality the Stoics insisted that every individual was unique and had its own proper formative quality, its "private whatness". Life is a higher form of "tension", and the highest of all manifestations of the Divine Fire is Reason, the Ruling Principle in man, by the possession of which he literally and physically has a share in the Divine Nature. The universe, too, has its Ruling Principle, the Divine Fire manifesting itself in the fulness of its rational energy, which is located either in the luminous æthereal region of the stars, or in the sun, the "Ruling Principle of the universe" according to Cleanthes; this latter doctrine was the foundation of the solar theology of the last ages of Græco-Roman paganism.

The passive matter of the universe is itself generated from the Divine Fire and periodically re-absorbed in it. The universe is thus not eternal or indestructible, but is eternally destroyed and re-created in an endless series of cycles. First, fire condenses into air and air into water, in which a seed of fire remains, the Seminal Logos of the universe which forms and develops all things. When the end of the cycle is reached there is a universal conflagration, when the Divine Fire or God re-absorbs all things into himself and remains for a time alone, occupied with his own thoughts. Then the whole process starts again; there is the Apokatastasis, the Restoration of all things, which means that the whole previous universe repeats itself again exactly in every detail and every event; there will be another Socrates and another Zeno, teaching exactly the same things to exactly similar pupils; and so it will go on for ever. For the Stoics there is no room for improvement in the divine universe, because it is divine and the ultimate reality. There can be no change, nothing really new, and every detail in the universe is exactly determined by Fate, which is the Divine Will, which manifests itself above all in the heavenly bodies, the living and intelligent fiery beings which are the visible rulers of the Cosmic City. The Stoics accepted with enthusiasm the horrible Eastern superstition of astrology, along with all forms of divination, as perfectly corresponding to their view of the cosmos. They were prepared to accept all the gods of mythology, too, as aspects of the one divine principle.

In all this Stoic physical theology there is a peculiar dynamic-vitalistic way of looking at the formative and ruling principle of the cosmos, bound up with strong moral and religious pre-occupations, which had much influence on later Greek thought. We may say, perhaps, that it resulted from a translation of Plato's doctrine of Divine Providence in the visible world, together with a good deal of Aristotle, into the language of the primitive Pre-Socratic doctrine of the "living stuff", which was attractive to non-metaphysical minds. The result is something new, not like Plato or Aristotle and still less like Pre-Socratic philosophy, yet I think almost entirely explicable in terms of its Greek inheritance; if we are prepared to grant the Stoic philosophers themselves a little real originality there is not much need to seek for Stoic origins in Syria or beyond.

6. Stoic Ethics are firmly rooted in this Stoic physical theology. The two are linked especially closely by the Stoic doctrine of the soul. The rational soul of man is, as we have seen, a fiery breath which is part of the Universal Fiery Breath, the Divine Reason or God which pervades, controls and determines everything in the universe. Therefore man's whole end and object in life must be to live in absolute conformity with this reason or Ruling Principle of his which is a part of the Divine Reason. In any case he will ultimately be forced to obey the decrees of the Divine Reason, which is Fate, determining everything in the universe; but he can choose how he will obey. He is, they said, like a dog tied to a moving cart, who can either trot along cheerfully or be dragged along uncomfortably, but must go along with the cart in any case. Ready and joyful assent to the decrees of the Divine Reason within us is then the whole duty of man. This is reason and this is virtue. Rational action and virtue are one and the same thing,

to act in accordance with our Ruling Principle; and this is the absolute and only good. Furthermore, the fiery rational soul of man is one, and is all reason. The passions then and the emotions and desires are not inferior activities of the soul to be controlled by reason. They are perverted reason, "irrational reason". They are wrong judgments about what is good and bad for us, just as virtue consists in right judgments of the reason about what is universally good and bad. (We must never forget that, for the Stoics, Reason is also a dynamic material force, the principle of action and life.) The passions and emotions, then, are not to be controlled but utterly eradicated. The ideal is Apathy, freedom from all passion, emotion, affections, from all the ways in which things can affect the soul whose reason is perverted. So we arrive at the grim figure of the Stoic Sage, their ideal of humanity, who is utterly indifferent to all external things, to riches, health or power, and utterly without any trace of irrational affection for family or friends, whose every action and thought is pure reason and virtue, in complete accordance with his Ruling Principle. To glorify him they heaped up paradoxes; he alone was truly king, truly rich, truly healthy. He was superior to all the changes and chances of life, unassailable by fortune, possessing all things in possessing virtue, the only thing worth having. From the beginning they admitted that the ideal was rarely attained, and they soon came to regard it as practically unattainable by man. But it remained their only ideal; and for these older Stoics there was no half-way house between good and bad. Either you were a Sage, living perfectly by the Reason within you, or you were utterly wicked and foolish. Moral progress, short of perfection, made no difference. "A man can drown as well a few inches under water as in the depth of the sea."

The Sage alone, the Stoics said, lives "consistently" and "according to Nature". To live "according to Nature" in their system meant, as we have seen, the same thing as living according to Reason or to God. In this way the Cynic "life according to Nature" acquired a deeper meaning, and the Stoics modified very drastically in other ways the original extreme Cynic conception of the "natural". They kept, of course, the intransigent Cynic declaration that virtue was the only thing that mattered and that nothing else was a good, at least in the same sense. There were always many Stoics who recognized the Cynic way of life as a true vocation to which the philosopher might be called (though there are also clear traces of an anti-Cynic attitude among some members of the school). Antisthenes and Diogenes were canonized as Sages along with Socrates. Zeno himself adopted the Cynic dress and diet, though he did not wander about supporting himself by begging in the true Cynic manner, and he indulged in drastic criticism, on Cynic lines, of all existing laws, customs and institutions. But, generally speaking, the Stoics fitted in with the society in which they found themselves. Their idea of life according to Nature or Reason did not necessarily require the Cynic asceticism, the cutting loose from everything and cutting down of wants to a minimum subsistence level. It could, and more usually did, fit in with a full normal civilized life, with all its duties and responsibilities. The Stoic philosophy encouraged public activity, and became popular among the Romans for that very reason. The element in their moral theory which accounts for this is their doctrine of things "preferred" and "deprecated" and of "suitable" actions. This goes back to Zeno, though it was developed and elaborated by Chrysippus. It amounted to this, that though virtue was the one and only good and no external things could be considered strictly as "goods" at all, yet it was reasonable, where virtue was not concerned, to regard some external circumstances as preferable to others. Thus a Stoic might regard health as preferable to sickness without prejudice to his philosophy. All external circumstances were classified into " preferred", "deprecated" and "absolutely indifferent". Life and death were among the things absolutely indifferent. From this followed one of their most famous doctrines, and one which they not infrequently put into practice. This was, that when the wise man found that the proportion of undesirable circumstances in his life was permanently greater than that of desirable circumstances he would leave life by committing suicide, as a man leaves a room full of smoke or a child a game of which he is tired. This easy advocacy of suicide is one of the most striking distinctions between Stoic and Platonic morality; the Platonists, true to the teaching of the "Phædo", absolutely forbade it. The Stoic can then, within the bounds set by reason and virtue, pursue the "preferred" objects and shun their opposites. He will also perform the actions which are "suitable" or "becoming" to the state of life in which he finds himself, to the part on the stage of this world which the Divine Reason has given him to play (a metaphor borrowed by the Stoics from the Cynics, and continually used by both). These actions when performed by ordinary imperfect people are "suitable" or "becoming" and nothing more. But when performed by the Sage, whose interior dispositions are perfect and who does everything in accordance with Reason and Virtue, the same actions become genuinely "right". It is the inward state, the motive, which makes the difference.

7. The Stoics as a result of these doctrines had a solid theoretical foundation for public activity, and we find them playing a very considerable part in the political life of the Hellenistic and Roman world. On the whole there was nothing very revolutionary about Stoic political influence. One Stoic, Blossius of Cumae, is known to have taken part in the revolt of Aristonicus which was one of the only genuine popular social revolutionary movements of the ancient world; and perhaps he was inspired by the fierce criticism of existing institutions, including slavery, to be found in the Cynics and in Zeno's "Republic". But in general Stoicism was far less "popular" than Cynicism, and tended to follow the normal way of Greek philosophy and address itself almost exclusively to the small educated upper class. The Stoics were cosmopolitans in the sense that they held that the whole Cosmos was one society, whose King was Zeus, the Divine Reason; and though only gods and wise men were true citizens of Cosmopolis, yet all men were its inhabitants and partakers in the Divine Reason and the philosopher had a duty to practise benevolence to all. This cosmopolitanism turned them away from the old world of the city-states to the new Great Powers of the Hellenistic world and later to the universal Empire of Rome. An idealized monarchy, "the rule of the best man", was on the whole the constitution they preferred. They consequently acquired much influence at the courts of Hellenistic monarchs, and it was something of an historical accident that so many of the Republican Opposition at Rome, that pig-headed body of aristocratic reactionaries, were Stoics. In the second century Principate Stoic influence at Court increased, culminating in the reign of the Stoic Emperor, Marcus Aurelius, of whom I shall say a little more later.

The most important expression of Stoic cosmopolitanism was their doctrine of "natural law" the universal decrees of the Divine Reason which are the same for all men and with which all positive law should correspond. The idea of unwritten divine laws superior to human law goes far back in the Greek tradition. We can find it in the fifth century most nobly expressed in the "Antigone" of Sophocles, and as we have seen the idea of an absolute moral law discoverable by reason is the foundation of the ethics of Socrates and Plato. But it was the Stoics and Cynics in their different ways who presented it first as a universal law, the law of the City of the Cosmos, the same everywhere and superior to merely local custom and tradition. This idea had a great future before it in Christian thought, but in the hands of the Stoics it did not produce any very startling consequences. Stoic morality normally made people who professed it perform the duties of their state of life somewhat better, but it did not make them seek to transform the whole basis of society. Stoicism was the most practically influential philosophy of the ancient world, but both the range and the effects of its influence were very limited. Alexander the Great held a wider, more generally all-embracing idea of the Brotherhood of Man than any Cynic or Stoic, and his ideal had much more practical effect. Perhaps the most notable service rendered to the ancient world by the Stoics, apart from the great degree of support and comfort their creed afforded to individuals, was the influence which their conception of natural law had in humanizing and universalizing classical Roman Law under the Empire, though the exact extent of this influence is not quite certain.

XII

Hellenistic Philosophies (2). Epicureans and Sceptics

1. WITH the Epicureans we find ourselves back in a thoroughly Greek milieu, and one in which a good deal of the old Ionian spirit survives. Epicurus himself was the son of an Athenian colonist in Samos. He was born in 341 B.C., came to Athens in 323, founded his school or philosophical community, the famous "Garden," about 307–6, and died in 270. His disciples came mostly from the Greek cities of the Asia Minor coast, and the only earlier philosophy of which he made any use was that of the Atomists, the most Ionian of all the Ionians. Epicurus was like the early Stoics a most voluminous writer, and is credited with producing three hundred rolls or volumes. All have perished except three "open letters" to disciples, two (to Herodotus and Menœceus) certainly genuine and one (to Pythocles) probably a compilation by a later Epicurean; a collection of forty short statements called the "Principal Doctrines" which Bailey well describes as "a practical manual of guidance for life intended for the professed Epicurean"; and a large number of fragments, some of them important. The two genuine letters are very valuable summaries of the most important parts of Epicurus's philosophy. We have also some very useful later sources of information about Epicureanism, of which far the most important is the great poem "On the Nature of Things" by the Roman poet Lucretius, a contemporary of Cicero, a devout and impassioned apostle of Epicureanism, and the only European writer who has ever put a philosophical (as distinct from a theological) system into supremely great poetry.

There is no ancient philosophy whose character has been so generally and completely misrepresented as the Epicurean. The ordinary man's view is, I suppose, that summed up in Horace's joking line about a "plump sleek pig from Epicurus's herd," a comfortable sensual hedonism combined with a crude atheism. In fact what we find when we examine the real evidence about Epicurus and his school is a small exclusive group of austere refined quietists, of the highest moral character (we can disregard the irresponsible mud-slinging which was a normal part of ancient philosophical controversy), with an extraordinary devotion to their founder and a most attractive theory and practice of strong and loyal friendship. We find that the Epicureans had a real, though extremely odd, religion. Epicurus himself was much more careful about external religious observances than the great Platonic mystic Plotinus. And both Epicurus and still more Lucretius display a moral earnestness worthy of any Victorian agnostic. Epicureanism was extremely unpopular in the ancient world, and its influence was extremely limited. Its teachings ran clean counter to that whole development of late pagan religious thought to which Stoics, Platonists and Aristotelians all contributed in spite of their violent disagreements and from which Christendom has inherited so much. The distorted picture of it which still survives in common speech and thought is a result of this singularity and unpopularity. But though its influence was limited it was not the worst who felt it. A philosophy which could deeply affect the mind of the young Virgil was not a philosophy for pigs.

2.   The Epicureans, on account of their devotion to their founder, made very little change in his teachings. There was no development of doctrine in their school as there was in Stoicism and an account of Epicurus's own teaching as far as we know it will therefore be an account of the teaching of the school as long as it survived. Like the Stoics, Epicurus divided philosophy into three parts, Canonic, Physics, including psychology and theology, and Ethics. Like the Stoics, too, Epicurus is a thoroughgoing materialist in the sense that for him only bodies are substantially real and capable of acting or being causes. And like all philosophies of the Hellenistic age, Epicureanism is, above all, a rule of life based on reason, whose end is the attainment of that imperturbable tranquillity which Epicurus calls "ataraxia," by the secure possession of which the wise man is proof against all the troubles of the world. These common characteristics of the philosophy of the age are essential features of Epicureanism. But it is equally important, if we are to understand Epicurus rightly, to realize the originality of his system, and in particular how completely he differed from the Stoics in his relation to previous philosophies and in the spirit, aim and most of the content of his teaching. Stoicism as we have seen was to a great extent a translation of certain Platonic and Aristotelian ideas into the language of the primitive Ionian belief in a "living stuff," a translation

which produced very original results. Epicurus owes little or nothing to Plato or Aristotle and the only earlier philosophy which made any important contribution to his teaching was Atomism, that final expression of the Ionian spirit which had broken away from the idea of "living stuff" and which stands rather apart and isolated among the philosophical developments of the fifth century. As regards the spirit and aim of the two philosophies, while both sought imperturbable tranquillity, the Stoics sought it in absolute self-identification with operative Providence, the Divine Fire by which everything in the universe was determined, the Epicureans in denial of any sort of Divine Providence or Fate at all, because belief in any such thing would disturb their minds and prevent them from assurance that tranquillity was something man could attain by himself, by his own resources, without reference to any outside power. Epicurus saw tranquillity negatively, as freedom from pain and trouble, and it seemed to him that the worst of pains and troubles was fear; and that the worst of all fears were the fear of the gods, the fear of arbitrary divine interference with our lives, and the fear of death and the life after death with its possible punishments and sufferings. Once freed from these by a rational theory of nature which excluded divine activity and asserted the materiality and mortality of the soul, the wise man could be self-reliant and at peace. Epicurus's whole philosophy is designed to serve this end. It is therefore not at all scientific in spirit. Epicurus is not in the least concerned to find the one true explanation of phenomena, but only to exclude from among the possible explanations any which imply divine activity. His system is even more obviously than that of the Stoics a structure hastily run up, out of what seemed to him the best available materials, to provide a secure refuge for the soul among the storms of this troublesome life.

3.   The first part of Epicurus's philosophy, Canonic, is concerned exclusively with the canons, criteria, or tests of truth. It thus differs from Stoic logic, since it pays no attention to the analysis of propositions, the forms of valid argument, or the art of disputation. In accordance with the whole spirit of his philosophy the object of Canonic is to supply tests of truth which will be certain, easy and obvious, derived from our immediate experience. The criteria he admits are four in number; (i) feelings of pleasure and pain, the ultimate criterion in ethics, (ii) sensation, (iii) concepts, (iv) the act of intuitive apprehension by which we grasp certain

sorts of concepts. These four are all forms of immediate physical experience. They represent ways in which our material souls are physically affected by other material things. The meaning of the first two criteria is obvious. Epicurus insists very strongly that sensation is always infallible. Error only comes in when we make judgments about what our senses show us. If, for instance, we see a tower in the distance and decide from its distant appearance that it is a small round one, and then find when we get closer that it is in fact a large square one, our senses have not deceived us. It is our judgment which is at fault. The tower did really look like a small round one, but we should have waited for the confirming evidence of a close and clear view before deciding that it was so in reality. Epicurus allows the necessity of this confirmation by the testimony of a closer inspection in the case of distant and obscure perceptions, though he sometimes seems a little unhappy about it, as tending to conflict with the absolute infallibility of sense-perception. When no closer inspection is possible, as in the case of astronomical phenomena, our judgment is sufficiently confirmed if we can find no evidence against it in our sense-experience. This rule applies also to judgments about things which are necessarily obscure, of which we can have no direct sense-experience, notably atoms and void, belief in whose existence is, of course, absolutely necessary to Epicurus's system.

What Epicurus meant by his third and fourth criteria can only be properly understood if we know his view of how sense-perception works. It is a simple and amusing conception. Everything, in the physical system he borrowed from Democritus, is composed of atoms and is continually giving off and taking in streams of atoms as long as it remains in being. The atoms given off are the outermost layers of the objects, which keep the shape and all the characteristics of the object which gives them off. These hollow, insubstantial, outline-reproductions of the objects, the "images", float through the air till they come into contact with a perceiving subject. Those composed of larger and less subtle atoms make an impression (an actual physical impression) on the appropriate sense-organ and so are perceived by the senses. Those made of very fine and subtle atoms penetrate through our pores directly to the mind (which is itself material, made of very small round atoms) and produce mind-pictures and in particular the visions which we have in sleep. Sometimes the "images" get distorted or mixed with each other in their passage through the air.

For example, the image of a man may get mixed with the image of a horse, and the mixed image may penetrate into our minds and cause us to dream about a centaur. In this way not only fantastic dreams, but every sort of hallucination and delusion, can be explained without departing from the fundamental principle that everything which we perceive has in some way a real material existence. The importance of this doctrine of "images" for Epicurus's theology is very great, and we shall discuss it later.

The third and fourth criteria depend on the doctrine of "images". A concept for Epicurus is simply the impression of a general notion produced by a constant influx of images of the same character. As a result of the continual reception of the images of men we have the impression formed in our mind of the general idea or concept "man". A concept is thus the immediate result of physical experience. It is to help to preserve this immediacy that Epicurus insists that words must always be used in their first and most obvious meaning and altogether rejects logic. Concepts are criteria because obviously without them we cannot form judgments on the things we perceive. The fourth criterion, the "act of attention" or "apprehension" of the mind, is not explicitly stated to be a test of truth by Epicurus himself, though he sometimes seems to be using it as one, and it is not very easy to see what he or the Epicureans who made it a criterion meant by it. Perhaps it was something like this: a mental process, analogous to the close inspection or "confirmation" which certifies the truth of our sense-impressions, by which we apprehend very subtle images (like those of the gods) or grasp certain concepts as clear and self-evident scientific truths as opposed to mere opinions. It was possibly because Epicurus felt a little uneasy about this, as he did about "confirmation" in the sphere of sense-perception, that he never explicitly made it a criterion.

4. The physics of Epicurus is simply the Atomism of Democritus, with some very curious adaptations to make it fit in better with the ends of his system. He maintains according to the teaching of Democritus that all things consist of Atoms in perpetual motion in the Void. There is no moving cause and no ordering intelligence, no room for divine activity anywhere. Worlds (cosmoi) and the individual things in them are simply chance collections, nebulæ as it were, of atoms coming together in the void and, after a time, breaking up again. Many worlds can exist at once (the contrast with the unique divine universe of the Stoics is striking). The Void

and the number of atoms are both infinite, and the variety of different atomic shapes indefinitely large. All this is taken straight from Democritus. Epicurus's own most notable contribution is the doctrine of the "swerve" (parenklisis or clinamen). He was as anxious to destroy the notion of an impersonal Fate and to affirm human freewill as he was to deny Divine Providence. Fate and Providence were for him only two ways of expressing the same fettering, perturbing, terrifying delusion. And he saw that Atomism as it stood led to a physical determinism as destructive to his system as the Stoic doctrine. The modern revival of Atomism has, of course, been closely linked with a strong belief in determinism, in the all-controlling mechanism of "natural law". The doctrine of the "swerve" is Epicurus's way of insuring against any sort of determinism creeping into his system. It requires first of all the assumption of absolute direction in space; that there is in some sense a real "up" and "down". The atoms, then, normally fall in a straight line downwards, carried by their weight. But every now and then, quite arbitrarily, without any possible reason, some of the atoms swerve slightly, slant aside from their straight downward fall. Then, of course, they collide with other atoms, and from the first collision and all the counter-collisions and entanglements to which it gives rise, a world and all its contents comes into being. Thus all existence depends in part, not on a divine will or a rigid mechanical law but on absolutely undetermined movements, and in a world constituted by such movements there is no reason why absolutely undertermined movements of atomic compounds, i.e. free human actions should not exist. Of course, there remains a background of absolute necessity. It is absolutely necessary that atoms and void should exist and that atoms should behave according to their nature. But Epicurus recognizes arbitrary undetermined Chance as a separate principle alongside physical Necessity.

Epicurus also, as we have seen, departed from Democritus in assuming the absolute trustworthiness of the senses. This got him into considerable difficulties over the question of how we know that atoms and void exist, which his doctrines of "absence of contrary evidence" and the "act of apprehension by the mind" are very far from solving. In his psychology he follows Democritus closely, holding that the soul is composed of the smallest and most subtle atoms, and making a distinction between the vital principle (the "anima" of Lucretius), which is diffused throughout the body, and the mind ("animus" of Lucretius) an aggregate of especially pure and subtle soul-atoms situated in the breast. Epicurus's theology seems to be quite original. It is surprising, in view of his anxiety to exclude divine activity from the universe, that he finds it necessary to postulate the existence of gods at all, but, given the assumptions of his system, he has good reasons for doing so. His great argument for the existence of the gods is that men have clear and distinct pictures of them in their minds, and in particular that they often have visions of them during sleep. Now every mental picture must be produced by an "image" flowing off from some existing body. The representations of the gods are presumably thought of as too clear and persistent to be the result of any sort of distortion of "images"; therefore the gods must actually exist. It is not altogether easy to see from our very scanty evidence what sort of beings Epicurus thought they were, but the most probable account seems to be this. The gods are eternal outlines into which a continuous stream of atoms ceaselessly flows, replacing the atoms which they continually give off in "images" and thus ensuring their immortality (other things cease to exist when the outflow of atoms is no longer balanced by the intake). The gods have the same sort of continuous existence as a waterfall, where the water is always new and the outline of the fall always the same. The gods, of course, take no part whatever in the affairs of the universe. They live in perfect tranquillity, neither troubling others nor being troubled themselves, in the "intermundia", the calm spaces of void between the worlds, exactly like a community of Epicurean philosophers in their garden. Like the philosophers, too, they converse in Greek! They represent in fact the ideal of human life, and the wise man who attains to perfect peace of soul will be living "a life worthy of the gods". In doing so he will be greatly helped by the contemplation of the "images" which the gods continually give off, very subtle images which he can only apprehend by that special faculty of "attention" or "apprehension by the mind". This is Epicurean religion, the contemplation and imitation of the divine life. And there is just a possibility of interpreting the existing evidence to mean that the gods recognize and "receive" true philosophers and willingly grant them communion with themselves by means of the "images" while they ignore the masses of the foolish and wicked; the philosophers, of course, remain mortal and their souls are dissolved at death like any other atomic compound. Thus the

Epicurean religious ideal is not, after all, very unlike that of other Greek philosophical religion. The Epicurean philosophers hope to attain in this life what Platonists hope to attain in the next and Stoics in this and perhaps in a limited immortality till the Conflagration, namely, to share the life of the gods as by right and through their own efforts and not by any divine grace. Gods and philosophers form a small, exclusive, privileged aristocracy in the universe for Platonists, Stoics, and Epicureans alike.

5. The basis of Epicurean ethics is to be found in the first criterion. It is our feelings of pain and pleasure which are the test by which we determine what is bad and good for us. But Epicurus understands pleasure very differently from the ordinary sensual man or the Cyrenaic Hedonists. It does not consist in the largest possible sum of individual, momentary pleasures of the highest possible intensity, but in absolute freedom from pain and perfect tranquillity. The worst pain is fear, fear of death and what may happen after death and fear of the gods. From this we are freed if our reason is enlightened by the Epicurean dogmas about the universe. But excessive and inordinate desire will also produce pain. Therefore we must distinguish between desires which are natural and necessary, desires which are natural but not necessary, and desires which are neither natural nor necessary. We must confine ourselves as far as possible to the first class and have nothing to do with the third; the desires of the first class are simple and easily satisfied. Therefore the life of Epicurus himself and of the true Epicureans was an ascetic one, based on the reduction of desires to the simplest minimum. And Epicurus himself, in the painful illness which ended his life, proved that, as he taught, the philosopher who has attained to tranquillity of mind can bear bodily pain with the utmost courage and cheerfulness (though he also taught that normally the foundation of all happiness was the "pleasure of the belly" i.e., a good digestion and something satisfactory to digest).

As a basis for social morality this doctrine which made human well-being consist in the pleasure of an austere tranquillity was not very adequate. Certainly Epicurus preached the importance of friendship to human happiness and he and his followers practised this doctrine and cultivated the art of friendship and all human affectionate relationships in a very attractive way. One of its chief manifestations was the devotion and religious veneration with which the Epicureans regarded their Master, Epicurus himself, a devotion which he seems to have deserved. The only fault which we can detect in his character is one common among ancient philosophers, an inordinate spiritual and intellectual pride which led him to cover all previous philosophers with abuse and contempt, even those from whom he had learnt much, Democritus and his school. The Epicureans, too, in their pursuit of tranquillity certainly gave no trouble to others. But they were equally not prepared to take any trouble on their behalf. Epicurus continually preached the desirability of avoiding public office and political life, and the Epicureans were quietists who withdrew from the world into their "gardens", their small exclusive circles of philosopher friends. It is impossible to imagine Epicurus preaching his doctrines in popular language in the market place like the Cynics and some Stoics. His appeal even more than that of the Platonists or Peripatetics was to a refined, select minority.

Justice was for Epicurus merely a matter of social contract, of agreement between men to avoid actions mutually disadvantageous. Hence it only applied within the limits of particular societies. There was no universal law of justice binding all men together, Greeks to barbarians. And, Epicurus said, the only ultimate reason why men ought to act justly is that the man who has committed an unjust action can never be quite sure that he will not be found out, and so the fear of possible consequences will always disturb his tranquillity.

6. The extreme dogmatism of the Stoics and Epicureans, who proclaimed absolutely contradictory doctrines resting on very shaky intellectual foundations with a narrow and quasi-religious fervour as the only possible and rational explanation of the universe, naturally produced a sceptical reaction. There were two sceptical schools in the Hellenistic Age. The name "Sceptic" (which simply means "thoughtful", "reflective") was only applied in antiquity to the followers of Pyrrho of Elea. He was approximately a contemporary of Zeno and Epicurus, his dates being about 365–275. He went East with Alexarchus, the companion of Alexander the Great, and met the Magi and the Brahmin ascetics whom the Greeks called Gymnosophists, and it is possible that he may have learnt something from these latter. His school almost died out with his disciple, the satirist Timon of Phlius, but was revived again by Ænesidemus in the first century B.C. and in the second half of the second century A.D., produced one of our most important source-books for the history of ancient philosophy in

the great work of Sextus Empiricus, who in order to show up the contradictions of the dogmatists put together a great deal of important information about the teachings of the various schools.

Pyrrho, like his contemporaries, sought for imperturbable tranquillity of soul, Ataraxy or Apathy. But he sought it not in a dogmatic theory of the universe and ethical system but in absolute agnosticism and suspension of judgment. All things, he said, were indifferent and unstable and undiscernible. None of our perceptions or thoughts is true or false. Nothing is really good or bad. We must not believe that anything exists or does not exist. We must not think anything definite or make any positive or negative statement. Silence and Suspension of Judgment are the ideal. And when we have attained to perfect suspension of judgment, when our minds are perfectly balanced so that we neither affirm or deny anything, then tranquillity follows inevitably "as the shadow follows the body". Pyrrho was first and foremost a moralist concerned with the end of human life and did not cultivate dialectic, though his disciple Timon satirized the dogmatists with vigour. But it seems to have been Ænesidemus who originated the formidable array of destructive arguments used against the dogmatic schools by the later Sceptics (Ænesidemus is sometimes regarded as belonging to the Sceptical Academy, and he certainly seems to have been a sceptic of the Academic rather than the Pyrrhonian type).

7. The other sceptical school were dialecticians and destructive critics from the beginning. To Plato's school, the Academy, with their tradition of really mature, serious and refined philosophical thinking, the argumentations and assertions of the newer schools, and especially the Stoics, seemed impossibly crude, feeble and uncultured. And under the fourth head of the school after Plato, Arcesilas (d. 241) they abandoned, as far as we know, their own positive metaphysical teaching and devoted themselves to a negative and destructive criticism in the spirit, as they thought of Socrates as he is presented in the early Platonic dialogues and basing themselves on his famous affirmation of ignorance. "I know that I do not know". Arcesilas himself wrote nothing, and we really know very little of his teaching as a whole; it might quite possibly have had a more positive side. But our scanty evidence shows it as an entirely negative scepticism, a deadly destructive criticism of the dogmatists, especially the Stoics who presented a large and vulnerable target. He is even said to have

carried his denial of the possibility of knowledge so far as to deny the positive element in Socrates's affirmation of ignorance. We do not even know that we do not know. He admitted some sort of "probability" or "reasonableness" as a practical guide to action, but we do not know exactly what he meant by it. Of the second great figure of this New or Sceptical Academy, Carneades (d. 129) we know a little more. He was again first and foremost a critic, especially of the Stoics ("If there had not been Chrysippus, I should not have been either," he said). But while he maintained the impossibility of absolute knowledge and the need to suspend judgment, he seems to have worked out a more comprehensive theory of probability than Arcesilas, and to have made probability, or "persuasiveness" a guide to thought as well as action. After him the Academy, as we shall see, moved back to a more positive metaphysical teaching. We may sum up the difference between the two sceptical schools by saying that while Pyrrho's scepticism was a real despair of human knowledge resulting in a pessimistic passivity, a complete withdrawal from human thought and action, that of the Academics was inspired by a delight in intellectual subtlety for its own sake and an impatience with the stupidities of the Stoics. They give the impression of having thoroughly enjoyed their destructive criticism, and indeed it is very good fun—as long as the thought does not cross your mind that it is the duty of the philosopher to make some positive contribution to the difficult business of living well, and not merely to knock away the intellectual supports, however poor, which less gifted mortals devise for their well-intentioned activities. However, the Pyrrhonian Sceptics, and still more the New Academy, did perform a very useful service in the development of Greek philosophy, clearing the ground and preparing the way for a new positive teaching very much profounder and more valuable than that of Stoics or Epicureans.

XIII

The Philosophy of the Earlier Roman Empire. The Revival of Platonism

1.   F R O M the point of view of the later history of philosophy, and especially of the traditional philosophy of Christendom, by far the most important development of Greek thought in the first century B.C. and the first two centuries A.D. is the revival of Platonism, that modified later Platonism which is the parent of Christian philosophy on the Hellenic side; this revived Platonism contained a large Aristotelian element, and during the centuries in which it was growing up the study of Aristotle in the Peripatetic school itself seems to have been pursued with a revived vigour. The greatest of the Aristotelian commentators, Alexander of Aphrodisias, who influenced in one important way the greatest of later Platonists, Plotinus, lived about A.D. 200. But before discussing this linked Platonic-Aristotelian revival and the closely related movement of Neo-Pythagoreanism, it will be necessary to say something about the later history of Stoicism, which also had its contribution to make to that final synthesis of ancient thought in which the revival of Platonism culminated, the Neo-Platonism of Plotinus and his successors. Of the later history of the other schools not much need be said. Epicureanism had a period of great success at Rome in the first century B.C. when it produced Lucretius and influenced many notable people. Thereafter the Epicureans went on repeating the doctrines of their founder and making few but devout disciples (hardly any cases are known of conversion from Epicureanism to any other philosophy) till they finally disappear quietly from view. The revived Scepticism of Ænesidemus kept up its formidable attack on the dogmatists of all varieties till the beginning of the third century A.D. and had a considerable influence among medical men. But the main interest of the period lies in the interactions and reactions between Platonism, Aristotelianism, and Stoicism which led up to the Neo-Platonic synthesis.

2.   In the last two centuries B.C. Stoicism underwent a process of humanization. Its teachings became gentler and more reasonable and certain of the harsher and more grotesque doctrines were quietly dropped. In this process of humanization it drew nearer

to Platonism in several important ways, just as the revived
Platonism more than once showed itself ready to take over a good
deal of Stoic doctrine. There are in fact signs of the emergence, not
of a common and universally held philosophy, but of a certain
body of ideas held by most thinking men who were not Epicureans
or Sceptics. We should not, however, I think, talk too loosely
and generally about Eclecticism as the general characteristic of
Græco-Roman philosophy in this period. The different schools
continued to exist and to engage in vigorous polemic against each
other, even though there was a certain amount of interpenetration
of doctrines. And we must distinguish carefully between the attitude of mind of a cultivated Roman gentleman well read in
philosophy like Cicero, who was a ıeal Eclectic, that is, not a
systematic thinker but one who collected little bits and pieces of
whatever pleased him in the teachings of all schools, and that of a
professional philosopher who would hold to the system of one
school however much he might be affected, consciously or unconsciously, by the teaching of others. This latter type of thinker
is not really an Eclectic in the usual sense of the word, though he
is sometimes called one by modern historians of philosophy, and
it is often convenient to use the word, as long as we clearly understand its meaning in this connection. The philosophical un-
denominationalism which is what we usually mean by Eclecticism
prevailed in some circles of high Roman society, though there too
we can find vigorous adherents of particular schools. But
denominationalism was still the order of the day among those
who took philosophy more seriously, and the final outcome was
not a fusion in which all the schools became indistinguishable,
but a complete victory over all the other schools for a Platonism
which had absorbed important Aristotelian and less important
Stoic elements.

The first of the old Stoic doctrines to be dropped was that of
the Conflagration, the absorption of all things in the Divine Fire
and their subsequent restoration, which made the history of the
universe an endless series of cycles. This seems to have disappeared
quite soon after Chrysippus, certainly by the middle of the
second century B.C. In its place the Stoics accepted the doctrine
common to Platonists and Aristotelians of the eternity of the
cosmos. By abandoning their older, more dynamic world-view
of the Divine Fire alternately creating and destroying all things
out of its own substance, while retaining and strengthening their

belief in the organic unity of the universe and the control of every detail in it by Divine Providence, these later Stoics made an important contribution to that view of the eternal, static cosmic order which is an essential element in late pagan thought. Two very "Oriental" Stoics, Diogenes of Babylon and Bœthus of Sidon, were responsible for abandoning the Conflagration, but a much more important philosopher who shared their views was Panætius of Rhodes, who carried the toning down of Stoicism a good deal further. He came to Rome in 143 B.C. with Scipio Africanus, through whom he came into contact with the circle of Roman aristocrats who were vigorously and successfully setting about acquiring Greek culture; and it was he more than anyone else who transformed Stoicism into a belief suitable for Roman gentlemen. Besides giving up the Conflagration he doubted the validity of divination, belief in which was very closely bound up with the Stoic idea of Fate or Providence. On the ethical side he laid more emphasis on at least the relative value of external goods and pleasure than the older Stoics; this may well be because he was more interested in the state of those making moral progress than in the ideal of the perfect Sage. It is possible that his difference from his predecessors was more one of tone and emphasis than a change of fundamental doctrine; but he was certainly regarded as gentler and more human, and his less rigid presentation of Stoicism helped a great deal to extend its influence over the minds of aristocratic Romans.

3. A different turn was given to the development of Stoicism by the great Greek-Syrian Stoic of the next generation, Posidonius of Apamea (130–46 B.C.), who also had a great influence at Rome. He was by far the most notable figure in the intellectual life of his age, a distinguished geographer and historian as well as a philosopher, and a voluminous writer. But his works have unfortunately perished, and it is difficult to know how much of the bold reconstructions of his philosophy made by modern scholars is really likely to belong to him. He certainly adopted a good deal of Platonic doctrine. His most notable certain borrowing from Plato is the tripartite psychology, the division of the soul into rational, emotional and appetitive parts (of course, he still thought of the soul as material). This was a startling breach with Stoic tradition, and it meant a humanizing of the older morality. Man's duty if the tripartite psychology is accepted is to keep his emotions and passions under control, not to eradicate them utterly. Perhaps

too, Posidonius stressed the transcendence of the Divine Fiery Breath as Operative Providence, seated in the æthereal regions and especially the sun, and held that the rational part of man's soul, the intellect or ruling principle, was an emanation from the divine substance in the sun, descending to the sublunary world by way of the moon, and at last after purification ascending again to a blessed immortality in the place of its origin. He greatly stressed the organic unity of the world and the universal sympathy which binds all things together, and originated the idea of the scale of different kinds of unity, culminating in the perfect unification of the organism, which Plotinus developed further. Posidonius first, too, stated clearly the idea, implicit in much earlier Greek thought, of man as a "bridge-being", intermediate between the two worlds, higher and lower, between the animal and the divine, which became of very great importance in later thought. We may mention here two ideas which seem to belong to the world of thought of Platonized Stoicism, or Stoicized Platonism though they cannot be attributed to Posidonius himself. One is the idea of "astral immortality", of the return of the souls of good men to the æthereal regions of the Upper Cosmos whence they came, where they spend a happy immortality contemplating the workings of the Divine Reason as manifested most perfectly in the movements of the heavenly bodies—in other words watching the stars go round (this idea may be Neo-Pythagorean). The other is the curious identification by some Stoics (and probably by Antiochus of Ascalon) of the Platonic Ideas with the immanent wisdom in the mind of the Divine Fire-Reason conceived as Providence operating in the upper, æthereal, regions of the Cosmos. These ideas fit very well into the common world-view which took shape in the last centuries B.C. and dominated later pagan thought, the view of the eternal cosmos, a single organism, ruled by a divine power residing in or manifesting itself through the bright fiery regions of the upper atmosphere, in the visible gods, the sun and the other heavenly bodies, with which divine power the highest parts of men's souls were naturally akin, so that they might hope to return after death to the æthereal regions, their true home.

For the latest Stoics and the ones whom we know best, since their works or full reports of their teaching have survived, philosophy is before all else a way of life. The great Stoics of the first two centuries A.D., Seneca, Musonius Rufus, Epictetus and

Marcus Aurelius are almost exclusively concerned with moral and spiritual direction or that self-examination which was a regular practice of the good Stoic. Seneca, the millionaire tutor and minister of Nero, is, as we might expect, the most superficial. In philosophy he is a complete eclectic, who though a professed Stoic, admires and frequently quotes Epicurus. His extensive writings on philosophy are all essays or lay sermons on practical moral topics. The Puritan and upholder of the old Roman moral tradition Musonius Rufus is an attractive figure in many ways with his preaching of humanity, chastity, the importance of marriage and the family and of agricultural life as best suited to a philosopher. But by far the greatest of these late Stoics are Epictetus and Marcus Aurelius. Epictetus is a conservative in philosophy, going back to the old traditions of Zeno and Chrysippus. But he is before all else a moral and religious teacher. This freed slave and cripple proclaims better than any other Stoic the essence of Stoic religion, the joyful resignation to the will of a Divine Providence which becomes for him a personal transcendent God rather than an impersonal Fiery Breath. And his morality is a high one, though disfigured to Christian thinking by a certain spiritual pride and hardness. The Stoic Emperor, Marcus Aurelius, finally, has left us in the twelve books of his self-examination, written in Greek and entitled "To Himself", a most moving record of a sensitive, profound, scrupulous, sometimes too consciously superior, but very admirable man. His thought is based very largely on that of Epictetus, but he is more of an eclectic, and in particular derives a great deal from Plato, who was much admired and read by late Roman Stoics. He does not, however, share the confident Platonic belief in immortality, but follows the Stoic tradition which regarded the survival of the soul as doubtful at best. The general impression left by these two last great Stoic writers is a saddening one. They preach magnificently the nothingness and futility of all earthly things. Epictetus pushes his doctrine of indifference to all possessions, external goods, and human affections to a Cynic extreme. And though Marcus Aurelius is the most loyal and loving of men to his family, friends and teachers, yet he too feels the futility of all the things with which men busy themselves; and he has nothing quite positive enough to put on the other side. He is a man deeply weary of life. One of his last sayings is "You are only a little soul carrying a corpse about". It is interesting to read the letters of the early second-century martyr St. Ignatius the Godbearer, Bishop of Antioch, alongside the writings of Epictetus and Marcus Aurelius, and especially to contrast their attitude to death, in order to realize the difference between the temper of the two religions, the new fire breaking out on the earth which is Christianity and the grey light of the end of Stoicism.

4. The return to positive and dogmatic teaching in the Academy began with Philo of Larissa, who succeeded Clitomachus, the pupil and expounder of Carneades, in. the headship. He definitely abandoned scepticism by teaching that things were comprehensible in themselves, even if the Stoic doctrine of "gripping representation" was invalid. He paid much attention to the history of his school and its doctrines, and as he maintained that there had been a real continuity in its teaching it is possible that he held the theory which we meet in Cicero and St. Augustine (and which may just possibly be true) of an unbroken tradition of dogmatic teaching preserved behind the outward scepticism of the New Academy. A much more important figure than Philo is his successor, Antiochus of Ascalon. He is philosophically a most curious person, for he reacted so thoroughly from the Sceptical Academy's attack on dogmatism that he maintained that Zeno was really a reforming Platonist and that Stoic teaching was identical with that of Plato! In this way he probably hoped to unite all the forces of dogmatism to resist the sceptical attack. His own teaching, as far as we can reconstruct it, was, in spite of his professed Platonism, in almost all respects a Stoicism of the eclectic type introduced by Panætius and Posidonius. In fact, it seems quite possible that there was less which was genuinely Platonic in the thought of the "Platonist" Antiochus than in that of the Stoic Posidonius. Antiochus is perhaps the philosopher who best represents that general world-view or body of ideas about the nature of things which I sketched above, and his influence was probably very wide. During the period between his leaving the Academy at Athens after a quarrel with Philo and his return there as Philo's successor, he taught at Alexandria and left behind him there a group of pupils who carried on the tradition of his particular sort of eclecticism. The later Eclectics of Alexandria in the time of Augustus, Potamo and his school, also modelled themselves on Antiochus. Among these Alexandrian Eclectics not only were Stoicism and Platonism combined, but also important Aristotelian and Pythagorean elements appear in their

philosophy. A more important Alexandrian eclectic philosopher than Potamo and his followers was Arius Didymus, the friend of Augustus. He was not really an eclectic in the true sense, for he seems to have been definitely an adherent of Stoicism, though willing to learn from other schools. But his importance is not as an original thinker but as a doxographer, a writer who collected and arranged systematically the opinions of the leading thinkers of all schools on the most important philosophical topics, grouping them according to the recognized divisions of philosophy, Logic, Physics, Ethics, etc. It is likely that his writings had a considerable influence on the later development of Middle Platonism.

5. This kind of doxographic writing and the other great activity of philosophical scholarship, the production of commentaries on Plato and Aristotle (which begins in the first century B.C. and goes on to the end of the history of pagan Hellenic philosophy and beyond), provide the learned environment in which the characteristic doctrines of Middle Platonism grew up. And Antiochus and his followers provided an outlook much more favourable to this scholarly study of philosophy, of which Alexandria was the most important centre, than the older, narrow and exclusive dogmatisms. After Antiochus and the Middle Stoics, philosophers of one school would sometimes at least read the writings of great thinkers of another school with respect and in the hope of learning something from them, and not merely for controversial purposes. It is in his return to positive teaching from negative criticism and his introduction into the Academy of this new attitude of appreciation of the positive teachings of other schools that Antiochus's real importance lies. But the actual development of Middle Platonist doctrine followed lines very different from those on which Antiochus started. When it becomes clearly visible in the second century A.D. it is neither a formless eclecticism nor Stoicism masquerading as Platonism. It is genuinely Platonic doctrine, differing in many important ways from the teaching of Plato himself, and showing many signs of the influence of Aristotle and of other schools, but going back in many essential points to Plato's own pupil Xenocrates.

It is not possible here to discuss the obscure and rather confused development of Middle Platonism from the first century B.C. to the second century A.D., nor even to give a detailed account of the teachings of every individual Platonic philosopher of any importance in the great age of Middle Platonism. What is essential for our purpose is that we should form as clear an idea as possible of at least the main outlines of the philosophy taught as Platonism by the Middle Platonists of the second century A.D., in order that we may be able to see how much this philosophy influenced the first Christian philosophical theologians and how far it provided a foundation for the infinitely greater and profounder philosophy of Plotinus. This is vital to our whole study, for the whole of traditional Christian philosophy and philosophical theology derives on the Hellenic side either from Middle Platonism or from Plotinus. It will not be altogether easy to get this clear view, for Middle Platonism is not at all a coherent philosophy; but I shall do my best to sketch it comprehensively, noting the most serious inconsistencies and divergences between different philosophers.

In the development of Platonism after its revival we can trace from the first century B.C. onwards an important conflict of opinions about the value of the teachings of other schools. One group of Platonists, perhaps centring round the Academy at Athens, regarded Aristotle and his teaching with hostility and were much influenced by Stoicism. Their most notable representative known to us was a certain Atticus, a person of remarkable intemperance of language. Another group was hostile to the Stoics (though not altogether uninfluenced by them) and was very thoroughly under the influence of Aristotle, especially of his logic and metaphysics. This latter group, whose best representative for us is the second-century philosopher Albinus, was considerably more important in its influence on later thought, though Plotinus, in spite of the great amount of Aristotelianism which his philosophy contains, follows the tradition of the first group in some ways, especially in his criticism of Aristotle's logic. A third important influence besides that of Aristotle and the Stoics was that of the revived Pythagoreanism which begins to appear in the first century B.C. Neo-Pythagoreanism might mean nothing more than astrology, occultism, and twaddle about the mysterious properties of numbers. But it might also be quite a serious philosophy, and from Eudorus the eclectic Platonist of Alexandria down to Numenius at the end of the second and beginning of the third century A.D. we meet philosophers, sometimes calling themselves Platonists, sometimes (like Numenius) Pythagoreans who emphasize certain doctrines which can be regarded as characteristic of this revived Pythagoreanism.

6.   Middle Platonism, like nearly all the philosophies and pseudo-philosophies of its age, was first and foremost a theology and a religious way of life. Its primary objects were knowledge of the truth about the divine world and "the greatest possible likeness to god". The personal religious attitude of its adherents varied considerably, from the superficial, emotional, rather bogus religiosity of Apuleius or Maximus of Tyre to the deep and genuine piety of Plutarch, the ascetic other-worldliness of Numenius or the detached, rational outlook, with little sign of deep religious feeling of a scholarly Platonist like Albinus. And for our purpose of tracing the history of traditional European philosophy it is the theology or metaphysics of Middle Platonism, with its views on the nature and destiny of the human soul, which is of primary importance. The first and in many ways the most important of its distinctive theological doctrines is the placing of a supreme Mind or God at the head of the hierarchy of being, as the first principle of reality. Of this Supreme Mind the Platonic Forms are represented as thoughts; they are not only its content and the object of its thinking, but it is actually their cause. This is a considerable development from the teaching of Plato as I have represented it, following the evidence of the dialogues as I understand them. But if we glance back at the philosophy of the generation after Plato we shall see plenty of precedent for it.

Xenocrates, it will be remembered, identified the Good, the first principle of the World of Forms with the Monad or Primal Unity (as Plato had apparently done) and with Mind. Aristotle, though he rejected the Forms and consequently could not place them in the Divine Mind, yet makes a transcendent Mind his first principle of reality. And an interesting confirmation of this tendency in the philosophy of the period is the teaching of Eucleides of Megara, Plato's contemporary and co-disciple of Socrates that the Good was one thing with many names and could be appropriately called "intelligence", "mind" or "god". Though, as we have seen, Plato himself speaks of the Good in a way which makes it legitimate for us to call it God, he does not represent it as a Mind of which the other Forms, are the thoughts. And neither for Aristotle nor for Xenocrates are the Forms actually in the Divine Mind; Xenocrates placed them in the companion of his Mind-Monad, the Indefinite Dyad and for Aristotle of course they are not there at all. But at least we have found, contemporary with Plato and among his own disciples, three very different thinkers who made Mind the first principle of reality: and one of them, Xenocrates, actually derived the Forms from this supreme Mind. Other fourth-century Platonists may have approached the Middle Platonist doctrine even more closely, but the evidence is not quite sufficient to be certain.

The Middle Platonists follow Xenocrates in identifying their supreme Mind or God with Plato's Good. The eclectic Eudorus also follows him (under the influence of Neo-Pythagoreanism) in calling it One; but he differs from him in making this One a supreme Unity which is before the One and Indefinite Dyad which are the elements of number and so generating principles of the Forms. This explicit identification of the Supreme Principle with the One which is of such importance in the philosophy of Plotinus, does not appear again before the end of the second century, but Neo-Pythagorean influence was certainly one of the causes responsible for the extreme stressing of the transcendence and remoteness of the Supreme Principle which we find more or less in all the Middle Platonists, and which is particularly marked in Numenius, who called himself a Pythagorean. In Numenius's insistence, however, on the repose of his First God and his freedom from all external activities we can see another most important influence which led the Middle Platonists to assert the utter transcendence of the Supreme so strongly—that of Aristotle's conception of his remote, self-thinking Unmoved Mover, who has no active concern with the affairs of the universe. Aristotle's influence, too, probably had a good deal to do with the placing of the Forms in the Divine Mind. Both his conception of the Unmoved Mover with its immanent, self-contained activity of thought, and his psychology, with its intimate correlation of thought and object of thought (which plays a very important part in Plotinus's later development of the doctrine) affected Middle Platonist thinking. But the form of the doctrine found in the Middle Platonists, with its very definite priority of the Supreme Mind as cause of the Forms is less Aristotelian than that which we shall find in Plotinus. It probably derives mainly from Xenocrates's identification of Mind and Good and may have been influenced by the curious middle Stoic doctrine which I mentioned earlier in this chapter, which identified the Forms with the thoughts of the Stoic Divine Fire-Reason. All the same, the Middle Platonist conception of the remote transcendent Supreme Mind and Good has nothing at all Stoic about it and is often presented (notably by Albinus) in a way which shows very clearly the influence of Aristotle. It is a complex and rather confused conception, showing very clearly the several strands of philosophical tradition which are loosely entangled rather than securely interwoven in it, but it is of the greatest importance for all later philosophical theology.

7. This remote transcendent Supreme Mind, though it is still a Mind and not as in Plotinus That which is beyond Mind and is its source, is exalted to such a height that it cannot be thought of as in direct contact with the material world or accessible to the human soul in this life, except in occasional flashes of illumination. To the Middle Platonists the Supreme God is not beyond all hierarchy, but is the head of the hierarchy of being and so is very far away from us and from our world, and only to be reached through intermediaries. Albinus, it is true, identifies his Supreme Mind with the Craftsman of the "Timæus", the former and orderer of the material world; but he is not at all consistent and elsewhere presents us with two intermediary powers between the Supreme and our world, the "Second Mind" or "God" and the Soul of the World, also taken from the "Timæus". These the Supreme Mind actualises and brings into effective existence by awaking them, as it were, from a sleep (a conception probably widely current among the Middle Platonists). The "Second Mind" in Albinus is given a very Aristotelian character, being the Mind or moving Intelligence of the First Heaven, which is moved by desire of the Supreme. This hierarchy of three principles, First Mind or God, Second Mind or God, and World-Soul, reappears in Numenius with the important difference that he identifies his Second God with the Craftsman of the "Timæus", drops the Aristotelian idea of the movement by desire of the Supreme, but makes his Supreme God rather more Aristotelian than Albinus, as being free from all outward activities like Aristotle's self-contemplating Unmoved Mover. In the more popular and superficial writers, like Apuleius and Maximus of Tyre, the intermediaries are the gods of mythology, the divine heavenly bodies, and on a lower level the "dæmons", supernatural beings not impassible nor according to some accounts necessarily immortal, of varying nature and disposition, who act as intermediaries between gods and men. Belief in these dæmones goes back to the beginning of Greek myth-making, to the "Theogony" of Hesiod. Plato makes use of it in his myth of Eros

in the "Symposium", but it is in the period which we are now dealing with that the belief becomes of primary importance in philosophy and theology. Among other things, it provided pagan theologians hard pressed by Christian apologists with a convenient explanation of the discreditable stories told about the gods and the unpleasant rites with which they were sometimes worshipped. These, it could be held (when no profound allegorical significance could be detected in them), were really concerned with the "dæmones" and not with the gods at all. Of course, Albinus and Numenius believe in the gods and dæmones as much as the more popular writers; and these latter accept the doctrines of the transcendent Supreme and the Platonic Soul of the World. If, then, we are to give a generalized picture of reality as seen by the Middle Platonists it will be something like this. At the head of the hierarchy stands a Supreme Mind or God, ineffably remote and exalted, combining Aristotle's Unmoved Mover with Plato's Form of the Good. Then come intermediary beings—the Second Mind, the lesser gods, the stars, the dæmones—ruling and ordering and some of them inhabiting the visible universe which is itself as in the "Timæus" a living being animated by a World-Soul.

As regards the formation of the visible universe the Middle Platonists were divided. As we have already seen, Plato's "Timæus" had a great influence on their thought and many important features of their theology derive from interpretations of parts of Plato's great myth, consciously or unconsciously influenced by later philosophy. Now the "Timæus", if taken literally, seems to imply the formation of the visible universe at a definite moment in time, and some of the Middle Platonists, notably Plutarch, accepted this. Others, however, strongly maintained the purely symbolical character of the "Timæus" narrative and so held to the eternity of the world, and it was this view which finally prevailed. It was, of course, that which modern scholars attribute to Plato himself, and it had been held (as had also the opposing view) in the Academy from the beginning and would derive further support from Aristotle's very strong insistence that the visible universe was necessarily without beginning and without end. Of course, neither side in the debate had any idea of creation or of eternity (as opposed to everlastingness) in the sense which Christian theology gives to the words; and consequently they could not arrive at anything like St. Augustine's magisterial solution of the difficulty about what God was doing before he made the world.

Another point disputed among the Middle Platonists was that of the source of evil. A very widely held belief among second-century Platonists, shared among others by Plutarch and Atticus, was that the cause of evil was an evil Soul immanent in matter and having the whole material universe under its domination. For Numenius matter itself was evil and the active enemy of God and of all good. Albinus does not take so pessimistic a view of the material universe, and does not identify matter and evil or assert the existence of an evil cosmic soul; but he has no better alternative explanation to offer, though, like all Platonists, he insists that the evils which affect us are the necessary result of embodiment and that God is not responsible for the evils that men suffer. The idea of an evil World-Soul is, of course, a development of suggestions made by Plato himself in the "Timæus" and the "Laws". The idea of matter as not merely passive but recalcitrant, thwarting the intentions of the good, forming, ordering principle is also in Plato and even sometimes appears in Aristotle. But the identification of matter and evil is Neo-Pythagorean rather than Platonic; and the dualism characteristic of these later Platonic systems seems to be influenced by that Persian dualism whose influence is even more apparent in Gnosticism.

8. So great was the distance separating the Supreme Mind from this our life in the visible world that the Middle Platonists thought that the most we could hope to attain in this life was a very rare and short-lived direct intuition of it. The remoteness of the Supreme, its characteristic of transcending our thought, is expressed by Albinus by the use of a crude and undeveloped form of the "negative theology" which is of such importance in the thought of Plotinus and in all later philosophical theology of the central tradition. I shall discuss this more fully when we come to Plotinus, but it is worth remarking here that the early history of this "negative theology"—the description of God by saying what he is not rather than what he is—is bound up with a particular interpretation of Plato's most difficult dialogue, the "Parmenides" which was accepted by all later Platonists and finds defenders even now. This indirect knowledge of God by negation is very far from the direct contemplation or full and clear intuition which is what Platonists mean by knowledge. This latter, the Middle Platonists held, we could only enjoy in a few brief flashes of

intuition until we were liberated from the body and returned to our proper god-like state. We find this sort of illuminism, the belief that very occasionally in this life the momentary vision of the Supreme breaks upon the soul like a blaze of light, not only in that very inferior thinker Apuleius but in the first Platonist writer against the Christians, Celsus, and among the Platonists whom Justin Martyr knew. But it is important to realize that there is no trace of true mystical experience among the Middle Platonists, and though there is plenty of silly, empty, rhetorical false mysticism in the philosophical underworld of the time, the Middle Platonists are on the whole very free from it. Albinus seems to have had little religious feeling, and Plutarch, whom we know as a man far better than the others from his voluminous works which have survived, had a very deep, sober, genuine piety without mystical pretensions or pseudo-mystical corruptions. There is one Platonist and one only in the whole history of pagan Platonism who is certainly a genuine mystic, and that is Plotinus. The religion of a Middle Platonist consisted of a remote intellectual devotion to the remote Supreme, to the vision of whom he hoped to attain in the next life and perhaps for a few rare moments in this, combined with a vigorous practice of the normal pagan piety towards the inferior gods, the star-gods and the other deities of mythology and public cult, who administered the affairs of the visible universe and with whom in this life we were most closely concerned.

9.   The Middle Platonist original contribution to other parts of philosophy was not considerable, and I do not propose to say very much about it. The Aristotelian party took over Aristotle's logic bodily as an indispensable preliminary to the study of Plato's philosophy, and the anti-Aristotelians correspondingly made it one of the main objects of their attacks. In ethics and psychology the Middle Platonists remained on the whole faithful to the Platonic tradition, though they did not escape considerable Stoic influence on their ethics, especially strong among the anti-Aristotelians, and there are some signs of Aristotle's influence (not however very marked) on the other side. But their general conception of the nature of man and of the good life was thoroughly Platonic. The human soul was a divine being which had been sent by God or had descended of its own free will into the body and the object of man's life is to purify himself by philosophy and so prepare for final disembodiment, a return to the life of the gods,

and the vision of the Supreme. It is a conception of man's life and destiny which has never been without influence, not altogether good, on Christian thinkers.

But the main Middle Platonist contribution to traditional philosophy was made in the sphere of theology. It was of enormous importance, to begin with, that they started the idea that it might be possible to reconcile and bring into harmony the ideas of Plato and Aristotle about the universe and about divine things. By bringing together Aristotle's Divine Mind and Plato's Good, First Principle of the World of Forms, and by placing the Forms in the Divine Mind they prepared the way for a more satisfactory conception of the Divine Being than had yet been arrived at. The making of the Forms the "thoughts of God" was in particular a development of the utmost importance. Their doctrine of intermediary powers and their false and inadequate exaltation of the Supreme Principle had very considerable influence in their own time and the period immediately following. But these doctrines involved a conception of the primal Divinity which Plotinus found it necessary to go very considerably beyond and which was quite incompatible with Christian theology, and therefore their influence was very much more restricted. The error, as I see it, in their conception of Divine transcendence is that they put God at the head of the hierarchy of reality, according to the general Hellenic tradition, and so make Him remote and inaccessible to its lower members. Actually, as Plotinus began to see, God is not at the head of the hierarchy. He is beyond all hierarchy, and therefore most intimately present to each and every member, high or low, of the hierarchy of derived realities, according to their capacity to receive Him.

10. Before ending this account of the development of philosophy from the first century B.C. to the beginning of the third century A.D., I must go back to the beginning of the period and say something about the activity of Cicero (106–43 B.C.) as translator and transmitter. Cicero himself was not an original philosopher and contributed nothing to the development of ancient thought. He was a great orator and statesman for whom the study of Greek philosophy and the setting down of those ideas of contemporary and earlier philosophers which interested him in admirable Latin was an absorbing, refreshing and comforting spare-time occupation. He says of his own philosophical works. "They are copies, made with very little trouble. I only supply the words, of

which I have plenty" (ad Atticum 12.52.3). He does sometimes elsewhere lay claim to rather more originality: but it can hardly be said to amount to more than a refusal, in the spirit of the New Academy, to commit himself completely to any particular opinion, a tendency to seek for compromises between opposing views, and a very Roman emphasis on the importance of practical morality. But his "copies", with their very fair setting out of the opposing views of the great schools, are copies or rather adaptations of originals now lost to us and are one of our main sources of knowledge about the philosophy of the period. And for many students of later ages who spoke and read Latin, notably St. Augustine, Cicero's works were the first introduction to ancient philosophy and their influence on Latin Christendom, especially on its moral, social and political ideas, was very great. The words, too, which he supplied were excellent ones. He is the creator of Latin philosophical language, and his work in this way has been of the greatest importance to the West. It is to him, for instance, that we owe "matter", "quality" and "quantity" (*materia* in its philosophical use, *qualitas* and *quantitas*).

XIV

The Beginnings of Greek-Christian Thought. Philo. The Apologists

I. STRICTLY speaking there can hardly be said to have been such a thing as Christian philosophy as distinct from Christian theology before S. Thomas Aquinas. Some very eminent authorities, indeed, deny with much vigour that it is legitimate to speak of "Christian philosophy" at all; but this debate about whether there is such a thing as Christian philosophy lies, fortunately, quite outside the scope of this book. There is no dispute about the historical fact that, though the division had been beginning to appear well before his time, it was S. Thomas who first clearly established it as legitimate and delimited two separate spheres of intellectual activity for Christians, philosophy and theology, and that this distinction has regulated the arrangement of the higher studies of Catholics, and especially of the clergy, since his time. Whether the effects of this sharp division have been good or not is another discussion upon which the limits of this book prevent us from entering. We must, however, have quite clear in our minds that within the period covered by this book and for centuries afterwards the Thomistic distinction of two well-defined separate kinds of mental activity is not made or thought of. What the Fathers of the Church and those early medieval thinkers who follow the tradition of the Fathers, right down to S. Thomas's great contemporary S. Bonaventure, are concerned with is the pursuit of what Maritain calls Christian Wisdom. That is, they are trying to apply all the resources of minds trained according to the methods and familiar with the traditions of Greek philosophy to the interpretation of the data of Revelation, to the explanation of the Scriptures and the deeper understanding of the doctrines handed down in the Church. In doing this much of their activity was in the strict sense philosophical and they by no means despised reason or denied the possibility of reasoning from naturally known first principles; but their philosophy and theology can never be clearly separated, because their reason throughout depends consciously on divine faith and grace. There were two motives which inspired their work, the first, apologetic, to make the truths of Christianity more

comprehensible and attractive to those educated in Greek
philosophy and the second the more genuinely theological desire
to use whatever was usable in the wisdom of the Greeks in order to
co-ordinate the traditional truths, to understand their inter-
dependence and to penetrate further into their meaning; in other
words to build up a real theology in the new Christian sense of the
term, containing or at least implying a philosophy, but a philosophy illuminated by faith.

It is very necessary, I think, that we should realize how this new
kind of intellectual activity, theology in what for traditional
Christian thinkers is the most usual sense of the word, differs from
the theology of the Greek philosophers and from the Natural
Theology which S. Thomas makes a part not of theology proper
but of philosophy. The theology of the Greek philosophers was
one section, that which dealt with divine, unchanging, everlasting, realities, of what claimed to be a complete account of
reality arrived at by the use of the human reason with no assistance from other than human sources. Christian theology is also
concerned with divine reality in itself and its relations with man
and other existing things; and it attempts to give as complete an
account of this as is possible for the human mind. But it insists
that divine truth is beyond the grasp of the unaided human
intelligence and that in order to give even the inadequate account
of it possible to us we need God's help in the form of grace and
also information supplied by God, i.e. Revelation. Natural
Theology according to S. Thomas bears more resemblance to
Greek theology in one way, since it consists of that amount of
truth about divine reality which can be known by the unaided
human reason; but it differs from Greek theology in insisting that
its truth is not the whole truth about the divine, even as far as
human reason here and now can know it. The truth which can be
known by unaided reason in the sphere of Natural Theology is
only a small fragment, incomplete at every point, of the truth
which can be known by Revelation and studied by Theology
proper.

Now that we have arrived at some understanding of the difference between pagan Greek and Christian theology, and have
understood that up to S. Thomas or shortly before him Christian
thought means Christian theology, we can go on to consider the
origins and nature of the earliest Christian thinking. But first it
may be as well to explain why I have thought it desirable, if this

Christian thought is as I have said theology rather than philosophy, to say anything at all about it in what purports to be a history of ancient philosophy. The reasons are, first that any survey of the thought of the Græco-Roman world which left out early Christian theology would be absurdly incomplete, and then that the influence of Christian theology on later European thought has been very great, and it is therefore absolutely necessary for a historian of ancient philosophy to give some account of that theology's beginnings. It was after all through Christian theology that Greek philosophical ideas were transmitted to the Middle Ages (there were, of course, other channels of transmission, but theology was by far the most important) and from the Middle Ages, to a greater extent than is sometimes realized, to the Renaissance and to the philosophers of later times. The persistence of this indirect Hellenic influence through the theological tradition alongside the direct influence of the works of the Greek philosophers themselves when they became known again in the West is a very interesting and important phenomenon in the later history of philosophy.

2.   The Hellenic philosophies which influenced this early Christian thought were naturally those of most importance in the Græco-Roman world, Middle Platonism and Stoicism. But beside this direct Hellenic influence, and perhaps in some ways more important than it, there was a less direct connection between Greek thought and early Christian theology through the Hellenized Judaism of Alexandria, and above all through the work of that remarkable personage Philo Judæus or Alexandrinus. Philo of Alexandria was born some time about the beginning of the reign of the Emperor Augustus, and died probably soon after A.D. 40, when he took part in an important embassy from the Jews of Alexandria to the Emperor Caligula. He was, as this episode shows, a leading figure in the Alexandrian Jewish community, and his writings are our best evidence for its culture and intellectual outlook. The Jews of Alexandria were the most thoroughly Hellenized of all the Jews of the Dispersion. They read the Scriptures in their own Greek translation, the Septuagint, and produced a considerable religious literature in Greek, including one of the latest books of the Old Testament Canon, the theologically very important "Wisdom of Solomon". The young men of their leading families were educated in Greek philosophy, of which Philo has a very extensive, if not always profound knowledge.

But in spite of their Hellenization the Jews of Alexandria remained practising and fundamentally orthodox Jews, and Philo is no exception. His extremely voluminous writings are all commentaries on the Jewish Scriptures and his thought, though it is so lacking in clearness and coherence that it is difficult to generalize about it, is essentially Jewish rather than Greek. He was, however, deeply influenced by his study of Greek philosophy and very anxious to find some way of interpreting the Jewish revelation so as to bring it into harmony with the teachings of the Greek philosophers. The results of this are curious. The method which Philo employs to bring the Scriptures into conformity with those Greek philosophical doctrines which attracted him is one very common in his period and for long afterwards, that of allegorical interpretation. It was a method extensively used by Stoics and Platonists alike in order to get some philosophical sense out of the very unphilosophical stories told about the gods by Homer and the other ancient poets, and was particularly useful to the later Neo-Platonists in their gigantic effort to bring all the pagan myths and rites into one coherent theological system capable of standing up against the attacks of Christianity. Philo applies it to the Scriptures in the most spacious manner and with a fine disregard for consistency, so that the literal meaning disappears completely in his exegesis. The book of Genesis in particular is not considered by him as a record of historical fact, but as a kind of Platonic myth describing the creation of Intelligence, higher and lower, and Soul by God together with the intelligible and sensible worlds, a Platonic "fall" of the intelligence seduced by the senses, and the ways by which it can return to its original state. This allegorical method as used quite recklessly by Philo is not likely to be attractive to modern readers, and, when employed as it often has been by Christian commentators from Origen onwards, its effects on the understanding of the Scriptures have generally been unfortunate; it should not, of course, be confused with the "typological" method of spiritual interpretation used already in the New Testament, in which Old Testament figures and events are seen as types of Christ and his redeeming action.

By means of his unbounded allegorizing Philo succeeds in reading into the Scriptures every doctrine of contemporary Greek philosophy which he finds attractive. Cynic ethics, Stoic physical theology and psychology, and a great deal of rather blurred Platonism, jostle each other in his interminable expositions of the

Septuagint texts. The mixture is all too liberally seasoned with
vast quantities of speculation about the mystical properties of
numbers in the worst-Neo-Pythagorean vein (this taste for the
dreary perversities of numerology was unfortunately shared by
the Christian Fathers and medieval theologians). Mingled with
this confused Hellenism there is a strong strain of genuine Jewish
speculation, and underlying all Philo's thought and never completely lost sight of is the great Jewish doctrine of God the Creator
and Ruler of the universe.

3. So far the impression conveyed by what I have said about
Philo must be that of a thoroughly tiresome and muddle-headed
person unworthy of any serious philosophical consideration, and
this indeed is how some serious students of the history of Greek
philosophy regard him. Muddle-headed and inconsistent he
certainly is, but in the rich confusion of his writings there can be
found, certainly not a coherent philosophy, but some ideas which
are permanently valuable and others which are at least of
historical interest. First of all we may consider what is probably
the most historically important group of Philo's ideas, those which
result from the interaction in his mind of the Jewish doctrine of
God with the sort of Platonic speculations about the transcendence and remoteness of the First Divinity which I have
described in the last chapter. The Jewish doctrine shows God as
intimately concerned with this world which He has made freely
by an act of His Will and continually governs. The Platonic
doctrine certainly insists very strongly on the divine governance
and divine formation of the world, and both Plato and the Middle
Platonists leave some room for the operation of the Divine Will in
this activity of formation and ruling; they do not, that is, as we
shall see that Plotinus does, represent it as a necessary, automatic
reflex action springing without thought or will from a higher contemplation. But Middle Platonism differed from Judaism in
recognizing a hierarchy of divine beings and its tendency was
as we have seen to remove the Supreme Good or God, the First
Principle or Mind, to a very great distance from the visible world
and to consider this latter as being ruled and generally also formed
by lower, intermediary divine powers. In Philo we find an
attempt to reconcile these two conceptions. There is only One
God who is active Himself in creating and ruling the cosmos. His
transcendence is however very much stressed and He does not act
directly in creating and ruling, but through the medium of various

intermediary powers. These powers Philo describes very confusedly, and does not make their status in reality at all clear.
Sometimes he speaks of "the Powers", sometimes of two Powers in
particular, the Creative and the Royal, but most often and most
strikingly of a single great intermediary, the Logos. Philo's
"Powers" hardly seem to be distinct beings, but rather God's
operations which appear to us as separate from God himself;
there are passages (Quæstiones in Genesim IV, 8. De Abrahamo
121ff) where Philo says that this appearance is due to the weakness of our normal intellectual vision and that in the highest
mystical contemplation the Powers disappear and we see God
One and alone. The question of the separate existence of the
Logos is a more difficult one. Philo unites in his descriptions of
this mysterious being the most diverse and contradictory images
and concepts. Now it is symbolized by the Jewish High Priest,
now it is the principle of division and separation, of the separate
existence of individual things (a Stoic idea) now it is the Platonic
World of Forms. In this last capacity it is represented by Philo
as being a sort of architect's plan or preliminary pattern which
God makes first in order to create the world according to it.
(De Opif. Mundi 17–25.) The function of the Logos is instrumental and intermediary. It is the instrument by which God
makes the world and the intermediary by which the human
intelligence as it is purified ascends to God again. The exact degree
of its independent existence must remain doubtful because Philo
is so vague about it, and it certainly cannot be said to be a person,
still less a Divine Person. Thus it differs entirely from the Logos
of St. John's Prologue, an actual historical Person who is also
Divine, and the once fashionable theory that the beginning of the
Fourth Gospel is a reflection of the ideas of Philo is hardly tenable
and is very much less widely held than it used to be. The Powers,
even the Logos, have really in Philo's mind no existence apart
from the functions they perform. His conception of them is
affected by contemporary Greek ideas, but perhaps they really
belong to that mysterious class of instrumental and subordinate
quasi-beings, which accompany the Divinity in Semitic and
Persian thought, the Angel, the Wisdom, the Breath of God
in the Jewish Scriptures, the Uncreated Law of the Rabbis, the
Spirit of Muhammad and the eternal Koran and other still
odder entities in Islamic thought, and the quasi-personified
Divine virtues or attributes of Persian (Zoroastrian) theology, the

Amesha Spentas. God's actions, thoughts, manifestations, and revelations seem to be thought of as so concrete, so intensely actual, that they become as it were distinct substantial beings; and in this, of course, there is a primitive foreshadowing of very profound truths (and on the other side a link with a still more primitive animism).

The most important feature of Philo's Logos-doctrine as far as Christian thought is concerned is his identification of the Logos with the Platonic World of Forms and his idea of the use made of the Logos under this aspect by God in His work of creation. This bringing into connection, however confusedly, of the Platonic doctrine of archetypes, of a spiritual world which is the pattern of the visible, with the Jewish doctrine of God the Creator, led to very great developments in the thought of the Fathers and mediæval theologians (and, incidentally, to a great deal of misunderstanding about the original meaning of Plato's "Timæus"). Other Philonic doctrines which seem to have had an important influence are his idea of "pneuma" and his doctrine of mystical union. Philo's idea of "pneuma" appears in his exegesis of Genesis 2, 7 (*e.g.* Quod Det : Potiori Insid: Soleat 80–84). It is a Divine communication, a free creative inbreathing by God of part of the Divine substance into man, where it becomes the highest part of the soul, the Intelligence of the Platonists or Ruling Principle of the Stoics. This inbreathed Divine pneuma is the image of God in man. We have here an explanation, which was probably widely current in the Alexandrian Jewish schools, of the Jewish tradition about the Breath of God in terms of the idea which is common in contemporary Greek philosophy of the highest part of man's soul as a portion of the divine substance, an idea characteristic of the Platonized Stoicism and Stoicized Platonism which we considered in the last chapter. The Jewish-Alexandrian doctrine keeps however two non-Greek characteristics, the idea of a free creative act of inbreathing by God instead of a necessary participation, and the idea of the highest part of the soul, the inbreathed pneuma, as the image of God. It is from this tradition that the use of "pneuma", which we find in St. Paul for the human "spirit", the highest part of man, superior to the "psyche" (soul), derives; and the idea of the "image of God" was of immense importance in later Christian thought. St. Paul and the Christian tradition, however, drop the materialistic Stoic idea of the "pneuma" in man being an actual portion of the Divine substance, a physically conceived "out-flowing" which is veɪy evident in Philo.

Philo stands alone among the writers of his time (the non-Christians at least) in having a real mystical doctrine based apparently in part at least on genuine experience. He describes how the humɑn spirit or intelligence may even in this life be rapt by Divine possession beyond its normal activity of intellectual contemplation (Quis rer: divin: heres sit 264–5), may attain to the mystical union and the direct vision of God in His simple unity instead of in the multiplicity of the Powers. His doctrine in the form in which he states it has clear connections with the ancient Greek conception of "enthousiasmos", possession by a God, but its deeper roots are to be found in the tradition of the Hebrew prophets. It has some remarkable likenesses to the mystical doctrine of Plotinus, but there are also important differences, and there can be no question of any direct influence of Philo on Plotinus. Philo's importance for the later development of Christian thought lies here as elsewhere in his bringing into juxtaposition, if not into organic and coherent connection, of Jewish and Greek ideas.

4. The first group of Christian writers who employ Greek philosophical ideas for the elucidation of their theology are the Apologists of the second century. The purpose of these writers is indicated by their name. They were concerned to defend Christianity against pagan calumnies, and, more positively, to present it in such a way that it would be attractive to educated men. The upper classes by the middle of the second century were beginning to take an interest in Christianity, but it was generally a distinctly hostile one. The series of works of anti-Christian apologetic begins with a book by Fronto, the tutor of Marcus Aurelius, which, like its successors by Celsus, Porphyry and Julian, has unfortunately perished. (We can reconstruct a good deal of the contents of the books of Celsus and Julian from the refutations by Origen and St. Cyril of Alexandria which have survived.) The object of the second-century Apologists was not however so much to answer these particular attacks by rhetori-cians and philosophers as to make Christianity attractive and comprehensible to the cultured world in general, and in particular to the Antonine Emperors and their circle. It was for this reason that they used the language of philosophy, Stoic or Platonic, which the readers they hoped for would understand. This led

to important developments, for the meaning of the philosophical terms used was necessarily altered when they were employed in a Christian context, and Christian theology underwent considerable developments, and sometimes distortions which later and more expert theologians had to rectify, under the influence of philosophical language and the ideas which it brought with it.

The first Apologists wrote in Greek. Latin Christian apologetic begins at the very end of the second century with Minucius Felix and Tertullian. Among the Greek Apologists, Aristides, the author of the "Letter to Diognetus", St. Justin Martyr, Tatian, Athenagoras and St. Theophilus of Antioch, by far the most important theologian, and the only one who is of any great interest for our present purpose is St. Justin (converted about 130, martyred at Rome, where he taught, about 165). We can take his thought as an example of that of the whole group, noting certain differences, and remembering that he is a good deal profounder and better philosophically equipped than the others. Like all the Apologists he is a theologian and not a philosopher, using the words in their Scholastic sense, because he bases all his doctrines, not on reason but on God's revelation of Himself in the Word made Flesh. St. Justin had known and been deeply impressed by Platonists who taught a doctrine like that of Apuleius and Celsus mentioned in the last chapter, that the human soul can by its own natural powers attain in flashes to a vision, a Platonic "noesis" or illuminated intuition, of the Supreme God. This Justin as a Christian denies. We can, he says, know by reason that God exists; but this is not what the Platonists meant by the knowledge of God, and Justin, like all other Christian writers, denies that the full immediate contact and vision which they hoped for is possible except through the operation of Divine Grace, and teaches that in this life the way to intimate personal knowledge of God is only through faith in the Revelation of the Incarnate Word, to be found in the Scriptures and the teaching of the Church. The way in which St. Justin relates this Revelation to the teaching of the philosophers and explains the resemblances between the two which sometimes appear is interesting and important. The other Apologists are generally satisfied to denounce paganism and all its works, including philosophy (which did not prevent them from being sometimes deeply affected in their own thought by Platonic or Stoic doctrines) and to explain resemblances in the doctrine of God by the unsatisfactory hypothesis of borrowing, direct or indirect, by the philosophers, especially Plato, from the Jewish Scriptures; an idea, incidentally, which the pagan Numenius seems also to have accepted. Justin sometimes uses this idea of plagiarism, but he has too fine a mind to be altogether content with it, and his attitude to the Greek philosophers, especially Plato and the Platonists, is very friendly and not at all denunciatory. His theory is that of the "seminal Logos", a Stoic term which he perhaps used to impress the Emperor Marcus Aurelius, but which he employs in a very un-Stoic sense. Justin's Logos is not the immanent Divine Fire-Reason of the Stoics, but the transcendent Word of God, who implants fragments or seeds of the truth in the minds of all men of good will, so that all the great philosophers have lived and taught to some degree according to the Logos and everything that is true in their teaching comes from Him. But the Christians, says St. Justin, have not merely seeds, fragmentary portions of truth implanted by the Logos, but the Logos Himself, the whole Logos Incarnate; and therefore the Christian Revelation transcends the teaching of the philosophical schools. It must be clearly perceived that St. Justin, though his thought is generally much more Platonic than Stoic, is not simply substituting a transcendent Platonic Logos for the immanent Stoic Logos. He is making the Logos a Divine Person who became incarnate on earth, taking a particular human nature at a particular time; this is Christian, and incomprehensible and repulsive to the Greek philosophers, for whom the higher divine powers were impersonal and universal.

St. Justin's predilection for Platonism slightly affects his theology on one point. He holds very clearly the Judæo-Christian doctrine of God as transcendent Creator, bringing all things into being out of nothing by a free act of will; and he holds also firmly the traditional doctrine of the Trinity, not yet formulated with complete clearness and precision, but which taught quite definitely that there were three Divine Persons, the Father, the Son or Word, and the Holy Ghost, and yet there was only One God. St. Justin's Platonism shows itself in a slight concession to the doctrine of intermediary powers, by which he brings the generation of the Word into close connection with the creation of the world, and presents the Word very much as the instrumental Power through Whom the Father made the world. Others of the Apologists pushed this "subordinationist" tendency very much further. They explained the visible manifestations of God in the Old Testament by saying that it was not the Father who appeared; He remains invisible and transcendent, like the Supreme God of the philosophers; it was the Son who appeared acting as His intermediary and messenger to men. This explanation of the Divine appearances is used by Justin, though with much discretion. But he avoids the statements made by his heretical disciple Tatian and others that the Word was only brought forth when the world was created to act as the intermediary in its creation, and the inept use of the Stoic idea of the " immanent " and "uttered" Logos to distinguish between the two states of the Word, latent in God up to the Creation and thereafter uttered or expressed.

XV
Tertullian. The School of Alexandria

1. O F the early Latin theologians Tertullian (155-60—222-3) is far the most philosophically interesting, because he is, as far as I know, the only Christian materialist. In spite of his ferocious contempt for the philosophers and for all professed and conscious attempts to adapt Christianity to pagan philosophy he was himself very deeply affected by Stoic thought, and like the Stoics is unable to conceive of any kind of real substantial being which is not body; therefore as God and the soul are undoubtedly real and substantial they must, for Tertullian, be bodies. Of course he also maintains, in accordance with the authority of the Scriptures, that God is a "spiritus". But "spiritus" for him is simply the Stoic "pneuma", an especially fine and subtle sort of matter which is alive and intelligent but genuinely corporeal. This Stoic vital materialism has its effect on his presentation of the doctrine of the Trinity. On many points he is perfectly orthodox and distinctively Christian. He teaches with the utmost clearness that God is eternal and infinite, and that He is not an immanent forming-force but a transcendent Creator creating all things, including primal matter, out of nothing. This doctrine of creation, with the sharp dividing line which it implies between the Divine Creator and all other things which are created, not divine by nature, and so differing from the Godhead not by a difference of degree but by an infinite dissimilarity in kind, is the most important distinguishing mark which separates genuine Judalo-Christian from genuine Hellenic thought. For the Greeks the universe is co-eternal and co-necessary with God, and there is a hierarchy of beings divine by right of nature reaching down to and including the human reason. All the Apologists, and also Tertullian, are on the Christian side of this division ; and they all, again including Tertullian, differ from the later Arians in holding quite unmistakably that the Son and the Holy Ghost are Divine, are on God's side of the infinite gulf between Creator and creation. Tertullian's Stoic materialism comes out in his account of the relations between the Divine Persons, which is very much like a translation into Christian terms of that materialistic theory of emanation which has been mentioned as possibly due to Posidonius, and which we shall meet again when we come to discuss Plotinus. The

Apologists and the School of Alexandria, like almost all religious thinkers of the first three centuries A.D. delight in "emanation-metaphors", the Sun and the Ray, the Source and the Stream, etc., which they use to describe the relations between the Divine Persons. St. Justin is the only one who avoids them, deliberately, because they seem to him to compromise the essential equality of the Persons. Tertullian uses them with the utmost vigour and indiscretion, and in a way which suggests that he holds the materialistic idea of the Persons as portions of the Divine Substance. The emanation-metaphor as generally used implied that the emanant was less than the source, and Tertullian is extremely Subordinationist in his theology. It is to him that we owe the clearest expression of the misleading idea that the Father can be identified with the "God of the philosophers" and the Son with the God active on earth and in constant intercourse with men, sometimes appearing to them visibly, who is revealed in the Old Testament.

Tertullian was a very much greater and more important figure than this account would suggest, but his amazing Latin style, his contributions to the development of Latin theology both on the side of language and content, his moral rigorism, controversial methods, and final heresy, belong to the history of Latin literature, of the Church, or of dogma, and cannot on any pretext be brought into an introduction to the history of ancient philosophy. The treatment of the next group of thinkers, the School of Alexandria, will for the same reasons be even more inadequate, and any student of the Fathers who may happen to read this chapter will be well advised to remember the limitations imposed not only by its scale but by its point of view.

2. The Christian teachers of the School of Alexandria differ from the Apologists in being concerned not only to commend the Faith to educated pagans or Jews, but to construct a real sacred science, a theology proper which would give an account of the truths of Faith intellectually satisfying to intelligent Christians. The Alexandrians attempted, with some success, to build up a real school of sacred science equal in intellectual quality to the best pagan schools of philosophy, and all later Christian theologians and philosophers owe them a considerable debt, both for their conception of how the intellect should be used in the service of the Faith and for a good deal of work of permanent value which they, especially Origen, did in trying to carry out that conception.

The school of Alexandria begins some time after the middle of the second century A.D. with Pantænus, of whose teaching we know nothing certain. He travelled in the East before becoming the first head of the School, and is said to have visited India. It is tempting to imagine that some influences from Indian thought may have penetrated through him into the school of Alexandria and reached Origen, whose own thought is sometimes more like that of the Indian philosophers than anything in the West (it has more real affinity to Indian speculations than anything in Plotinus). But this cannot be regarded as anything more than rather hazardous speculation, especially as the probabilities are on the whole that Pantænus's thought was more like that of his immediate successor, Clement, than like that of Origen.

Clement of Alexandria was born about 150, and died before 215. He is greatly inferior to Origen as a philosophical theologian, but is perhaps the most complete representative of the School of Alexandria and what it stood for. We possess his three main works, which form a progressive series giving a complete instruction in Christian life and doctrine, the "Protrepticus", the "Pædagogus" and the unfinished "Stromateis" or "Patchwork". Clement combines a vigorous Christian orthodoxy and respect for tradition with an unbounded admiration for Greek philosophy. He insists with the utmost emphasis on the transcendent unity of God, the Divinity of Christ from Whom all truth and all possibility of goodness come to men, the unity of the Church and the superiority of the revealed doctrine, handed down in her from the Apostles and their successors, to all human wisdom. But at the same time he maintains, in opposition to Christians (like Tertullian), who held that all pagan philosophy was a delusion of the Devil and treated it with fierce contempt and hostility, that Greek philosophy is in its way and place most excellent, and a most valuable preparation and assistance in attaining the final truth of the Christian revelation. He uses and develops St. Justin's image of the seed of truth sown by the Word in all men's hearts; but his idea of the function of the Hellenic philosophies is more dynamic. It is not a question just of scattered fragments of the whole truth, but of active help given towards its attainment. All that is good in philosophy for Clement comes from Christ and leads to Christ.

Clement is before all else concerned with the good life, the life of moral and spiritual purification and ascent to God. He is thoroughly Christian in making this life depend altogether on

Christ and His grace and teaching, but his way of conceiving of its stages is often very Platonic, and he also in his moral teaching borrows a good deal from the later Stoics, especially from one of the most attractive and human of them, Musonius. The language in which he speaks of the Divine unity and transcendence echoes contemporary Platonism, but his most striking importation of Hellenic ideas into Christianity is his sharp division of Christians into two classes, the ordinary faithful and the "gnostics" or intellectual élite. This idea, in much cruder and more fantastic forms which Clement rejects, is also to be found among the heretical Gnostics, with whom however Clement has nothing else in common. The ordinary Christians, according to him, live only by faith, the "gnostics" have attained to a higher wisdom by which they have not only faith but knowledge of divine things, and access to a secret tradition handed down from the Apostles of which the ordinary Christian knows nothing. This distinction in Clement's view, will persist even in the next world, and he describes with some satisfaction the suffering which the common herd will undergo, even in heaven, from regret at being deprived of the superior happiness to which they see that the "gnostics" have attained, whom perhaps they despised and distrusted when on earth. It is not a doctrine which has commended itself to the Church or found its way into the general Christian tradition. It is rather related to the Greek idea of a small exclusive intellectual aristocracy, who alone attain to wisdom and therefore to true happiness in this world and the next.

3. Of all the Christian theologians before the fourth century Origen is the one with the greatest intellectual power and the one who, with the exception perhaps of St. Irenæus, exercised the widest influence. He is incomparably the greatest figure of the School of Alexandria, though the influence of his teaching was more powerful in Syria and Asia Minor than in Egypt. He was an Egyptian, born of Christian parents in 185–6. He succeeded Clement as head of the Catechetical School at Alexandria at the age of eighteen; later, after a dispute with his bishop, he went to Cæsarea in Palestine, where he taught for the rest of his life. He suffered imprisonment and torture for the Faith in the persecution of Decius, and died as the result of his sufferings in about 254–5. There is no space here to tell in full the story of his life; but it is perhaps worth saying that no one can study it without being impressed by his ascetic holiness, attracted powerfully by his

character, and convinced of his entire and passionate fidelity in
intention to the Church and the Catholic Faith. The startling
unorthodoxies into which he sometimes falls in the pursuit of his
great enterprise of constructing a really comprehensive philosophical theology are put forward always as nothing more than
suggestions or personal opinions, and are submitted fully to the
judgment of the Church. That judgment has been unfavourable
on certain important points, but no competent historian of
theology would deny the greatness of the debt which later
theologians owe to Origen. Of one most important side of his
activity, his work on the text of the Scriptures and his tremendous
labours as a Biblical commentator of the allegorical Alexandrian
school we can say nothing here, though his Biblical commentaries
have probably had the widest and most lasting influence of all his
works. But we must confine ourselves to considering him as a
philosophical theologian.

Origen's system is a most original and interesting attempt to
adapt Platonism to the requirements of Christian theology, with
some traces of Gnostic and perhaps even of Indian influence. It
has interesting points of likeness with the philosophy of his contemporary Plotinus, also an Egyptian and educated in Alexandria,
and still more interesting points of difference from it. Origen's
starting point is, of course, quite different from that of Plotinus
or any other pagan Greek philosopher. He is before all else a
Christian teacher, and he begins with the data of Revelation,
which far transcends all philosophy. From Revelation he receives
the traditional presentation of One God in Three Persons, freely
creating all else that exists out of nothing and revealing Himself
in the Incarnate Word, and to this central Christian tradition he
always remains faithful. He did a very great service to the Church
in his exposition of the doctrine of God by insisting on the Divine
spirituality; God is, he demonstrates clearly, following the true
Platonic tradition, absolutely immaterial. This was important,
and Origen realized it. The example of Tertullian has shown that
there was a real danger of Christian materialism developing under
Stoic influence. Origen keeps the line between Creator and
creature very clear, in a way which is Christian and un-Platonic,
but in his account of the relations of the Three Divine Persons
he departs very far from the normal Christian tradition and
introduces ideas which are to be found in Plotinus and the later
Neo-Platonists. Origen is an extreme Subordinationist. The Son

is lower and less than the Father both in the order of being and of knowledge, and the Holy Spirit lower and less than the Son. The Son and the Holy Spirit are intermediaries between the Father and the world of created spirits. We can ascend in our knowledge of God from knowing the Father in His Image, the Son, to knowing Him as He is in Himself. This Alexandrian doctrine of the Image of God plays a great part in Origen's thought, whether he is thinking of the Eternal Image, the Son, or of created images, rational spirits. The Father, Origen says, is absolutely one, the Son at least virtually multiple. This is strikingly like Plotinus's distinction between his First and Second Hypostases, the One and the Divine Mind. Another of Origen's distinctions between the Persons anticipates an important doctrine of later Neo-Platonism, when he says that the power of the higher is wider in scope and extends further down the scale of being than that of the lower. The Father's power as Creator extends to all created things; the Son's only to rational beings; the Holy Spirit's only to a limited number of rational beings whom He sanctifies.

4. The first creation according to Origen was that of a community of rational disembodied spirits, all equal and possessed of free-will. Origen was deeply concerned to reconcile Divine Justice with the inequalities of the fortunes which befall men, apparently through no fault of their own. He solved the difficulty by accepting whole-heartedly the Platonic and Pythagorean doctrines of the soul's pre-existence and pre-natal fall, in a form which also strongly suggests the Indian doctrine of Karma. The spirits of the first created community sinned and fell in varying degrees and according to their degree of sin they became angels of the various hierarchies, men, or devils. Thus all the inequalities between created spirits are due not to direct Divine arrangement but to the fault of the spirits themselves, whom God from the beginning only deals with according to their merits. The material universe, Origen held, was only created after this primal fall to provide penitential dwellings for fallen spirits, who are assigned to bodies of more or less dignity according to their deserts. Even the sun and the other heavenly bodies are purgatorial vehicles in which are embodied spirits which have sinned. The whole material creation is thus a direct result of sin, its purpose is to serve as a purgatory, and it would have been much better if there had never been any need for it. This is closer to Gnosticism than either to Plotinus or to the true Christian view; though, of course, Origen

differed from the Gnostics in holding that the material world was not evil in itself and that it was created by God, not by an evil power.

Origen followed Platonic tradition in believing in reincarnation. The fallen spirits were to pass through long series of lives moving up and down the scale according to their merits in each successive one, so that an angel might become a man, or even a devil, and a devil might eventually rise to be an angel; and this would go on not only through the lifetime of one universe but through cosmic cycle after cosmic cycle, as world succeeded world, not one repeating the other as in early Stoicism, but each one different (the scale of the imagination here again suggests India). At last would come the Apokatastasis, the Restoration of All Things, when all spirits at last returned to their first purity and equality, none, not even the devils, being excepted.

In this vast cosmic imagination there seems little room for traditional Christian dogma, but Origen remains a passionate Christian believer, and all the work of redemption of the spirits is accomplished by Christ, who, he thinks, must have passed through all the angelic hierarchies, taking the nature of each and redeeming them before becoming incarnate on earth. And for the life of man the Church and the Sacraments are all important and Origen's teaching about them is orthodox and profound. As might be expected he has an intensely vivid sense of the Communion of Saints, of that heavenly community of spirits to which we truly belong, and of the importance of the Angels in our spiritual life. And in his ascetical teaching and doctrine of the soul's ascent to union with God Christianity and Platonism are brought very close together. He shares Clement's idea of inner mysteries of the Christian faith accessible only to a select few, but not his idea of a permanent separation in the next life between "gnostics" and the rest. For Origen every created spirit may some day attain the highest and be perfectly united to God. The Platonic framework which Origen devised did not fit the Christian Faith very well; it was discarded and many of his opinions condemned. But we must recognize in him a figure of much importance in the history of Christian thought and life, the first great Christian Platonist, a man loyally Catholic in intention, and an heroic confessor of the Faith.

XVI

Plotinus (1). Writings and Life. The One. The Divine Mind

1. THE revival of Platonism reaches its highest point in the third century with the philosophy of Plotinus, who is with Plato and Aristotle one of the three supremely great masters of pagan Hellenic thought, and whose influence on later thinkers of many different schools has been very considerable. We have a certain amount of reliable information about him, for his disciple and editor Porphyry, who was intimately associated with him for many years, wrote a life of his master to introduce his collected edition of Plotinus's works. This edition, the "Enneads" has survived complete. It consists of fifty-four treatises of varying lengths, arranged rather artificially by Porphyry in six books, each of which is an "Ennead" or group of nine treatises dealing with different aspects of a single subject. These treatises were written by Plotinus in the last fifteen years of his life, and are based on the lectures and discussions which took place in his school at Rome. In many of them we seem to hear him thinking aloud, answering objections, modifying and developing his ideas as he writes. But the treatises all belong to a time when his system was already fully formed in his mind, and though we know the chronological order of them from Porphyry's "Life" (ch. 4–6) it is not possible to trace any very large-scale development, still less to observe any radical change in Plotinus's thought as expressed in the Enneads. The treatises do not provide a systematic and ordered exposition of Plotinus's philosophy. Rather they return again and again to the same subject or group of related subjects, retouching, adding details, throwing new light from different points of view. It is consequently very easy to find inconsistencies in the Enneads, and every intelligent interpreter of Plotinus is brought up sooner or later, as we shall see, against certain great antinomies or tensions in his thought. But the inconsistency of Plotinus is the inconsistency of a great mind, and is something very different from the incoherence of the Middle Platonists or Philo, mediocre men who never properly mastered their material. Plotinus sees too much for even his powers to be able to bring all the truth he sees into a fully consistent system.

He combined profound original insight with the inheritance of a rich and confused tradition to which he is always loyal in intention. But if he sometimes saw more truth than would go into his system that is a tribute to his intellectual honesty and powers of insight, and perhaps to even higher gifts, and it is a characteristic that has greatly increased the influence of his writings. But it does not make them easier to read. Plotinus is the most difficult of Greek philosophers, and his style does not help matters. He was completely indifferent to all considerations, not only of literary form, but also of grammar and spelling, and he never revised what he had written (Life, ch. 8). The thought was all that mattered to him, and he bent to its expression an extraordinary power of intellectual concentration, which we can feel throughout the Enneads. He could, Porphyry tells us (Life, ch. 8), break off his writing and carry on a conversation without any sign of abstraction while keeping his mind all the time busy on the theme on which he was engaged, so that he could go straight on with his writing as if there had been no break as soon as the conversation was over. Not infrequently, in spite of his carelessness about style (or perhaps because of it, for the stylistic fashions of his age were artificial and exaggerated to the last degree) the power of his thought forces him to a great magnificence of expression. There are passages in the Enneads which rank with the greatest philosophical writing of any age and country and which in some ways go beyond the range of Plato himself.

It may be useful to conclude this account of Plotinus's writings by giving an indication of the principal subject-matter of each Ennead; though it must be remembered that Plotinus sees his philosophy as an organic whole with all the parts closely interconnected and that consequently there is a great deal of overlapping, because he never treats any subjects in isolation from the rest of his system, and it is never possible to be sure that you have all the evidence about his thought on any particular point unless you have looked all through the Enneads for it. Porphyry's divisions by subject are, however, a useful indication of where the fullest information about Plotinus's thought on any particular topic is likely to be found. The First Ennead, then, is concerned principally with ethics, the Second and Third with philosophy of nature and the material universe, the Fourth with Soul, the Fifth with the Divine Mind, and the Sixth with the First Principle, the One.

2. Before going on to attempt some account of Plotinus's philosophy there are a few facts of his life which it is necessary to record. He was born in A.D. 205 and died in 270. He thus lived through one of the unhappiest and most chaotic periods in the history of the Roman Empire, but the confusion and distress of the outside world has left little trace in his writings, which give the impression of one utterly withdrawn from the world and the affairs of common men. He was an Egyptian of Greek speech and culture, but nothing certain is known about his race or parentage, for he was, Porphyry says, "like a man ashamed of being in the body" (Life, ch. 1) and would never speak of such things. He went to Alexandria for his philosophical training and after some disappointing experiments with the best-known philosophers of the city, he finally found satisfaction in the teaching of Ammonius Saccas, and remained with him for eleven years. Ammonius Saccas is the most tantalizingly mysterious person in the whole history of ancient philosophy. He is said to have been a renegade Christian, and to have been entirely self-taught, having started life as a porter. He must have been a remarkable person to have influenced and impressed Plotinus so deeply, but of the actual content of his teaching we know practically nothing, and it is impossible to assess the extent of Plotinus's debt to him, to know what in the Enneads comes from Ammonius and what is original Plotinus. There is, however, no real doubt that Plotinus is a great original thinker and that he at least very considerably developed any doctrines which he may have taken over from Ammonius. We know that Ammonius claimed to have "reconciled Plato and Aristotle" and the fusion of Platonic and Aristotelian elements is as we shall see very characteristic of the philosophy of Plotinus. But we have already seen that it is also characteristic of the philosophy of the preceding age, the Middle Platonism of the second century A.D. and without further evidence we cannot tell in what the originality of Ammonius's reconciliation consisted.

When he left Ammonius Plotinus went East with the unsuccessful expedition of the Emperor Gordian in the hope of studying Persian and Indian philosophy. When Gordian was murdered by his own soldiers at the instigation of Philip the Arabian Plotinus only just escaped with his life to Antioch. He then came to Rome and established his school there in 244-5. He taught there for the rest of his life, gathering round him a body of devoted disciples, male and female. In 270 he died of a painful illness (probably a form of leprosy) very bravely borne. Porphyry's description of his character perhaps makes him rather more of the conventional ascetic philosopher-saint of the period than he actually was. But it does succeed in showing him as not only the venerated philosopher, the Adept, the man who had attained the ultimate vision, but as a person of very great charm and practical kindliness. It was as the Adept that his friends and disciples almost worshipped him, but he condescended from the heights to give them much spiritual and material help: he saved Porphyry from suicide by very this-worldly and sensible advice and he acted as the loyal, beloved and practically efficient guardian of the children of many of his friends. On the other side, the most we can say against Plotinus is that both in Porphyry's biography and in the Enneads we can perceive a superiority which is a little too conscious for our taste and a lack of sympathy for the desires and ways of common men untempered by the charity and humility which Christians regard as essential virtues even when they practise them considerably less than Plotinus. But these are defects of character common to most ancient philosophers and a good many modern professors.

Plotinus's establishment of his school at Rome had important consequences for the later history of philosophy and theology. It meant that his doctrines were well known in the Latin West, better known and more highly valued in the century after his death than they were in the Greek East. The Western Neo-Platonist tradition deeply influenced St. Augustine, who read the Enneads in a Latin translation by Marius Victorinus, and principally through him the thought of Plotinus exercised a great and fruitful influence on Western Catholic theology and philosophy.

3. The philosophy of Plotinus presents us with a great ordered hierarchical structure of spiritual reality, a cosmos, which though it is static and eternal is no dead mechanical pattern, but living and organic. In this cosmos there are two movements, one of outgoing or descent, the automatic creativity of the higher which generates the lower as a necessary reflex action of its own contemplation. This is the proper cosmic movement by which the various levels of reality are eternally brought into being. Then there is the movement of return, ascent and simplification by which Soul, the traveller of Plotinus's universe, passes up through all the stages of being to final union with the First Principle. This is the

movement of the spiritual life. The first, the cosmic movement, is one away from unity towards an ever-increasing multiplicity; the second, the movement of the spiritual life, goes from multiplicity back to the perfect and originating unity and the highest possible degree of unification. Plotinus sometimes concentrates his attention on one of these movements and sometimes on the other, with consequent important differences and even inconsistencies in his account of the various spiritual realities which he is describing. But it would be an undue simplification to reduce his thought simply to an account of two movements, one of outgoing and one of return, which might be considered as a single circular movement with its beginning and end in the First Principle. The cosmic movement is itself a complex one, production being a necessary reflex of contemplation; and at each stage of Plotinus's account of the cosmos there are to be found other tensions and complexities in his thought. These complexities and tensions can partly be accounted for by the extremely complicated tradition which he inherited, in which very large Aristotelian and Stoic elements were combined with Platonism. Plotinus uses Aristotle and his commentators consciously and directly a great deal, though he disagrees with the Peripatetic tradition very sharply on some points. He is a good deal less friendly to the Stoics, but he by no means altogether escapes the indirect influence of Stoicism. Another cause of the complexity of Plotinus's thought and of certain of its great antinomies is his own profound and subtle analysis of the mental and spiritual life of man which, as I have already suggested, sometimes leads him to conclusions which he cannot completely integrate into a system. We must, however, always keep in mind the double character of his philosophy, the cosmic and the religious. It aspires at once to give a complete account of reality and to be a guide to the spiritual life. Of course, the two aspects cannot be sharply separated. They cannot in any great religious philosophy, and least of all in that of Plotinus, who inherits to the full that self-confident Hellenic theological rationalism, that belief that a human philosopher can by his own powers give a satisfactory account of divine things, which has its roots in the conviction that man himself is by nature divine. So Plotinus's whole spiritual life is determined by his conception of the structure of reality, and his conception of the structure of reality is deeply affected by his spiritual life. The Enneads are not a book of devotion or a treatise on mysticism, nor are they a series of speculations made by a philosopher to whom the Divine is not conceived as a matter of personal concern but simply as an eminent and eminently interesting object of speculation. Plotinus's religion is his philosophy and his philosophy is his religion. It is, however, possible and sometimes necessary for a clear understanding of his thought to consider the two sides of it separately, and I shall sometimes do so on each of the levels of reality in Plotinus's system. This I propose to consider in the order in which it seems to me most easy to make it intelligible, beginning at the top with his First Principle, the One or Good, and proceeding downwards through the two other great realities of the intelligible universe, the Divine Mind and Soul, to the lowest level of reality and the frontier of non-existence in the visible universe.

4. At the head of Plotinus's system stands the transcendent First Principle which he most usually calls the One or the Good. Sometimes he speaks of It as the Father—not, of course, in the Christian sense—but he very rarely calls It God. Porphyry, however, does so without hesitation, and the One is nearer even to what we mean by God than anything else in Plotinus's system, perhaps than anything else in Greek philosophy. Plotinus's conception of the One is a very complex one and has been very variously interpreted. It is here perhaps more than anywhere else that we can see the great tensions or antinomies in his thought. The Middle Platonists, it will be remembered, had recognized a First Principle of extreme transcendence and remoteness; but they spoke of it quite definitely as a Mind, and their conception of it was very much influenced by Aristotle's description of his Supreme Being or God, the Unmoved Mover, the transcendent, self-sufficient, perfectly realized Intelligence which has no outside activity but is absorbed in its own self-contemplation. Plotinus, on the other hand, places the One or Good beyond Mind and beyond Being. It is the source of the Divine Mind and the World of Forms which is its content, but the One Itself is neither a Mind nor a Form. A number of different routes led Plotinus to this idea of the absolute transcendence of the One, and he consequently presents It in a number of different ways. One way of approach is Neo-Pythagorean. The One is Unity-Absolute, from which all number or plurality proceeds, that is all reality looked at from a Pythagorean standpoint. When Plotinus is considering the One in this way his reasons for placing It beyond being are logical. We cannot predicate being of the One, we cannot say

"The One is" without introducing at least a duality between subject and predicate, and there can be no duality in the primal Unity, Unity-Absolute, which is the principle of unification to everything else. Very closely related to this Pythagorean way of approach is the quite illegitimate interpretation of Plato's dialectical exercise on the subject of the One in his dialogue "Parmenides" which had been current among Platonists and Pythagoreans since the first century B.C., and which Plotinus, the later Neo-Platonists and some modern writers accept. According to this interpretation the first hypothesis about "the One", which Plato probably intended to show that if you posit an absolute unity in the strict sense all sorts of impossible consequences follow, is a description of a transcendent Unity, the First Principle of all things, which can only be described by negations. As a result of this way of thinking we find Plotinus using sometimes about the One the language of what I have called elsewhere "the negative theology of flat denial", in which all determination, all predication is refused to the One for fear of compromising Its unity, which is the principle of unity and so of existence to everything else; for it is a cardinal doctrine of Plotinus derived from Middle Stoicism, that a thing only exists because and in so far as it is a unity, a single coherent whole; and for any Platonist the principle of all incomplete unities, unities-in-multiplicity, wholes of parts, must be a Unity-Absolute.

This very negative way of looking at the One, however, is not the whole or even perhaps the most important part of Plotinus's thought about It. He has another much more positive way of approach. We must remember that the First Principle is not only the One for him, but also the Good. And he very often represents the One-Good as That to which no predicates and no determinations can be applied because It is more and better than the reality of which It is the source, and Its excellence goes beyond the resources of our thought and language. It is absolutely single and simple because It is infinitely perfect. It is That which is wholly beyond and surpassing the hierarchy of limited realities which we can know and describe. The World of Forms which is the formative content of the Divine Mind is only an imperfect imaging in multiplicity of the single Good; and from the Good an added, we might almost say a supernatural radiance, falls upon the proper glory of the Forms, a "grace playing upon their beauty" (Enn. VI. 7.22). This phrase of Plotinus brings home very strikingly the difference between him and Plato. For Plato the One or Good, the First Principle of the World of Forms was itself a Form and a substance, the all-inclusive Form containing all the others. It had not this unique transcendence and otherness which Plotinus gives the One. When Plotinus speaks of the One in this positive way It comes nearer than anything else in Greek philosophy to what we mean by God. We have taken over Plotinus's "negative theology of positive transcendence" and speak of God by negations to show that He is more than and cannot be contained in the inadequate words and thoughts which we apply to Him and that He is different in kind to the realities we know. And Plotinus alone of the Greeks makes his First Principle something more than the supreme Intellect, head of the hierarchy of reality and differing in degree rather than in kind from the other beings of the intelligible world. In stressing this positive God-like aspect Plotinus says that the One is pure will and loves Itself and is the cause of Itself (VI.8.15,18). And, though he is concerned to exclude from It any sort of thought within the range of our intellect, because it involves the duality of knower and known, even when the two are only two aspects of one reality as they are in the Divine Mind, yet he is also anxious to show that "absence of thought" in the One is not mere unconsciousness, that the One is above, not below thinking. So he speaks of It as having a "super-intellection", an immediate self-awareness which is Itself (V.4.2). Plotinus's positive descriptions of the One sometimes seem to bring It back very close to the Divine Mind; and it is true that the levels of reality are not sharply cut off from each other in his thought as they are in the rigid classifications of the later Neo-Platonists. But the distinction always remains clear for him. The complex reality of the Divine Mind is in principle intelligible; its transcendent source, the One, is beyond the reach of thought or language in Its infinite simplicity.

The positive and negative aspects of the One both appear in the religious as well as the cosmic side of Plotinus's thought. The positive aspect predominates in the Enneads as is natural, for whether the One is thought of as the First Principle of reality or the final term of the spiritual life it is difficult not to speak of It in positive terms, to consider It as a reality, however transcendent, and the fullest and richest of all realities. The negative aspect, however, is always there and the two aspects are never completely separated from each other; if Plotinus is speaking in terms of one, the other is always in the back of his mind. A link between them is furnished by the idea, very important in Plotinus, that it is precisely as Unity-Absolute, as principle of number and measure, that the One is First Principle of reality; for to be to a Neo-Platonist is to be in some sense a unity, and the degree of unification of anything determines its place in the scale of reality.

5. The religious side of Plotinus's thought about the One is that which has always most deeply impressed his readers, but it has been very variously interpreted. Most readers of the Enneads would agree that Plotinus had attained to a genuine mystical experience; Porphyry definitely states that he did, and even without Porphyry's evidence there are many passages in the Enneads where Plotinus speaks of union with the One in language which has the ring of personal experience and is very close to that used by other great mystics. Whether Plotinus's mystical experience was genuinely supernatural or was a very high form of "natural" contemplation is a much debated question into which there is no need to enter here. But I do not think that anyone who really studies the Enneads without prejudices or preconceptions can deny that it was genuine and that it was good and valuable, and not a pathological state or a psychological aberration. There is no doubt, too, that it had a very important influence on his conception of the One. The divergence between the interpreters begins when they try to determine exactly what results this influence produced, what Plotinus's thought about the spiritual life and its goal actually was. Some make him an extreme pantheist and anti-rationalist for whom the end of the spiritual life is the denial and repudiation of all distinct reality and clear thought and the dissolution of the self into a formless nothingness, a One which is indistinguishable from primal matter. Others see in him a close kinship to Hindu thought and think that for him the summit of the spiritual life was the realization of our pre-existing identity with the One, the supreme and absolute Self. We *are* the One, and have only to realize it by our own efforts, and in attaining the One we attain the supreme self-realization. Others again regard his thought as beings closely akin to that of the great Christian and Moslem (Sufi) mystics and therefore consider that those passages in which Plotinus speaks of union with the One as a union in love with the transcendent Good in which soul and Good are perfectly "oned",

as a medieval English mystic might say, but are not the same represent his true thought. The first view seems to me absolutely unjustified and contrary to the whole spirit and teaching of the Enneads. The second has some evidence to support it; it seems that Plotinus did occasionally think of union with the One in this way, as the supreme self-realization. It is a way of thinking which is in accordance with Platonic tradition in some ways, though opposed to it in others; it brings the Supreme into organic and unbroken connection with the lower levels of reality and makes the mystical experience the climax of the long process of intellectual purification by which man realizes his own divinity; though neither the placing of the supreme experience beyond thought and knowledge nor the idea of an Absolute Self are Platonic.

The third way of thinking, however, seems to me to be Plotinus's normal one. The passages in which he suggests a real identity between the human soul and the One are very few and his usual teaching is quite opposed to such an identification. He very often insists on the identity of the highest part of the soul with the Divine Mind. We are more than "man" and more than "soul". In our return to the highest we can put off our lower humanity and become what we are by right and in a way have never ceased to be, the Divine Mind which is also the All, the boundless totality of real being. "Thou wert All, but something else beside the All was added to thee, and thou didst become less by the addition" (VI. 5. 12). But to become the All is not the same thing as to become the One in Plotinus's usual way of thinking, though sometimes he speaks as if it were. The One or Good is transcendent in both the religious and cosmic orders. It is "light above light" (V. 3. 12) and even the Divine Mind itself can know it only by leaving itself behind, going out of itself in ecstasy. Its normal divine intellection gives it only that pluralized image of the One which is the World of Forms, its proper object and content.

This last way of thinking about the mystical union as union with a transcendent Good which is more and other than ourselves is obviously the religious side of that positive attitude to the One which I have discussed above in its cosmic aspect. But the negative way of looking at the One, which was already in the tradition which Plotinus inherited (in which the two kinds of negative theology of denial and of transcendence or analogy were already distinguished by Albinus), and was not alien to his own personal experience, also helps him to distinguish the One from our selves at their highest, on the level of the Divine Mind. It is because of the absolute simplicity of the One, which he sometimes speaks of in terms of extreme negation, that It must be wholly other than all things. To say that It is no thing because there is in It no plurality with its accompanying limitation or that It is no thing because It is other and more than all things are both true but inadequate ways of speaking of the ultimate source of reality attained in the mystical experience (Plotinus insists repeatedly on the inadequacy of all ways of speaking about the One, his own included). So in the mystical union the antinomy between the positive and negative approaches to the One is reconciled. And the double affirmation of the transcendence of the One thus secured would seem to clear Plotinus of any suspicion of pantheism (he certainly is not a pantheist in any ordinary sense of the word). But it remains true that for him our selves have no fixed upper limit short of the final goal; we return to the One from Which we came out, and between ourselves in their last degree of purity and simplification and their infinite ground no clear frontier can be drawn, and in the union all sense of distinction disappears. Yet it is also true that even in union the distinction remains which is established by the original creative impulse which gives us power to return; we are always mind and soul and are not annihilated into the original unity. So I am inclined to think, after much reflection, that the "Absolute Self" presentation of Plotinus's mystical doctrine does not adequately represent the true thought even of his most pantheistic-sounding passages.

6.   From the One proceeds in order the whole of derived reality, the Divine Mind, Soul and the material universe. This procession is necessary and eternal; for Plotinus, as for later Greek thought in general, the universe as a whole in all its levels, spiritual and material, is eternal, and it is impossible to conceive of any part of it not existing or existing otherwise than as it is. The manner of this procession is rather loosely and inadequately described as "emanation". The background of Plotinus's thought at this point is certainly a Middle Stoic doctrine of the outflow of intellect from a divinity conceived as material light or fire, and his favourite metaphor to describe the process is that of the radiation of light or heat from sun or fire. This was consecrated for him by Plato's

analogy between the Sun and the Form of the Good in the
"Republic", and further commended to him by his own doctrine
of the special status of light in the universe as the incorporeal
energy of the luminous body: other comparisons which he uses are
the diffusion of cold from snow or scent from a flower. But he is
not content merely to use this traditional analogy and leave it at
that, to allow the generation of spiritual beings to be thought of
in terms of a materialistically conceived automatism. Mind
proceeds from the One (and Soul from Mind) without in any
way affecting its Source. There is no activity on the part of the
One, still less any willing or planning or choice. There is simply a
giving-out which leaves the Source unchanged and undiminished.
But though this giving-out is necessary, in the sense that it
cannot be conceived as not happening or as happening otherwise,
it is also entirely spontaneous; there is no room for any sort of
binding or constraint, internal or external, in Plotinus's thought
about the One. The reason for the procession of all things from the
One is, Plotinus says, simply that everything which is perfect
produces something else. Perfection is inevitably productive and
creative. And, as it is one of the axioms which Plotinus assumes
without discussion that the product must always be inferior to
the producer, what the One produces must be that which is next
to It in excellence, namely the Divine Mind.

Plotinus, when he gives a more precise account of procession,
introduces a psychological element which goes beyond his Stoic
emanation-metaphors. He distinguishes two "moments" in the
process, the first in which the lower is radiated as an unformed
potentiality and the second in which it turns back to the higher
in contemplation and so is informed and filled with content. In
this second part of the process the higher is Form, in the Aristotelian sense, and the lower Matter. In fact the whole doctrine is an
application on a universal scale of Aristotle's theory of knowledge in
which the mind becomes what it thinks, receiving and being informed by the forms of the objects it knows. And we see here another
of the great principles of Plotinus's philosophy; that all derived
things depend for their existence, their activity and their power to
produce on their contemplation of their source. Contemplation
always precedes and generates activity and production.

7.   The double rhythm of outgoing and return which appears in
the Aristotelian way of looking at the relations between the
levels of being is very important for the later Neo-Platonists.

(Of course, it must be clearly understood that return does not succeed outgoing in time; the two movements are timeless and simultaneous.) It can be seen most clearly in Plotinus's account of the second great reality in his Spiritual world, the Divine Mind, the One-Being or One which Is or the All (the first One, as we have seen, is the One Beyond Being). This account is a wonderful and successful blend of Plato, Xenocrates and Aristotle, with a small Stoic element. The Divine Mind is the World of Forms because it thinks them. There is a perfect unity-in-duality of thought and object of thought. The Mind cannot exist without its Object or the Object outside the Mind. It may be asked why, in accordance with the general Plotinian rule that the lower contemplates the higher and is informed by it, the One rather than the World of Forms is not the object of contemplation and informing principle of the Divine Mind. The answer is to be found in the extreme transcendence of the One, which the Divine Mind cannot attain except in ecstasy. Its normal intellectual contemplation is indeed an effort to return to the One, but it cannot reach that absolute and unthinkable Simplicity and has to be content with a manifold image, the World of Forms. Something resembling this idea appears already in Philo, and in a modified form it plays a great part in later Christian theology.

The World of Forms as Plotinus describes it differs a good deal from Plato's. Its organic character as a single living reality is greatly stressed, probably as the result of Stoic influence. There are Forms of individuals, in which neither Plato or Aristotle believed. Here again there is probably some Stoic influence, and Plotinus's concern with personality is also apparent. Socrates must be himself in that other world as he is here, and not somebody else or an undifferentiated universal. But though there are forms of individuals, the total number of Forms in the spiritual world is finite for Plotinus (not, however, for his disciple Amelius). The Divine Mind is infinite in power and beyond all external measuring and limitation; but its contents form a finite whole. None the less, the acceptance of Forms of particular things in all their particularity is an important change. It was this Plotinian form of the doctrine, in which the World of Forms contains the archetypes of all individual things that are, have been or will be, which passed to the Christian philosophers and theologians to be still further developed by them. Another important development is that the union of Mind and Forms in the Divine Mind-

World is so close that the Forms are themselves living intelligences
and everything There is awake and alive. And, being live intelligences, by the laws of Aristotelian psychology they interpenetrate.
Each Form-Intelligence thinks the whole World of Forms and so
becomes it; so that There the part is the whole and the whole is
in every part, and there is no separation or division. The doctrine
that soul or intelligible or spiritual being is not divisible, but is
always present "the whole in the whole" is not peculiar to
Plotinus but common in later Greek thought. Plotinus's application of it, however, in conjunction with Aristotelian psychology
to the interrelation of the Forms in the Divine Mind is original
and is one of the most profound and valuable parts of his
philosophy. It enables him to present his Mind-World as perfectly unified, containing real diversity but no separation. It
makes the Forms really part of the Divine Life and not static
objects of contemplation; and it has permanent value in the clear
and vivid realization of the nature of spiritual being and its freedom from spatio-temporal limitations which those passages in
the Enneads in which Plotinus describes the Forms in the Divine
Mind bring to those who read them with understanding. The
Divine Mind is the supreme reality, the highest level of being
(for the One is beyond being) and the quasi-realities of the visible
cosmos are only shadows and far off imitations of it. But it cannot,
I think, be described as "Plotinus's God". In the process of ascent,
the order of the spiritual life, the Divine Mind is ourselves at
our highest. It is the level at which we attain to our full self-
realization. We are only fully ourselves when we escape from the
bounds of our lower, limited ego, our soul concerned with the
body, and pass beyond Soul to recover our consciousness that we
are, and have never really ceased to be, Divine Mind in all its
multiplex universality. But even when we have realized our
identity with the Divine Mind our ultimate Good which is also
the First Principle of reality, the One, still lies beyond. Later
theologians applied to God much of what Plotinus says about the
Divine Mind. But it remains true that in the Enneads it is the
One rather than the Divine Mind which corresponds most
closely to what we mean by "God". Of course, not only the
Divine Mind but also Soul are "gods" in the Greek sense, and our
own intelligence is for Plotinus a god within us.

XVII
Plotinus (2). The Soul and the Material Universe

1. FROM the account which I have given of the two highest principles in Plotinus's system, the One and the Divine Mind, it should be clear that they do not correspond to the two highest principles of the Middle Platonists, though Plotinus's thought about them derives a great deal from Middle Platonism. Perhaps the best way of describing what Plotinus at this point in his thought has done with the philosophy of his immediate predecessors is to say that he has split up the confused mass of attributes, transcendence, priority to the Forms, self-contemplating intelligence, supreme unity and goodness, which the Middle Platonists had applied to their First Principle, and refers some of them to the One, some to the Divine Mind, with a good deal of development in both cases. One result of this is that the Divine Mind which is also the World of Forms itself attains a very high degree of transcendence which is appropriate to its origins. It is as remote from the material universe as Plato's Forms or Aristotle's Unmoved Mover. The link between the higher, spiritual, and the lower, material, worlds (the third of the Great Hypostases), is called by Plotinus, as it was by Plato, Soul. Plotinus's doctrine of Soul, however, though it derives from Plato and remains genuinely Platonic in its essentials is very much more elaborate than the doctrine of the "Timæus" or the "Laws". The realm of Soul extends from the World of Forms in the Divine Mind down to the last shadow of reality in bodies, and its frontiers on the side of the Divine Mind are not at all clearly defined. Soul in Plotinus has to fulfil the functions both of the Second Mind or God and of the Soul of the World in the Middle Platonists (that is, of Plato's Great Craftsman or Providence and of his World-Soul) and is consequently divided into two, higher Soul and lower Soul, or Nature. Though Plotinus sometimes denies that these are really distinct he does as a matter of fact present them as two different realities, the lower emanating or proceeding from the higher.

2. The relations of the higher Soul to the Divine Mind are in some ways closely parallel to those between the Divine Mind and

the One. Soul is emanated or radiated from Mind as Mind is from the First Principle, and Mind is the source of Soul's reality and of whatever is good, beautiful and intelligent in it. Soul returns upon the Divine Mind in contemplation and Mind acts as Form of Soul's Matter. Soul receives Mind according to its capacity, in a Soul-like way, just as Mind receives the One according to its capacity in a Mind-like way, receiving (except in ecstasy when it is no longer Mind) the Absolute Unity not as It is in Itself but in a unity-in-diversity, the pluralized image which is the World of Forms. In the case of Soul's reception of Mind according to its capacity this means a still further departure from unity and descent towards multiplicity. Plotinus's system is based to a very great extent upon introspection. He sees the universe in terms of the life of the human spirit and the great levels of being which he recognizes are projections on to the cosmic plane of the stages of human consciousness (though they are a good deal more than this as well). Looked at in this way Soul is the realm of discursive thought, in which truths are known separately by a process of reasoning passing through distinguish-able stages, and Mind of intuitive, in which all truth is know· at once in a single flash of realization which comprehends the u ity-in-diversity of the Forms. The operation of the Divine M· d is Plato's "noesis", of the Soul Plato's "dianoia".

But there is more to be said than this about the relation of the higher Soul to the Divine Mind. So far the Mind has been thought of as a unity and the principle of Soul, which is quite separate and clearly distinguished from it on a lower level. But the Divine Mind is also a World, and of that world Soul is an inhabitant, though holding in it the lowest place. Soul's most important function, after all, is to be a link between the two worlds, the intelligible or spiritual and the material, to be that final development of spiritual being which not only rules and orders but gives life and reality to the visible universe. Therefore it must have a footing in the higher as well as the lower world. Material things are represented there by their archetypes, the Forms, but Soul is present itself. It is the only reality which inhabits both worlds. In its primary activity of contemplation it belongs to the world of the Divine Mind, in its secondary activity of ruling, ordering and informing bodies it is concerned with the material universe. In the two treatises on Providence (III 2 and 3) the higher Soul seems to be removed to a further degree of transcendence by the introduction of what appears to be a new distinct principle, the Logos, which is produced by "Mind and Soul disposed in accordance with Mind" (III. 2. 16) and which takes over all the functions of Soul in the material world, leaving to Soul proper only its higher activity of contemplation. This final elaboration belongs to Plotinus's last period, and is not paralleled anywhere else in the Enneads, but it is not really out of tune with the rest of his thought. Since Soul is the link or bridge-principle between the intelligible and visible worlds, Plotinus always recognized stages in its activity, contemplation, ruling, animating, etc., and was always rather inclined to attribute these different, higher and lower activities to different spiritual realities. The distinction of the higher and lower Soul is found throughout the Enneads, though the further distinction between higher Soul and Logos only occurs in the treatises on Providence. Of course all these different realities are regarded as being of the nature of Soul, and are not as sharply cut off and distinguished from each other as Soul is from Mind.

Plotinus's use of the word "Logos" should perhaps be explained a little further in view of the great philosophical and theological importance of the term. It derives from the philosophical vocabulary of both Aristotle and the Stoics and may possibly be influenced by earlier Alexandrian thought. A "logos" for Plotinus is an active formative spiritual principle. Individual Souls and the forming principles of bodies are "logoi". This use is Aristotelian-Stoic in origin. And when one spiritual principle is spoken of as the "logos" *of* another spiritual principle Plotinus means that it is the representative and expression of that higher principle on a lower level of being. So the universal Logos of the treatises on Providence is the representative of Mind, of the transcendent divine World of Forms, and of intelligent Soul, in the visible world, to which it is the principle of intelligibility and order, producing the highest degree of unity and coherence of which the material is capable. This has obvious analogies with the instrumental and intermediary part played by the Logos of Philo, though no direct influence of Philo on Plotinus is in the least likely.

3. In the rest of the Enneads (apart from the treatises on Providence) the higher Soul rules and orders the material world directly, and not through the intermediary of a Logos. Its rule is that of a being transcending the material though in contact with it, like Plato's God or gods. The immanent functions of Soul are

performed by the lower Soul. Universal Soul is in no way confined in or bound to body. Plotinus always likes to say that the
lower is in the higher rather than the higher in the lower (thus
Soul is in Mind). Soul therefore is said to contain body, not body
Soul (here Plotinus is developing a suggestion in the "Timæus").
The relation of Universal Soul to individual souls is complicated
and difficult to get clear. The individual souls seem to be
"Plotinian parts" of the Universal Soul, parts, that is, which in
the manner proper to spiritual being according to Plotinus have
the whole in a certain sense present in them and can if they wish
expand themselves by contemplation into universality and be
the whole because they completely share Universal Soul's detachment from the body which it rules. They are bound to occupy
and administer the bodies appointed for them by the plan of
Universal Soul. The soul, in Plotinus as in Plato, is in the body not
as a result of a fall due to sin but by the law of the universe. Yet
souls are sometimes illogically blamed for descending to animate
the bodies of non-human creatures, though it would seem that
they must do so according to the universal plan. The spiritual
state of the soul in body depends on its attitude. If it devotes
itself selfishly to the interests of the particular body to which it
is attached it becomes entrapped in the atomistic particularity
of the material world and isolated from the whole, and sinks at
last into brutishness. The root sin of the soul is self-isolation, by
which it is imprisoned in body and cut off from its high destiny.
But the mere fact of being in body (at least in a human body)
does not imply imprisonment in body. That only comes if the
soul surrenders to the body; it is the inward attitude which makes
the difference. It is always possible for a man in the body to rise
beyond the particularism and narrowness of the cares of earthly
life to the universality of transcendent Soul, and then to pass
beyond Soul altogether to recover his rightful place in the world
of the Divine Mind. For it is, as we have seen, one of Plotinus's
most important doctrines that we are more than "man" or
"soul", we are Mind; and "we do not altogether come down";
the highest part of our selves remains in the world of the Divine
Mind even when we are embodied (this true and higher self seems
to be identical with our original and archetypal Form of which
our soul is a Logos). And, still remaining in the body, when we
have again become Mind we may pass still higher and attain, if
only rarely, to that ecstatic union with the One in which Mind

attains to the highest by leaving itself behind. Here we can see how Plotinus's account of the spiritual life cuts across the levels of being in the cosmic order; there is a real tension in his account of soul and the life of man between the religious and the cosmic sides of his thought, between the free ascent of the philosopher's spirit to the Supreme and the careful demarcation of the levels of being and the proper characteristics of Mind and Soul respectively. But we must not exaggerate the opposition. As the doctrine of "logoi" very clearly shows, the levels of being are not to be thought of as rigidly separated, but as stages in the unfolding of a single life.

4.   The lower Soul or Nature is, as I have said, Soul immanent. It is the World-Soul of the "Timæus" and of Middle Platonism. It is a true emanation of the higher soul of which it is an image on a lower level and which irradiates it. It is truly Soul, though Soul at the lowest level, and therefore it has as its primary activity contemplation; this contemplation is, however, not rational but like that of a man in a dream. Waking, intelligent contemplation belongs to the transcendent spiritual world of the higher Soul and the Divine Mind. As a result of the weakness of this strange dream-like contemplation of Nature its products, produced as usual by automatic necessary reflex action, are "dead", incapable of contemplation or of producing anything below themselves. They are the final limit of the unfolding of being, the last trace or shadow of higher reality. These products of Nature are the immanent forms of bodies. Plotinus describes them as very like Aristotle's immanent forms, just as his conception of Nature may be regarded as an adaptation of Aristotle's Nature to his own very original development of Platonism with its doctrine of universal contemplation. But there is one important difference between Plotinus's immanent forms and Aristotle's. Aristotle's forms unite with matter to make up a single reality of which the two aspects are separable only by logical analysis. But in Plotinus matter remains unchanged by the forms imposed upon it. It is a formless darkness, negative and the very principle of negation; and its very negativity makes it the principle of evil in the material world. In this way Plotinus tries to combine Aristotle's idea of matter as a pure negation, a mere potentiality of becoming with Plato's idea of matter as recalcitrant, resisting the ordering and informing activity of Soul.

Though matter is evil for Plotinus, the material, visible universe most emphatically is not. He defends its goodness passionately against the Gnostics for whom it was not only evil but made by evil powers. For Plotinus it is a noble work of the higher Soul, ordered and ruled by it and held together in an organic unity by Nature, its universal principle of order and wholeness. Because it is material it holds the lowest rank in reality, on the borders of the darkness of non-being. But for Plotinus, as for both Plato and the Stoics, it is the best of all possible material universes, the best possible reflection on the material plane of the light and beauty of the material world, and is not only a work of Soul but itself an ensouled living being. Plotinus stresses very strongly the organic wholeness of the material universe which results from its being living and ensouled. In this he regards himself, quite truly, as following the teaching of Plato in the "Timæus", but a great deal has also been contributed to his picture of the organic universe by the Middle Stoics. From them he derives his idea of the universal sympathy, binding every part of the cosmos together which is the basis of Hellenistic magic and on which Plotinus founds an entirely magical theory of prayer, which is to him simply the setting in motion through the universal sympathy of a celestial force proceeding from a star-god, by means of an incantation or magical ritual. The whole process is automatic and has nothing to do with religion as either we or Plotinus understand it; he himself had little use for the external pagan cult, and is only interested in the magical side of it as illustrating his doctrines. The Wise Man, he says, is beyond the reach of magic because his soul dwells in the higher regions to which magical operations cannot attain. This reason for the Sage's immunity from magic is, of course, Platonic and not Stoic, and Plotinus again follows the Middle Platonists as against the Stoics in drawing a distinction between Providence and Fate, which he identifies with the operation of the higher and lower universal Soul respectively, thus preserving the hierarchical order of the different levels of Soul within the single organic universe.

Plotinus is closer to the Stoics again in his account of the order and harmony of the material universe and the way in which it affects human life. It is to him a Heraclitean harmony of clash and conflict in which material evil and suffering are the inevitable consequences of the working out of the pattern, the only kind of pattern, order and harmony which there can be in the material world, which represents the most extreme degree of disunity and separation which is compatible with any sort of existence. The individual who suffers in the clash and tension of the cosmic rhythm has, Plotinus says, no more right to complain than the tortoise who is trampled underfoot by the dancers as a great choral dance moves majestically to its climax. Suffering is a necessary consequence of embodiment. The wise man is beyond the reach of suffering not because his body cannot suffer but because he is utterly detached in spirit. The most important part of his self abides above, in the spiritual world, and does not come down into the conflict and turmoil of bodily life. For the ordinary man who is not a philosopher and cannot ascend by the power of his own spirit to that higher world Plotinus offers little hope. The weak and foolish as well as the wicked suffer in this world through their own fault and only get what they deserve, and they have no right to expect gods or good men to lay aside their own life and come to help them (Enn. III. 2. 9). Perhaps Plotinus here is alluding to the Christian doctrine of the Incarnation and Redemption. If so it is his only allusion to Catholic Christianity, though he attacks the Gnostics vigorously (in Enneads II. 9).

5. Plotinus's cosmology and his ethics are very closely connected and cannot really be separated. His views of the nature of the world in which we live, of the relations of soul and body and of the dependence of soul on the higher principles, the Divine Mind and the One, determine his views on how man ought to behave. Nor, of course, can Plotinus's morality be separated from his religion. The practice of virtue is for him a means to the spiritual ascent. Consequently, though there is a very strong Stoic element in his view of the material world and the moral law governing it, his Stoicism is always subordinated to his Platonism. And we can sometimes detect a conflict, not exactly between the Stoic and Platonic sides of his thought but between that attitude of respect for the visible world which is to be found in Plato's later writings, especially the "Timæus" and the "Laws" and which is powerfully reinforced in Plotinus by Stoic influence, and the sharply other-worldly Pythagorean temper, apparent in Plato's "Phædo", which regards embodiment as an evil, a falling below the highest, which becomes very prominent in the writings of Plotinus's last years. The idea of the visible universe as an organic whole belongs to the first way of thinking, and it logically demands that everything in the visible world should be regarded as noble and necessary in its place, since it is the best possible image of a

Form in the intelligible world; and that since it is Soul's business to animate and govern the material world as a whole and every part of it, and since individual souls animate different bodies according to the divine and universal law, embodiment should not be regarded as in any way a descent or an evil, and it should be no fault in a soul to animate and govern any body, even the lowest. In fact, we find that Plotinus is too much under the influence of the more Pythagorean side of the Platonic tradition ever to admit this, and this is the reason why he holds that only through its own sin can a soul be found animating any body lower than a human one and why in general he seems to regard embodiment as a natural but regrettable necessity, rather as the Victorians regarded a visit to the W.C. His whole moral teaching is directed to so purifying the soul that, though it must abide in body as long as its appointed term of embodiment lasts, yet it will live as though it were out of the body, utterly detached from material and earthly things and abiding in its proper place in the intelligible world. It is one of the most important parts of Plotinus's moral and religious teaching that we can and should live almost wholly in the higher realms of spiritual and intellectual life while still remaining in the body. This moral and religious outlook sometimes affects his cosmology by leading him to represent the material world, the realm of embodied soul, not so much as an organic whole as a series of layers, down to the ultimate evil darkness of matter from which it is our business to keep as far away as possible. This particular conflict or tension in Plotinus's thought is one which runs through the whole Platonic tradition. In the Enneads, thanks to the honesty of Plotinus's thought and the thoroughness with which he discusses his problems, we can understand it particularly clearly. But it makes that part of his thought which deals with the visible world and the relations of soul and body the least coherent and satisfactory part of his philosophy.

XVIII
The Later Neo-Platonists

1. PLOTINUS is incomparably the greatest of the Neo-Platonists and has had a far deeper and wider influence than any of his successors. Of these Porphyry (232–early fourth century), his intimate disciple, keeps very close to the philosophy of his master, his most important work being the editing of the Enneads. In him, however, certain tendencies begin to appear which develop enormously in the later Neo-Platonists. Plotinus quite often uses the method of allegorical interpretation, applying it to Plato's dialogues, but he never takes it very seriously. Porphyry takes it very seriously indeed, and uses it not only to elucidate Plato but to find deep philosophical meanings in Homer, and the pagan Platonists of the last period of the school, the successors of Iamblichus, exploit the method as remorselessly and with as far-fetched results as Philo himself. Again, Plotinus had practised vegetarianism but never thought it worth writing about. Porphyry wrote a treatise on it, and obviously considers it an important part of the philosophical life. In this he anticipates, though still at some distance, the morbid, more than Orphic scrupulosity about ritual purity and purification, which distinguishes the Neo-Platonists after Iamblichus. Plotinus is not deeply interested in contemporary religious cults, even the mystery religions, though he borrows images and even a few ideas from them; nor has he much use for the popular Platonist theology of gods and dæmones, though he accepts it as true as far as it goes. And he is not concerned to defend Hellenic, paganism as such against the onslaughts of orthodox Christianity, which he ignores except perhaps for the one remark already mentioned, though he is concerned to defend Platonism against the Gnostics, whose claims to superior wisdom he refutes crushingly in Enneads II. 9. Porphyry follows his master in his attitude towards outward religious practices. Religion for both of them is an entirely inward and individual affair, the ascent of the solitary spirit to the One. But Porphyry is very much interested in the dæmones, the crowd of spirits intermediate between gods and men, and has a good deal to say about them. And he is the first of the Neo-Platonists, the successors of Plotinus, to embark on a task with which the school became more and more deeply concerned, the defence of Hellenic paganism against Christianity

(a second-century Platonist, Celsus, had already written a work of anti-Christian apologetic which Origen answered). On the whole we may sum up Porphyry as very much the loyal disciple and devout follower, intelligent enough to appreciate and understand Plotinus but a lesser man altogether and without the creative ability to develop his master's doctrine.

A great change comes over the spirit of Neo-Platonism with Iamblichus the Syrian, who like Porphyry taught at Rome after the death of Plotinus but retired in later life to Syria, where he died about 330. From his time onwards the centres of Neo-Platonism are in the East, in Syria, at Alexandria, and at Athens where by the fifth century the Academy itself had become Neo-Platonist and the Diadochi, the successors of Plato (as the heads of the Academy were called) continued to teach Neo-Platonic doctrine until the school was closed by Justinian when the teaching of pagan philosophy was prohibited in 529. The Neo-Platonic tradition survived also in the West, but there the Christian Neo-Platonists, above all St. Augustine, are much more important than the pagans. These, men like Macrobius or Martianus Capella, are theologians, scholars and devout commentators on ancient texts and had little philosophical importance or interest; their thought remains close to that of Plotinus and Porphyry. Macrobius and M. Capella were much read in the Middle Ages, and their works form one of the channels (not by any means the most important) through which Neo-Platonic ideas were transmitted to the Christian West. Chalcidius, the fourth-century translator of a portion of the "Timæus" into Latin, whose version with its lengthy commentary had a great influence in the Middle Ages in the West, was probably a Christian and is certainly Middle-Platonist rather than Neo-Platonist in his philosophical outlook. Maximus of Madaura, St. Augustine's pagan correspondent, an attractive old gentleman, provides another instance of the survival of Middle-Platonist ways of thinking in the West long after the rise of Neo-Platonism. But it is with the Neo-Platonists of the Eastern half of the Empire, the Syrian and Athenian schools, that a historian of philosophy must be chiefly concerned. Among them the system of Plotinus not only survives but is considerably developed and curiously transformed.

2.   From Iamblichus onwards the pagan Neo-Platonists had two main concerns. First to provide the rapidly weakening and disappearing paganism of the ancient world with a complete and

coherent theology, which was something which it had never had before and which was totally foreign to its true nature. It was a theology based on inspired scriptures, on the Dialogues of Plato, above all the "Parmenides" and the "Timæus" and on an extraordinary farrago called the "Chaldæan Oracles" delivered by the gods, so the Neo-Platonists said, through Julianus the theurgist. Both these were divine and absolute authorities. This theological side of their activity, by which they provided an intellectual support for the last desperate rally of pagan religion and culture against the overwhelming force of Christianity, though very fascinating in itself, can only concern us here in so far as it affected their philosophical system. On the philosophical side they were concerned to elaborate and bring out the logical implications of Plotinus's rich and living, but not always very clear thought and to reduce it to an absolutely complete, watertight and rigid system. This was finally achieved, as far as it could be, by the greatest of the later Neo-Platonists, Proclus the Platonic Successor at Athens (410–485). After him the last notable pagan Neo-Platonist, Damascius, reacts to some extent towards a freer and more genuinely Plotinian kind of thought.

The assumption which underlies all the later Neo-Platonic elaboration of Plotinus is that the structure of reality corresponds so exactly to the way in which a late Greek philosopher's mind works, that there is a separate real entity which corresponds to every distinction which the mind can make. Plotinus had already recognized certain great distinctions in the spiritual universe corresponding to the levels of human thought and consciousness; the distinctions between the Divine Mind and Soul and between the different levels of Soul are of this kind. But the later Neo-Platonists, Iamblichus, Theodore of Asine, Syrianus and Proclus, lack Plotinus's sense of living reality and split up, subdivide and classify to such an extent that their entities become so abstract as to be hopelessly unreal. For Plotinus the Divine Mind-World of Forms was Being. That Which Is; it was also alive, Life itself, and Intelligence. But Being, Life and Intelligence are clearly distinguishable in thought. Plotinus had already recognized this, but had never gone so far as to break up the complex unity of the Divine Mind into three distinct hypostases. Iamblichus however did so, and the triad Being, Life, Intelligence, plays an important part in the later Neo-Platonic system (the first two form the transcendent source of the immanent intelligible content of the last, so that the Intelligible is not as in Plotinus completely correlated with the Intelligence but is outside it in one sense and within it in another).

And this is only the beginning of the complications of later Neo-Platonism. Iamblichus introduced some principles which, applied with remorseless logic, led to a truly fantastic elaboration. There is the "law of mean terms", according to which two doubly unlike realities must always be connected by an intermediate term which is like one in one respect and the other in another (A B must be connected to not -A not -B by either A-not -B or B-not -A) which forms a triad with them, and without this intermediate term they cannot be directly related. Then again there is the recognition on every level of the system of the triple movement of "remaining", "procession" and "return" by which effects proceed from their cause and return upon it again. This is implicit in Plotinus, but is not used by him as a rigorously applied structural principle. And besides these general principles of construction there is the need imposed by the task of constructing a pagan theology of finding a place in the system for every god, dæmon, hero or other supernatural being of late pagan syncretistic mythology and cult and of following up every suggestion arising from the allegorical interpretation of the pagan Scriptures, the Platonic Dialogues and the Chaldæan Oracles, and the ancient myths, Greek, Egyptian or Near Eastern. The result is a vast and elaborate map of the spiritual world, the outlines of which can be studied most conveniently in Proclus's "Elements of Theology", where the main principles are set forth, proved and applied to the proof of other consequent doctrines in a series of two hundred and eleven propositions, Euclidean in form. In this system reality is divided into a large number of superimposed and sharply distinguished levels, each of which forms an "order" whose complex construction is determined by the structural principles described above and others deduced from them. Each successive "order" is exactly similar in construction to the one above it, and the corresponding entities in the different "orders" form vertical descending "series".

At the head of the system, immediately below the One which remains the ultimate First Principle come the Divine Henads or Gods. These are one of the strangest of the later Neo-Platonic elaborations and seem to have been invented by Proclus's master Syrianus. On the theological side they represent the gods of the ancient pagan cults and myths, though it is hardly possible to imagine anything less like the human, vigorous and lively imaginations of Homer or the beings worshipped in the shrines of ancient Greece and portrayed in their great statues than these quite impersonal abstractions, each reflected on five different levels of reality in its appropriate descending "series". Philosophically they are an attempt to bridge the gulf between the One and the Many, to help to explain how the multiplicity of the world-order can proceed from the ultimate Absolute Unity; a not very helpful attempt, for it still remains to be explained how the complicated multitude of the Henads proceeded from the One; the mystery cannot be solved by any amount of interpolation of intermediate terms, because there can be no real intermediate between the Absolute One and other things. The Henads also, from a late Neo-Platonic point of view, complete the system tidily; just as there are many souls beside and subordinate to Universal Soul and many minds beside and subordinate to Universal Mind so there should be many Ones beside and subordinate to the Supreme One. Plotinus, of course, did not think at all like this. In his thought it is essential that the One should be alone and unique, and that multiplicity should begin with the Divine Mind; the introduction of the Henads really makes nonsense of his whole system. A curious feature of the doctrine is the relation of the Henads or gods to the divine attributes; they are not correlated singly so that each god has a proper attribute of its own but grouped so that a number of gods share one dominant attribute between them. Also, in a manner which contradicts the most fundamental rules of Proclus's own thought, single principles in the lower "orders" participate in groups of gods; thus "unparticipated Being" participates in the whole group of "intelligible gods" directly and "divine unparticipated Soul" participates in the group of "hypercosmic henads" at two removes, through two intervening "orders" or levels of reality.

3. In this amazing metaphysical museum, with all the entities and super-entities neatly labelled and arranged on their proper shelves, there is no room for the free spiritual life of Plotinus, the unfettered ascent from the realm of Soul through Mind to the possibility of union with the One. In Proclus's system no spiritual being can have direct contact with any other being higher than the one immediately above it in the hierarchy; it can

only reach beings higher still indirectly through the medium of all the intervening terms of its "procession". And though we find occasional pious allusions to the mystical union, from Iamblichus onwards it was no longer a part of experience or the centre of Neo-Platonic religion. The place of mysticism was taken by Theurgy, a collection of magical practices based on that doctrine of universal sympathy in which Plotinus, as I said, believed but which had nothing to do with his religion. The theurgist's aim was, through incantations and the mysterious properties of certain stones, herbs and other material substances, to set in motion a chain of sympathies running up through a whole "series" to the god he was trying to evoke, and so to produce a divine apparition and attain a sort of magical and external communion with the divine being. The practice of theurgy implied for the late Neo-Platonists a philosophical principle of some importance, namely, that the effects of a higher principle reached further down the scale of being than the effects of a lower principle and consequently that something very low in the scale of reality might participate in something very high with fewer intervening terms than were necessary in the case of a higher participating principle. Thus for Proclus matter (and consequently the material objects used by the theurgists) participated in the One through fewer intervening terms than the human soul or even intellect; and the most direct way to the divine was consequently through theurgy and not through philosophical speculation. (It would be an interesting and valuable exercise to work out the differences between this conception and Catholic sacramentalism.)

Proclus naturally, in conformity with this view, gives up altogether the view that matter is evil and the principle of evil which we find sometimes in Plotinus. For Proclus matter is given its quasi-existence by the power of the One; it is part of the universal order and therefore good. Evil for him is entirely negative, the absence or deficiency of good, and material evils and imperfections are necessary to the completeness of the universal order. This, of course, is the doctrine of later Christian thinkers, and is also to be found in the Enneads, but faithfulness to the Platonic tradition made Proclus also retain the other idea of matter as opposed to form and order and so the ultimate source of evil. Another important difference between Plotinus and Proclus which is bound up with the change of spirit I have noticed, the rigid hierarchic order and the impossibility for any spiritual being to transcend its limits, is that in Proclus the whole personality descends and is embodied. Nothing of man remains above, in the realm of the Divine Mind, as Plotinus had said it did.

4. This is a very summary and inadequate survey of post-Iamblichean Neo-Platonism as developed and perfected by Syrianus and Proclus, and one which has perhaps laid more stress on its perversities than its profundities. But Proclus, it is important to realize, is not a philosopher to be despised. His influence on the Byzantine world and on the medieval West was very considerable, especially through the writings of the Pseudo-Dionysius, which are very deeply influenced by him; and he often provides a most valuable commentary on the Enneads. He is not of the stature of Plotinus, but he is a most useful supplement to him. It is above all through Proclus's writings, the immense Commentaries on Plato, the Platonic Theology, and the hand-books and shorter treatises of which the "Elements of Theology" is the most important, that we know this later Neo-Platonism. Very little of Iamblichus survives, nothing of Theodore of Asine or Syrianus, and the theological effusions of the Emperor Julian, a devout Iamblichean Neo-Platonist, are not philosophically enlightening. Damascius, the last pagan Neo-Platonist in the unbroken succession, who was teaching when Justinian closed the School in 529, stands in some ways rather apart. He retains the whole monstrous system, but, so to speak, opens its doors and lets a free wind of spiritual life blow through them by his doctrine of the Ineffable First Principle, the Absolute which he will not even call the One. The pages in which he speaks of it at the beginning of his "Problems and Solutions" are among the most impressive in later Greek philosophy. It is beyond all resource of human language to express and utterly beyond the hierarchy of reality. And because It is outside and beyond all hierarchy, everything, and the soul of man, can participate in It directly and without intermediary though in an unspeakably mysterious way. Though there is no evidence that I know of that he had any personal mystical experience, his language comes closer to that of the "Dionysian" tradition of mysticism than even that of Plotinus, and certainly than anything in the thoroughly unmystical Proclus. It is a strange and impressive last word for pagan philosophy. Alongside of the original philosophical speculation of this last age the work of commenting on Plato and

Aristotle was kept up to the end. It is to this period that the great commentaries of Simplicius, the Neo-Platonist, on Aristotle belong. The Neo-Platonists of Alexandria, whose interests were more scholarly and less theological than those of the Athenian and Pergamene schools, were also active in the work of comment and produced a number of important commentaries on Aristotle. We do not find in them the complicated metaphysical theology of Iamblichus and his successors or the passionate hostility to Christianity that went with it; in fact some of them became Christians. Perhaps this work of comment had a wider and more lasting influence on later philosophy than the original treatises of Proclus and Damascius, though how wide and deep the influence of Proclus especially was both in East and West during the Middle Ages and the Renaissance is only now beginning to be realized.

XIX

St. Augustine and the Transmutation

of Ancient Thought

1. IN the last chapter we have been dealing with that amazing
hard and solid projection of pagan Hellenic thought into the world
of the Christian Empire which is formed by post-Iamblichean
Neo-Platonism. Now we may conclude this sketch by studying
the most striking and important example of how the Christian
contemporaries of the last pagan Neo-Platonists transformed
Hellenic philosophy and adapted it to the needs of the Christian
theological tradition, with far-reaching consequences for the
history of thought in general. This work had been started already,
as we have seen, by the Apologists and the School of Alexandria,
but the decisive steps in the process of transformation were taken
in the fourth and fifth centuries A.D. by a group of great
philosophical theologians, Eastern and Western, who make this
period one of the most fruitful in the history of Christian thinking.
One man stands out above all others of this time both in the
quality of his thought and its importance for the later development of philosophy. This is St. Augustine, and it is to his thought,
both as an original philosophy of great value and significance
and as affording excellent examples of the way in which the late
Hellenic tradition was transformed for Christian use, that I
propose to devote this last chapter. (Boethius, who is also in a
different way an important link between Neo-Platonism and
Western Christian thought, belongs more properly to the history
of mediæval philosophy.)

St. Augustine has been called the Christian Plato, and there is
some truth in the comparison. Like Plato he is a great originator,
who does not present us with a finished system but introduces
us into a landscape of living and growing, ceaselessly productive
ideas which cannot be reduced to a diagram. But though
Augustine's thought cannot be rigidly systematized it is very
homogeneous and forms a unity. There is not and cannot be,
as we shall see, any separation in St. Augustine between philosophy and theology, and all through his thought we find the
same great principles being applied in every part and to the
solution of every problem. And Augustine's thought derives this

unity and homogeneity from the fact that it springs so directly from his own personal experience. We cannot understand the thought without understanding the man or the man without understanding his thought. For this reason an indispensable preliminary to any study of St. Augustine must be the reading of his own autobiography, the "Confessions" (and, quite apart from the serious study of Augustine's thought, no-one who has not read the "Confessions", and read them right through, including the last three books, can regard himself as properly educated). The outward circumstances of Augustine's life are not perhaps of the greatest importance for our understanding of his thought, except in so far as they affected his intellectual and spiritual development. A few dates and facts are worth recording. He was born in 354 at Thagaste in North Africa, of a Christian mother, S. Monica, and a pagan father, Patricius. He was given a thorough rhetorical education, and became a brilliant and successful professional rhetorician, practising at Rome and Milan. At Milan in 386 he was converted and soon after ordained. He became Bishop of Hippo in North Africa in 396 and there he remained for the rest of his life. It is to this period of very active work as a diocesan bishop that the greater part of his immense literary output belongs. He died at Hippo in 430 while the Vandals were besieging the city.

2. Much more important for our understanding of him is the history of his inner development. We cannot really hope to understand the workings of Augustine's mind unless we realize that he knew the Christian Faith and Scriptures all his life, thought he had little use for them in his adolescence and early manhood and was not baptized and did not practise the Christian religion until the time of his conversion. Yet his knowledge of Christianity preceded his knowledge of philosophy and his mind was never altogether free from its influence. It is also essential for our understanding of his thought to remember that for some time he accepted Manichæism as giving the best possible explanation of the universe. Manichæism was the latest and most successful form of that sort of materialistic emanation-religion which was so popular in the early centuries of our era, especially in the Near and Middle East. It is related to earlier Gnostic systems, but is more sharply dualistic in the Persian manner; that is, it regards Good and Evil as two independent positive forces, sharply opposed and engaged in ceaseless conflict. Both according

to Manichæan doctrine are material, Good being material light and Evil material darkness. God is a vast luminous body abiding beyond the sky, from whom proceeds an elaborate hierarchy of emanations. The material world which we know is a kingdom of evil and darkness, created by the Evil Principle. Human spirits are fragments of the divine light imprisoned in bodies, from which they may be delivered after many incarnations by rigorous ascetic practices and a curious and complicated purgatorial machinery operating on them after death in the upper regions of the universe. Augustine was particularly attracted to Manichæism by the easy solution which it offered of the problem of evil, to which in later life he devoted much attention, and he was very deeply affected by Manichæan materialism. From this his mind was delivered by reading the Neo-Platonists, and especially Plotinus. It was Plotinus who convinced him that God was a spirit, not a luminous body, and he always remained grateful for this deliverance from the crude fantasies of the Manichees. It is also important to remember when considering Augustine's thought that he passed through a very painful period of scepticism or universal doubt, when he found himself forced into the Academic position without any of the pleasure which the Sceptical Academy seems to have felt in negative and destructive thinking. This accounts for the care and thoroughness with which in after life he refutes the sceptical position and discusses the problem of certainty which had tormented his own mind in a way which to some extent anticipates and undoubtedly influenced Descartes.

3. The only Hellenic philosophy which permanently influenced Augustine was the Platonism of Plotinus, and this influenced him very deeply indeed. He first came to know Plotinus at Milan, in the two years before his conversion, at the time when he was also acquiring a deeper knowledge of Christianity than he had ever possessed before by regularly listening to the sermons of St. Ambrose. He only at this time read a very few treatises of the "Enneads" (certainly I. 6 "On the Beautiful" and quite probably V.I. "On the Three Chief Hypostases"), in the Latin translation of Marius Victorinus. Victorinus was another convert Professor of Rhetoric, this time at Rome, who made a determined attempt to apply the principles of Plotinus's philosophy to the elucidation of the Christian dogma of the Trinity as against the Arians, with results which are interesting if not altogether theologically satisfactory. But his chief importance in the history

of thought is in the influence which his translation of the "Enneads" had on Augustine's mind. Augustine improved his acquaintance with Plotinus afterwards, and perhaps even in later life read some of the "Enneads" in Greek; he certainly also knew some of Porphyry's writings well. But it was the first impact of Plotinus's thought on his mind at Milan which was the decisive one. What impressed him particularly deeply and did more than anything else to prepare the way intellectually for his conversion was the very great degree of agreement which he found between the teaching of Plotinus and that of the Scriptures as expounded by St. Ambrose, above all the Gospel of St. John. It was their agreement that God is Spirit and altogether immaterial, as Plotinus so well explains, which liberated him from Manichæan materialism, and he also (mistakenly, though he never saw his mistake) thought that Plotinus's teaching about the Divine Mind was identical with that of St. John about the Divine Logos. Very soon after his conversion, and probably at the actual time, he was clearly conscious of certain fundamental differences between Plotinian Neo-Platonism and Christianity. He expounds the differences and resemblances as he came to see them magnificently in Confessions VII, 9, which, with Chapters 10 and 20 of the same book should be read by anyone who wishes to understand Augustine's own view of the relationship between his own thought and that of Plotinus. But he never abandoned the view that there was a great measure of agreement between Plotinus and Christian doctrine and for this reason, as we shall see, was very ready to allow his thought to be influenced by Plotinus in many important ways, within clearly defined limits set by the overriding authority of the Scriptures interpreted by Catholic tradition.

4. Before going on to discuss St. Augustine's thought it will be as well to note the character of the writings through which we know it. His works fill sixteen volumes of Migne's Patrologia Latina, and it would be impossible to give even a list of the titles of them all. The main bulk of his works, as with all the Fathers, consists of very detailed explanations of the Scriptures, either in the form of sermons preached to his people at Hippo or of commentaries on various books of the Bible. These expository works are of the very greatest importance for the right understanding of Augustine's thought, for, however important the influence of Plotinus on him may be, it is always from the Bible and not

Plotinus that he starts and the Bible remains the dominant influence. Among his most important works of this kind are the Homilies on St. John, the Explanations of the Psalms, and the commentaries on Genesis. Then there are a number of large-scale works on particular theological problems of which perhaps the most important and influential are the great treatise on the Trinity and the works on grace produced by the controversy with Pelagius. There is a mass of smaller works, moral, theological, philosophical, controversial, and one on æsthetics, the "De Musica"; a very interesting group are the works written just after his conversion during his retirement at Cassiciacum, which are of much importance for our understanding of the development of his thought. There are many Letters, some of which are really small treatises on moral or theological points. There are the Retractations, written towards the end of his life, in which he surveys and criticizes his earlier works. Then finally we must mention his two most widely read books, neither of which can be classified under any general heading, the "Confessions" and his great work on the philosophy of history the "City of God", a book controversial in intention but of a scope and importance going far beyond its immediate controversial purpose.

5. In trying to give some idea, however inadequate, of St. Augustine's thought the purpose of this book makes it necessary to concentrate on those elements in it which are of philosophical interest and importance and to leave in the background those which would nowadays be considered exclusively the concern of professional theologians. But we shall soon see that it is really impossible to separate Augustinian philosophy from Augustinian theology. We are dealing with a unity which depends throughout on the Christian Revelation. Neither for Augustine himself nor for any thinker in the Augustinian tradition is a true philosophy distinct and separate from theology even possible. The reason for this lies in what is perhaps the most important foundation principle of Augustinian thought, the utter helplessness of man to do anything right or think anything true by himself, without God. But before examining this principle more closely we must try to understand what St. Augustine meant by God. He meant, of course, the same as the other great Christian Fathers who were his contemporaries and immediate predecessors, and, in essentials, as all orthodox Christian thought before or since. But he meant something very different from Plotinus or any pagan Platonist.

The essential difference between pagan, Hellenic, and Christian thinkers is to be found in their different understanding of what is meant by "God" or "The Divine".

For the Christian, God is the single and only Absolute Reality. He is the fulness of Being (and therefore of Good, Truth, Beauty, Thought and Life) who is in Himself everything that relative and derived, created beings are and infinitely more. He is Absolute Unity, entirely single and simple, but this unity is not like that of the created unities we know. It is not the unity of a unit, a member of a class, an atomic individual, which is a mere negation of plurality; neither is it the composite unity-in-plurality of an organism, a structure, a genus or species, or any kind of class. It is a unity which lies over the edge of our thought so that our minds can never reach it but only approximate to it. It is an essential quality of all orthodox Christian thought about God that it sees in Him this transcendent perfection of Unity and Being which goes beyond all thought and all realities that the human mind can contain. All we can say is that He is absolutely One and that His Unity is a rich unity, in which are all realities that He creates and infinitely more, not existing virtually or potentially as in a seed, but raised to a higher degree of actuality than we can conceive; this is what we try to express by saying that the Forms of all things are in the mind of God, thought in a single and eternal Act and introducing no plurality into His transcendent Source-Unity. There is much more to be said (though it all in the last resort is nothing against the Reality), but it cannot be said here. Those who really want to know what Christians think about God must go to St. Augustine, St. Thomas and St. Bonaventure themselves, and not to second-rate textbooks.

As against this Christian idea of a single transcendent Divine Being the pagan Platonists, as we have seen, believed in a Divine World, hierarchically ordered, with a number of eternal beings, all divine but differing in their degree of divinity, and all deriving from a transcendent First Principle. It is true that Plotinus sometimes comes very near to the idea of a single transcendent Divine Being, and that he sees that if the First Principle of the divine hierarchy, the One, is to be adequate as a First Principle it must contain all and more than all which is in the subsequent divine beings, and that without prejudice to its absolute unity. But he is, as we have seen, never quite clear about this and its implications, and he certainly never sees that it would enable him to dispense with the hierarchy of subordinate divine beings which do not really help to solve the problem, necessarily beyond our minds, of how the Many come out of the One. But when the great Christian Platonists of the fourth and fifth centuries A.D. begin to apply the ideas of Plotinus about the divine to gain a deeper understanding of the Christian doctrine of God, what they do is precisely to drop the conception of the Divine Hierarchy, to see the whole of Divinity concentrated in the One, and to apply to the Trinity-in-Unity everything that Plotinus says about his divine hypostases. Thus the Fathers apply everything that Plotinus has to say about his Second Hypostasis, the Divine Mind or One-Being, either to the Godhead or more particularly to the Second Person of the Trinity, the Son, Who is the Divine Wisdom in Whom are all the Forms, the full, perfect, infinite and eternal Expression of the Divine productivity of the Father, on Whose eternal generation all creation of relative being outside the Godhead depends. The Fathers also apply a good deal of what Plotinus has to say about the activities of the higher Soul in the universe to the external activity of the Holy Spirit, though Plotinus, of course, can give them nothing to help them to express the place of the Holy Spirit in the inner life of the Godhead, as Substantial Love springing from the unity of the Father and the Son. The God of the Christian Fathers of this age, and of all orthodox Christian theology since, is absolutely One and is also Being, though transcending all the limited, relative and derived beings we know and differing from them in kind, not in degree (so that in this sense He may be said to be "beyond being"); thus He combines Plotinus's First and Second Hypostases, the One and the Divine Mind. And all the acts and attributes which Plotinus attributes to his various levels of divine being are attributed by the Fathers to the whole Trinity-in-Unity or to one of the Three Divine Persons in particular.

This transmutation of Plotinus's theology is particularly clear in St. Augustine, because his thought is at once so authentically Christian and so very close in some ways to Plotinus. His tremendous stressing of the Unity of God as the transcendent principle of all order and number and so of all being (for to be anything other than Absolute Unity is to be an ordered whole of parts and so in some sense a unity) derives from Plotinus. But in stressing the Unity he equally affirms the Being and the Trinity of God. In considering the Trinity-in-Unity he (and the whole West after him) certainly starts from and lays the first emphasis on the Unity of the Godhead and not, as the Cappadocian Fathers and the later East, on the Three Divine Persons. But neither St. Augustine nor any other of the Fathers nor any thinker in Augustine's tradition ever considers the Unity and the Trinity separately, the one as a goal theoretically attainable by the unaided reason in philosophy and the other as only knowable (in so far as it can be known) by the help of revelation in theology, as the Thomists do. For Augustine and his followers all true thinking begins and ends with the Trinity. It is indeed for them only as Trinity that God creates us and only as Trinity that we can approach Him. For He creates in and through the Son, the Divine Wisdom or Eternal Art in Whom are the Forms, and we approach Him only by being made like Him, which can only be through the same Son, the absolute and only adequate Image, the Likeness of the Father by Whom all else are made like Him. This idea of the Absolute Likeness by which things are made like, as they are made beautiful by Absolute Beauty, is again taken over from Platonism. Another point at which Augustine's (and all orthodox Christian) theology of the Trinity approaches very closely to the thought of Plotinus, yet with significant differences, is his insistence on God's absolute self-sufficiency, on the completeness and self-containedness of His inner life of love and knowledge and its absolute primacy over His external activity of creation. For the Christian theologians, as for Plotinus, an inwardly-turned love and contemplation is the essential Divine activity and all God's actions on the creatures he calls into being are secondary. But for the Christians, unlike Plotinus, creation is not an automatic reflex action of the Divine contemplation. It is an absolutely free and generous act of the Divine will. God is not compelled by any necessity to create. The Divine productivity is perfectly expressed in the Eternal Son. Creation and still more Redemption are extra and spontaneous overflowings of the single great stream of will and love with which God wills and loves Himself. And here is another difference from Plotinus. The Christians, at least of the older theological tradition, hold that we can only make such approach to an understanding of God's inturned love and contemplation as is possible to us when we realize that He is Three Persons in One, and that His Unity is not the bare negation of multiplicity of Plotinus's thought at its most negative.

6. This tremendous vision of the single Power and Act which is the Divine Being, infinite in all His perfections, has naturally made Christian theologians all the more intensely conscious of that absolute dependence of all created beings, including man, on God, belief in which they have received from the Jewish Scriptures. The consciousness of this is peculiarly vivid in St. Augustine, especially as it applies to man in his present fallen and sinful state. He knew only too well from his own long experience that he could neither see the truth nor act rightly when he had seen it by his own strength. Here Plotinus could not help him, for Plotinus like all the Greeks held that the philosopher could and must act virtuously, purify his life, know the truth and ascend even to the threshold of the final vision or union by his own strength and without any special Divine help. It was the Christian faith, and above all St. Paul, which taught Augustine to look for the answer to his desperate helplessness in Divine grace. And the absolute conviction of the insufficiency of all things created, their inability even to exist without God's sustaining presence, and above all of the utter helplessness of fallen man if left to himself is the deepest principle of Augustine's thought. We can see it at work in his account of the creation, in his theory of knowledge, and in that doctrine of the good life, of the way of return of the redeemed soul to God, which is the centre of his teaching and the end to which it is all directed.

Like all other Christian thinkers Augustine believes in the creation of the whole universe, spiritual and material, out of nothing, by God. God, that is, as Augustine makes very clear, creates not only the immanent forms in matter but the matter which they inform; the creation of form and matter is simultaneous, for matter cannot exist unformed, but the two stages, the creation of primal matter and its information, can be distinguished in thought. Augustine and all his followers accept Plotinus's teaching that there is "matter" in the philosophical sense of a potentiality capable of receiving form in the created spiritual world, the world of the Angels, as well as in the world of space and time. Augustine's description of the formative element in the created universe is thoroughly Platonic and Plotinian. All things only exist in so far as they are images of the Forms in the mind of God; they are more or less imperfect copies of God's perfection. And that which makes them images and so gives them such degree of being as they possess is the element of number,

order and rhythm in the created universe. Augustine often calls
the forms of created things "numbers", and he insists that the
universe and each and every creature in it only exist at all and
have any degree of goodness and beauty because they are ordered,
harmonious, and so in some sense unities. Everything that exists
is for Augustine good in so far as it exists, being made by a good
creator. Evil, he holds like Proclus, is not a positive force but
always negative, a defect, an imperfection, a lack of order; this
doctrine is that generally accepted by all Christian philosophers.
Augustine praises the beauty and goodness of the visible world as
magnificently as Plotinus and sometimes in language borrowed
from the Enneads, but sometimes with a deeper and more
intimate delight because he sees God's immediate presence in all
His works in a way in which Plotinus did not. Yet Augustine is
as clear as any Platonist about the necessity of transcending the
visible universe, of passing from body to spirit and from spirit
to God. The Christian doctrine of God and His relations with
man transforms, however, as we shall see, his whole conception
of this ascent of the soul.

Augustine's sense of the absolute dependence of creatures on
God appears in his account of creation in two ways. First, there
is the proof of the existence of God derived from the radical insufficiency of creatures to account for themselves. "All things",
he says, "cry out that they are made". If we really understand
what a created thing is, the essentially relative, non-necessary
and therefore dependent character of its being, we shall inevitably
perceive God as its cause and the support of its existence. The
second way is in his doctrine of the "rationes seminales". This
is an adaptation of the doctrine of "seminal logoi" originated by
the Stoics and radically transformed in a Platonic sense by
Plotinus. Augustine's form of it is Platonic rather than Stoic and
must come from Plotinus or some other Neo-Platonic source, but
it is modified in such a way as to make God the only real cause of
everything which happens in the created world. The "seminal
reasons" of Augustine are "numbers," i.e. formative principles
implanted in matter by God at the Creation like seeds, that is so
that they do not carry out their informing work and produce
fully-formed beings at once, but only after remaining latent in
matter for a period until the time ordained by God for the
emergence of those particular formed beings has come. Thus no
secondary, created cause in Augustine's universe has any real

originating power. Everything which emerges at a later stage of the universe's life was really directly created by God in His single original creative act.

According to Augustine the universe was created not in time, but with time. He answers the question "What was God doing before he made the world" quite simply by pointing out that there was no "before". God's life is eternal. There is no change, transition, developing imperfection, or incompleteness moving to its fulfilment in Him. Therefore there can be no time, because time is the way our minds measure change and motion. Only things created and so to some degree imperfect and changeable exist in time, and time came into existence with them. Augustine's psychological theory of the nature of time is interesting and important. Time is for him a mental phenomenon; it is in the soul that we measure time; it is a "stretching-out of the soul". The past is memory, the future expectation, the present attention; and if we consider time carefully we shall find that the present is the only one of its three dimensions which really exists, containing the past in present memory and the future in present expectation, and that this present is essentially impermanent, always vanishing away into the past. The world of time is a Heraclitean flow and only in God is there stability and permanence (cp. Confessions Book XI, 14 ff). Augustine altogether breaks away from the old Greek theory of cyclic time, the measure of the everlasting circular motion of the everlasting universe; for him time is the measure of a single, irreversible, unrepeatable, rectilinear movement of history; it is the measuring of history by human consciousness. This is the first philosophical theory of time inspired by the Christian revelation; it is thoroughly original and deeply affects St. Augustine's philosophy of history.

7. This theory of time illustrates very well the "inwardness" of Augustine's thought. The centre of all his thinking is God, and after God the human soul. Like Plotinus he tends to turn away from the external, material world and concentrate on the inner spiritual reality. The forms in matter are certainly for him likenesses of the Divine Ideas, but they are only "traces" (vestigia) of God, just as in Plotinus they are "indalmata", the last and lowest appearances of spiritual reality. The human soul on the other hand is for Augustine very much more than a "trace". It is an image of God. In this he is following the Jewish and Christian rather than the Platonic tradition (for the pagan

Platonists, of course, the soul was a divine being in its own right).
Augustine's conception of the soul is in some ways very Platonic.
He admits, as any Christian is bound to do, that the whole man
is not soul only, but soul and body. But he does not, like the
Aristotelians, define the soul as the form of the body, but like the
Platonists sees it as a separate, independent and complete spiritual
substance, though adapted by God to the function of using and
ruling a body which distinguishes it from other spirits. He defines
man as a rational soul using (or ruling, or simply having) a body.
In perception and knowledge he holds that the soul acts in a
Platonic and not an Aristotelian manner; that is, it perceives and
knows the form-element in things actively, by virtue of its kinship
with them, and does not, like the Aristotelian soul, passively
receive impressions, sense-impressions and mind-pictures, from
which by a rather elaborate process it abstracts its concepts. The
soul for the Platonists and for Augustine and his followers is never
passive and never really affected by the body. It is always active
and dominant, using the body and its sense-organs for its own
purposes. Furthermore, the content of its thought is not exclusively derived from sense-perception. It has some degree at
least of immediate contact with the intelligible. This dominant,
body-ruling Platonic soul is, however, for Augustine a creature,
and a fallen creature. It is therefore as a creature utterly unable
to exist or act without Divine support and assistance, while as a
fallen creature it is plunged in the utmost depths of misery and
indigence. A very striking feature of Augustine's thought is his
vivid sense of actuality, the care he takes always to keep close
to the real condition of man as he sees it. He does not, like
S. Thomas, draw a clear distinction between what man had by
nature before the Fall and what he had by grace, the supernatural
gifts which made him more than man. For Augustine man before
the Fall was simply man as he ought to be, man as designed by
God, with the supernatural gifts necessary to bring him to perfect
happiness. And after the Fall man is not simply deprived of the
supernatural while retaining his natural powers uninjured (St.
Thomas does not think this either, but there is no space to discuss
his doctrine here with the necessary precision). His whole being
was corrupted and vitiated; he was plunged into ignorance and
sin and is utterly incapable of knowing what he should without
Revelation and still more incapable of doing what he should
without the grace of the Redemption.

But though corrupted and vitiated, man's nature is not totally destroyed. God, St. Augustine says, has not completely withdrawn His gifts, otherwise we should simply cease to exist. The soul continues to exist, and to be able to operate. Therefore it receives Divine support in the way proper to its several operations. We can see very clearly in his theory of knowledge how even these natural operations of the human soul (which are by themselves quite insufficient to bring man to his true end and the happiness which he desires) depend absolutely for Augustine on continual Divine assistance. He begins his consideration of knowledge with that famous refutation of scepticism which anticipates Descartes. There is one thing, he says, of which I can be absolutely certain, and that is, that I exist. But why should I not be wrong even about this? Simply because, if I am wrong, then in order to be wrong I must exist. "Si fallor, sum" (De Civ. Dei XI, 26 cp. De Trinitate XV, 12, 21). This refutation of scepticism has important implications. First, it means that man has direct and immediate cognisance, not through the senses, of at least one spiritual reality, himself as a thinking subject. Augustine emphasizes this frequently; though he admits, unlike some later Augustinians, that we know external material objects through the senses and only through the senses, the highest and most important knowledge for him is that immediate contact of the mind with spiritual, intelligible reality to which the first step is our consciousness of our self as a living, thinking reality.

From it we can go on to further conclusions about the nature of our knowledge. In knowing our own existence we know a truth and, having once refuted the Academics and delivered ourselves from hopeless scepticism by arriving at this one absolute certainty, we shall be able to go on and find that we know other truths. Now truth has certain characteristics which it is surprising to find entering into the thought of a being in a world such as ours. It is necessary, immutable, eternal, always and universally true. Where, then, does it come from? Not from the Heraclitean flow of transitory mutability which is the visible world; and not from ourselves or any other created spiritual being, for all created things are transitory and changeable. (This is a most important difference between Augustine and pagan Platonism; for the pagan Platonists the human intellect at least, the highest part of the soul, was divine and partook of the eternal stability of the divine.) For Augustine knowledge of the truth means some sort of contact of the mind with the eternal and absolute Being of God, for it is only God who is Truth and Reality, whose Being is necessary and eternal. Whenever we make a true judgment it only derives its character of necessity and universality from some illumination of our minds by the Forms in the Mind of God. These Forms are in Christ, the Divine Wisdom. Therefore he is our Master, and our only Master, the only one who can teach us truth, in the sphere of natural as well as of supernatural knowledge. He leads our minds towards Him and teaches us about His own existence through our knowledge of the simplest truths, and then completes our knowledge and makes it sufficient for the attainment of our last end through Revelation.

Thus we find that, according to Augustine, in knowing ourselves and knowing that we know truth we prove the existence of God, for only God can be Truth and can account for the presence of universal truths in our minds. This "interior" proof of God's existence, which does not go outside our own intimate self-consciousness but leads us straight from the depths of our selves to God, is St. Augustine's favourite one. More than any other part of his thought, except perhaps his doctrine of grace, it shows his conviction of the absolute dependence of the creature upon God, so that if we really understand any creature, above all ourselves, of whom we have an immediate inward knowledge, we shall understand that it is a creature and absolutely dependent, and shall inevitably in the same act of comprehension comprehend that God is with it, supporting it in being and activity by His presence and power.

Augustine never describes or defines the illumination of the mind by the eternal truths very precisely, but there are one or two doctrines often attributed to him that he almost certainly did not hold. He certainly did not believe that we have any direct perception of the Forms in God, for that would mean contemplating the Divine Substance directly in this life, which like all orthodox Christians he holds to be impossible. Nor did he believe that God implants in us at birth all our true ideas ready-made ("innatism"). And it seems very improbable that he held that God works in our minds like the Aristotelian Active Intellect, abstracting our concepts for us, since he did not think of the mind in an Aristotelian way at all and does not seem to have been interested in the process by which concepts are formed. If we keep to Augustine, as distinct from later Augustinians, we can hardly go beyond the metaphor of "illumination"; in some way the Forms, the eternal truths in God, are the source of truth in our minds; exactly how Augustine does not tell us, but that the light of God does shine on our minds he is certain. This doctrine of illumination replaces in Augustine and his followers the Platonic doctrine of Recollection (anamnesis), to which nevertheless, in a modified form, Augustine was somewhat attracted, especially in his earlier years as a Christian thinker.

8. For St. Augustine the end to which all knowledge is directed is happiness. Man can only find his true happiness in attaining to union with God, Who alone can satisfy all his desires. Therefore the end and object of all thinking is the ascent of the mind to God and ultimate union with Him, for Augustine as for Plotinus, though their conceptions of God and of the way to Him differ very greatly. All knowledge and all speculation which does not help the soul on its way to God is to Augustine and his followers vain and harmful curiosity, and the centre and most important part of all his thinking is his teaching about the Christian life of increasing union with God by grace in supernatural charity. A full discussion of this, involving as it would a detailed consideration of St. Augustine's doctrine of grace and also his teaching about the Church, the Sacraments and Christian morality, would carry us too far outside the scope of what professes to be a history of philosophy. But there are certain points which we can and must consider, as they are of great importance for the later history of Western thought.

The first is the importance which Augustine, in accordance with the general Jewish and Christian tradition, but unlike the Hellenic philosophers, gives to the will, by whose act man chooses the object desired and sets all his energies in motion to attain it. It is the direction of the will which shapes and determines man's life. For Augustine the freedom of the will is established by the fact of choice. If we make real choices, as all our experience assures us that we do, then that fact establishes that our will is free in the usual sense of the word, for freedom is simply ability to choose. But, Augustine adds, if we make the wrong choice, are dominated by the wrong desire and moving to the wrong end, we are not really free at all, but enslaved. And if we are left to ourselves we always shall choose wrongly, that is, sin. Only God by His grace can give us the true freedom, which is not freedom to sin but freedom not to sin, or, in the highest degree, in Heaven, freedom from sin, inability to sin (De correptione et gratia XII, 33). We may perhaps say that Augustine realizes the importance of the will so vividly just because he is so intensely conscious that in himself and all fallen humanity the will left to itself works hopelessly badly. In our corrupt and ruined state we are impotent to do any good action at all or make any right choice without the grace which comes to us from Christ Incarnate who redeemed us by the Cross. It was the inability of the pagan Platonists to accept with humility the humiliation of the Word Made Flesh and dying upon the Cross˙ for our salvation which was in Augustine's eyes their fundamental error which ˙prevented them from reaching the God whom they saw far off. They could not cross the sea which lay between them and Him because they would not trust themselves to the wood of the Cross, the plank of His humiliation (Hom. in Joann. II, 4). In St. Augustine's tremendous emphasis on grace we see again his sense of the absolute dependence of the creature on God strengthened by his intense realization of the Fall of man and its effects.

The direction of the will, the way we choose, is the determining factor in the life of man and the driving force of the will is love. "Pondus meum amor meus; eo feror quocumque feror". "My love is my weight; by it I am carried wherever I am carried" (Confessions XIII-9, 10). Love moves the will, and so the whole man, as its weight irresistibly carries a body to its natural position. Therefore living rightly is loving rightly, delighting in and being altogether carried away by the desire of our proper object, which is God. And only God by His grace can give us that degree of delight in Him which moves our will to choose Him freely, love Him and seek Him in preference to all else; why He moves some and not others to this˙ effective delight in Him by which alone we can be saved is an impenetrable mystery of His justice. (The Church found it necessary later, as against distorted and exaggerated statements of Augustine's doctrine, to make very clear that God gives all men enough grace to be saved and that man can always refuse God's grace.) Without this grace we live wrongly because we love wrongly. That is, we enjoy and devote our whole energy to grasping as ends those partial, secondary earthly goods which we should only use as means to help us on our way to God. This enjoying as ends what we should only use as means, this perversion of the will, is the essence of sin according to St. Augustine (*cp.* De Doctrina Christiana I). We can only live rightly if we keep a right order in our love. "I think that a short and true definition of virtue is: it is the order of love" (De Civ. Dei, XV, 22). We should desire material goods less than spiritual and treat all created goods, which are transitory, partial, and can never content us, as 'means to attain God, who alone can satisfy the desire of man's soul completely and finally. In the conception of sin as primarily a wrong direction of desire to a lower good in preference to a higher Augustine is very close to the thought of Plotinus.

9. Love for Augustine is not only the driving force of individual, but also of social life. All societies and communities, he says, are constituted by a common desire. Those who seek the same object necessarily form a society to attain it; and it is the nature of the end which determines the character of the society (De Civ. Dei, XIX, 24). The great division of mankind as we have seen is between those who desire their proper end, God, above all else, and those whose desire is perverted so that they choose earthly goods as ends instead of means. And these two groups necessarily form two societies or "cities", which divide the human race between them, the City of God and the Earthly City, or City of the Devil. "Two loves make these two cities; the love of God makes Jerusalem; the love of the world makes Babylon." The City of God is in heaven, not on earth, and its citizens here are strangers and pilgrims with no permanent abiding-place. Angels as well as men are its citizens and it includes all the redeemed from the beginning to the end of the world. It does not therefore correspond to the Church on earth, which nevertheless stands in a very close relationship to it. The Church in this transitory and imperfect life is the representative, and the only representative, of the City of God and is endowed as a whole with supernatural holiness; but many of her members are no true citizens of the City, and there are many at any given moment outside who will be saved and become citizens. The City of God is Created Wisdom (Confessions, XII, 15) everlasting and belonging to the supra-temporal order. The Church is the society through which that supernatural order is made present to us in the manner appropriate to this life of passage and change.

The Earthly City or City of the Devil has no single kind of society which is its necessary embodiment and realization; but all temporal societies and States are parts of it in so far as they pursue purely worldly ends, power or glory or riches, and do not recognize the True God and subordinate themselves to attaining the ends of His City. If a State turns from the service of the devil and the pursuit of worldly ends and recognizes the salvation of man, his attainment of union with God and heavenly citizenship through the Church, as the supreme end of human life, it is of course no longer part of the Earthly City. And even an evil State, devoted to the service of the devil, can claim a certain degree of obedience from the citizens of the Heavenly City who live in it, as long as it commands them nothing contrary to the law of God, because it provides certain temporal goods, a degree of peace and order above all, which they need in their pilgrimage. The warfare between the Two Cities which St. Augustine sees dominating the whole course of human history, is something profounder and more universal than a struggle between Church and State (though it may often show itself in that form). It is the conflict between right love and perverted love, between true order and the false order which is really disorder, which lies at the root of human life and in which every man and every group or community must take sides.

With St. Augustine we end our survey of the philosophy of the ancient world. He makes a good stopping-place, for it is he more than any other one man who forms the link between ancient philosophy and the later thought of Western Christendom. In trying to tell so great a story in so small a space there must necessarily have been many errors and omissions, and a certain amount of disproportion. But the book is only intended to act as an introduction to the subject and to stimulate the interest of any readers it may have. It will have served its purpose excellently if it moves anyone to do some wider reading on his own account, and above all to read, in the original or in translation, some at least of the works of the greatest of those whose thought I have been trying to describe. If I have managed to persuade anybody that Plato and Aristotle, Plotinus and Augustine are something more than musty historical curiosities who can be left to the attention of specialists with nothing better to do, then I shall have done something well worth doing. After all, we may reject the conclusions of the ancients if we like, but their thought is of sufficiently high quality and has affected that of later ages sufficiently deeply to make it very unwise for us to ignore them completely in making our own decisions about what we believe to be true.

A Note on the Sources

We derive our information about the lives and teachings of the ancient philosophers from two kinds of sources. First, and by far the most valuable, there are the writings of the philosophers themselves, complete or fragmentary. We possess one or more complete works of: Plato, Aristotle, Epicurus, a number of Middle Platonists and late Stoics, Plotinus, Porphyry, Proclus and a number of other late Neo-Platonists, and the Christian Fathers. The amount preserved of each of these philosophers varies considerably, from probably the whole of the written works of Plato and Plotinus and the great body of Aristotle's mature output to the two letters and the collection of aphorisms which are all that is left of the extensive works of Epicurus. The fragments preserved of the other philosophers also vary considerably in length, the longest and most valuable being the extracts from the philosophical poems of Parmenides and Empedocles. They are embedded in the works of a great variety of later writers and it is often difficult to be certain whether what we have is a genuine quotation and, if it is, precisely where it begins and ends.

The second source of our information about the ancient philosophers is what other people in the ancient world wrote about them. Plato and Aristotle often refer to their predecessors, the Pre-Socratics. Plato makes the great Parmenides (with his disciple Zeno of Elea) and two of the older Sophists, Protagoras and Gorgias, the principal characters in the dialogues bearing their names, and often discusses Pre-Socratic and Sophistic teachings in other dialogues. But his accounts of the philosophers themselves and of their teaching are adapted to his own literary and philosophical purposes and are not meant to be and should not be taken as being historically accurate. Aristotle too when he writes about his predecessors does so in terms of his own philosophy and therefore inevitably often misrepresents them, making them appear to be concerned about problems which could actually never have occurred to them. Later philosophers when they write about earlier members of their own school or those whom they claim as its ancestors are determined to show that these earlier masters are supporters of the opinions which they themselves hold, which at least in a school like the Platonic, which developed greatly in the course of its history, is destructive of all historical accuracy. And when they write about their opponents (for example Plutarch on the Stoics and Epicureans) they do so as a rule in the thoroughly unscrupulous spirit of ancient controversy. The evidence of the ancient philosophers about each other can therefore only be used with extreme caution. The fairest and most objective reporter of other people's philosophic views in the ancient world is Cicero, who was not himself an original philosopher and was not a partisan of any school.

The greater part of our information, however, about the lives of the ancient philosophers and the teachings of those whose works have perished comes to us not from the surviving writings of other philosophers but directly or indirectly from the great mass of more or less scholarly writing about philosophers and philosophy which begins with Aristotle's Peripatetic disciples, notably Theophrastus and Aristoxenus, and goes on through the works of the

Hellenistic scholars of Alexandria right down to the end of the pagan world. From the writings of this tradition also originally derive very many of the direct quotations from the lost works of philosophers which make up our collections of philosophical fragments. There were several kinds of this writing about philosophy ; lives of philosophers sometimes with some information about their teaching; works on the dating of the various philosophers; histories of particular schools and the very artificial Successions of Philosophers (see Chap. XI); collections of philosophical doctrines arranged by subjects (doxographic writings) or by schools; and finally the great commentaries of the Roman period. (The Lives of Philosophers were for the most part particularly unreliable, being based more on legend and scandalous gossip than on serious and truthful historical evidence.) The earlier and probably better works, those by the Peripatetic and Alexandrian scholars, are lost and we know them only at several removes through later and generally inferior compilations. The most important example of the whole of this kind of literature that we possess is the book of Diogenes Laertius (3rd cent. A.D.) entitled " Lives, Opinions and Sayings of Famous Philosophers," in ten volumes, containing an amazing mixture of extremely valuable and totally worthless information from a number of sources. We have also important late collections of doxographic material in Pseudo-Plutarch's "Placita Philosophorum", a good deal of which derives through Ætius (A.D. 100) ultimately from Theophrastus, and the " Eclogæ " of John Stobæus (after A.D. 400). Much is also preserved in the writings of Porphyry and the great Neo-Platonic commentaries, especially those of Proclus and Simplicius, in the controversial works of Galen, Plutarch and Sextus Empiricus, and by Christian writers, notably Hippolytus (3rd century A.D.), Theodoret (5th century) and Nemesius (about 400); there is a certain amount in the literary miscellanies of Gellius (A.D. 150) and Athenæus (A.D. 200). The Christian Fathers continually quote the pagan philosophers, either directly or at second hand, for controversial purposes or to illustrate the preparation for the Gospel among the Gentiles.

A Short Book List

This list does not pretend to be anything like a complete bibilography of works on Ancient Philosophy. It is merely intended to provide some suggestions for further reading. I have not as a general rule included texts, but I have given the titles of some important collections of fragments and of some of the most important English commentaries, and also a number of translations.

I. GENERAL WORKS

A. *Collections of Select Passages*

DE VOGEL, C. J. Greek Philosophy. Leiden. Vol. I. Thales to Plato. 3rd Edition 1963.
II. Aristotle, the Early Peripatetic School and the Early Academy. 2nd Edition. 1960.
III. The Hellenistic-Roman Period. 1959.
(This supersedes all previous collections of texts: Vol. III, which contains a great deal of material which is very difficult to find elsewhere, is an indispensable help to the study of later Greek philosophy. Besides the Greek texts, the volumes contain valuable notes and explanations, introductions and bibliographies.)

B. *General Histories of Ancient Philosophy*

ARMSTRONG, A. H. (ed.). The Cambridge History of Later Greek and Early Mediaeval Philosophy. Cambridge 1966.
BRÉHIER, E. Histoire de la Philosophie. Vol. I. L'Antiquite. 2 pts. Paris, 1926–7.
BURNET, J. Greek Philosophy. Part I (all published). Thales to Plato. London, 1914. (Rpd. 1928)
COLEBURT, R. An Introduction to Western Philosophy. London, 1958.
COPLESTON, F. A History of Philosophy. Vol. I. Greece and Rome. London, 1946.
CORNFORD, F. M. Before and After Socrates. Cambridge, 1932.
CORNFORD, F. M. The Unwritten Philosophy. Cambridge, 1950.
GOMPERZ, J. Greek Thinkers. English Transl. by L. MAGNUS and G. G. BERRY. 4 vols. London, 1901–12. (Rpd. 1913–29).
GUTHRIE, W. K. C. The Greek Philosophers. London, 1950.
GUTHRIE, W. K. C. A History of Greek Philosophy. Cambridge 1962– Probably 5 vols.
KRANZ, W. Die Griechische Philosophie. Wiesbaden, 1950.
ROBIN, L. Greek Thought. English Transl. London, 1928.
UEBERWEG. Fr. Grundriss d. Geschichte d. Philosophie. Pt. I. Das Altertum. 12th Edition, by K. PRAECHTER. Berlin, 1926. (A complete guide to the subject, indispensable for serious study.)
ZELLER, E. Outlines of Greek Philosophy. English Transl. of 13th Edition, by W. NESTLE, by S. F. Alleyne and E. Abbott. New Edition revised. London, 1931.
ZELLER, E. Die Philosophie der Griechen. 3 vols. in 6. Last reprinted 1963.

C. *Works on Special Subjects and Related Themes (Ancient Science, Religion, Education in Relation to Philosophy.)*

CORNFORD, F. M. Principium Sapientiae. Cambridge, 1952.
DODDS, E. R. The Greeks and the Irrational. Cambridge, 1951.
DUHEM, P. La Système du Monde. I. La Cosmologie Hellénique, Paris 1913.
FERGUSON, J. Moral Values in the Ancient World. London, 1958.
FESTUGIÈRE, A. J. Personal Religion among the Greeks. Cambridge, 1954.
GUTHRIE, W. K. C. The Greeks and their Gods. London, 1950.
GUTHRIE, W. K. C. In the Beginning. Some Greek views on the origins of life and the early state of man. London, 1957.

Heath, Sir T. L. History of Greek Mathematics. 2 vols. Oxford, 1921.
Manual of Greek Mathematics. Oxford, 1931.
Jaeger, W. Paideia. The Ideals of Greek Culture. Engl. Trans. by G.
Highet. 3 vols. Oxford, 1943–45.
Marrou, H—I. History of Education in Antiquity. Engl. Trans. by G. R.
Lamb. London, 1956.
Nilsson, M. P. Geschichte der Griechischen Religion. 2 vols. (Handbuch
der. Altertumswissenschaft V.2). Munich, 1941–50.
Nock, A. D. Conversion. Oxford, 1933.
Sambursky, S. The Physical World of the Greeks. London, 1956 (reprinted
1960.)
Sarton, G. History of Science: Ancient Science through the Golden Age of
Greece. 1953.
Schrodinger, E. Nature and the Greeks. Cambridge, 1954.
Sinclair, T. A. A History of Greek Political Thought. London, 1952.
Snell, B. The Discovery of the Mind. Engl. Trans. by T. G. Rosenmayer.
London, 1953.

II. PRE-SOCRATIC PHILOSOPHY

A. *Fragments*

Cornford, F. M. Plato and Parmenides (contains translation of Parmenides
with running commentary). Cambridge, 1939.
Diels, H. Die Fragmente der Vorsokratiker. 3 vols. 10th Edition revised by
W. Kranz. Berlin, 1961. (Complete collection of all ancient information about the Pre-Socratics with German translation of the
fragments and very full indices.)
Freeman, K. Ancilla to the Pre-Socratic Philosophers (A complete English
translation of the Fragments in Diels, to accompany the same
author's Companion—see below). Oxford, 1948.
Kirk, G. S. Heraclitus. The Cosmic Fragments. (Text, translation,
introduction, commentary). Cambridge, 1954.
Kirk, G. S. and Raven, J. The Presocratic Philosophers. A critical history
with a selection of texts. Cambridge, 1957.
Lee, H. D. P. The Fragments of Zeno of Elea. Cambridge, 1936.

B. *Modern Works*

Burnet, J. Early Greek Philosophy. 4th Edition. London, 1930.
Cornford, F. M. See I.C. and II.A.
Freeman, K. Companion to the Pre-Socratic Philosophers. Oxford,
1946.
Guthrie, W. K. C. Orpheus and Greek Religion. 2nd Edition, London,
1952.
Jæger, W. The Theology of the Early Greek Philosophers. Oxford,
1947.
Raven, J. E. Pythagoreans and Eleatics. Cambridge, 1948.
Tannery, P. Pour l'Histoire de la Science Hellène. Paris. 2nd Edition, by
A. Dies. 1930.

III. SOCRATES.

The books on Plato listed in the next section also contain a great deal on Socrates.
A few works exclusively devoted to him are given here.
Field, G. C. Socrates and Plato. Oxford, 1913.
Gigon, O. Sokrates. Berne, 1947.
De Magalhaes-Vilhena. V. Le Probleme de Socrate. Socrate et la
legende Platonicienne. Paris, 1952.
Rogers, A. K. The Socratic Problem. New York, 1933.
Sauvage, M. Socrates. Eng. Trans. by P. Hepburne-Scott, London ,1959.
Taylor, A. E. Varia Socratica. 1st Series (all published). Oxford, 1911.
Taylor, A. E. Socrates. London, 1932.

IV. PLATO

A. Translations and Commentaries

Complete text and English translation in the Loeb Series (11 vols), complete text and French translation, often with valuable introductions, in the Bude Series (13 parts,); a number of good translations, sometimes with useful introductions and appendices, in the Oxford Library of Translations.

BLUCK, R. S. Plato's Phaedo. London, 1955.

CORNFORD, F. M. Plato's Theory of Knowledge. Cambridge, 1935. ("Theætetus" and "Sophist", translated with running commentary.)

CORNFORD, F. M. Plato's Cosmology. Cambridge, 1937. ("Timæus", translated with running commentary.)

CORNFORD, F. M. Plato and Parmenides. Cambridge, 1939. (Fragments of Parmenides and Plato's dialogue "Parmenides", translated with running commentary.)

CORNFORD, F. M. The Republic. Oxford, 1941. (Translation with introduction and notes.)

GUARDINI, R. The Death of Socrates (Extracts from the Euthyphro, Apology, Crito, and Phædo, with a running commentary). English Translation by B. WRIGHTON. London, 1947.

HACKFORTH, R. Plato's Examination of Pleasure. Cambridge, 1944. ("Philebus", translated with running commentary.)

HACKFORTH, R. Plato's Phædrus. Cambridge, 1952.

HACKFORTH, R. Plato's Phaedo. Cambridge, 1955.

JOWETT, B. The Dialogues of Plato. 5 vols. 4th Edition, revised. Oxford, 1953. (Complete translation with introductions.)

SKEMP, J. B. Plato's *Statesman* (translation with introductory essays and commentary.) London, 1952.

TAYLOR, A. E. A Commentary on Plato's "Timæus". Oxford, 1928. (Commentary only.)

TAYLOR, A. E. Plato's Philebus and Epinomis (translations and introduction; edited by R. KLIBANSKY, G. CALOGERO and A. C. LLOYD.) London, 1956.

TAYLOR, A. E. Plato's Sophist and Statesman (translations and introduction: edited by R. KLIBANSKY and E. ANSCOMBE). London, 1961.

TAYLOR, A. E. Plato, The Laws (translation, introduction and notes). London, 1960.

B. Modern Works

BARKER, E. Greek Political Theory. Plato and his Predecessors. 2nd Edition. 1925.

BURNET, J. Platonism. Berkeley, Cal., 1928.

CROMBIE, I. M. An Examination of Plato's Doctrines. 2 vols. London, 1962.

CROMBIE, I. M. Plato, the Midwife's Apprentice. London, 1964 (a short introduction for the general reader).

DIÈS, A. Autour de Platon. 2 vols. Paris, 1927.

FIELD, G. C. Plato and his Contemporaries. Oxford, 1930.

GRUBE, G. M. A. Plato's Thought. London, 1935.

LEVINSON, R. B. In Defense of Plato. 1954.

LODGE, R. C. Plato's Theory of Ethics. 1928.

LODGE, R. C. Plato's Theory of Education. London, 1947.

LUTOSLAWSKI, W. Origin and Growth of Plato's Logic. London, 1905.

POPPER, K. R. The Open Society and its Enemies Vol. I. The Spell of Plato. 2nd Edition. London. 1952. (A brilliant but unfair attack which has started a vigorous controversy. See the books of LEVINSON and WILD, which are replies to Popper and to other recent attacks on Plato.)

RITTER, C. Platon. 2 vols. Munich, 1910, 1923.

RITTER, C. Essence of Plato's Philosophy. Eng. Trans. by R. ADAM ALLES. London, 1933.

ROBIN, L. La Theorie Platonicienne des idées et des nombres. Paris 1908.
ROBINSON, R. Plato's Earlier Dialectic, New York and London, 1941.
ROSS, SIR DAVID. Plato's Theory of Ideas. Oxford, 1951.
SKEMP, J. B. The Theory of Motion in Plato's Later Dialogues. Cambridge, 1942. (Plato's doctrine of Soul as universal cause of motion.)
SOLMSEN, F. Plato's Theology. Ithaca. N.Y., 1942.
STENZEL, J. Plato's Method of Dialectic. Engl Trans. Oxford, 1940.
TAYLOR, A. E. Plato: the Man and his Work. 3rd Edition. Oxford, 1929.
TAYLOR, A. E. Platonism. (Our Debt to Greece and Rome.) 1924.
TAYLOR, A. E. Plato. (Philosophies Ancient and Modern.) 1922.
WILAMOWITZ-MOELLENDORF, V. von. Platon. 2nd Edition. 2 vols. Berlin, 1920.
WILD, J. Plato's Modern Enemies. Chicago, 1953.
ZELLER, E. Plato and the Older Academy. Translated from Vol. II of Die Philosophie d. Griechen, by S. F. Alleyne and A. Goodwin. London, 1888.

V. ARISTOTLE

A. *Translations and Commentaries*

The Oxford Translation of Aristotle (ed. J. A. Smith and W. D. Ross) is complete in 12 volumes. The text with English translation, and sometimes useful introductions, appendices, etc., is being issued in the Loeb Series, and with a French translation in the Bude series.

De Anima

HICKS, R. D. Cambridge, 1907. (Text, Translation and Commentary.)
ROSS, W. D. Oxford, 1961 (Text, Introduction and Commentary.)

De Generatione Animalium

PECK, A. L. Loeb Series. London, 1944. (Text, Translation, Introduction and important Appendices on *pneuma*, etc.)

De Generatione et Corruptione

JOACHIM, H. H. Oxford, 1922. (Text, important introduction on A's natural philosophy and commentary.)

Nicomachean Ethics

BURNET, J. London, 1904. (Text and Commentary).
RACKHAM, H. Aristotle's Ethics for English Readers. Oxford, 1944. (An abridged translation.)
JOACHIM, H. H. The Nicomachean Ethics. (ed. D. A. REES.) Oxford. 1951. (Commentary only.)

Metaphysics

ROSS. W. D. Oxford, 1924. (Text, Introduction and Commentary.)
WARRINGTON, J. Aristotle's Metaphysics (introduction by Sir D. Ross). London, 1956. (A new translation arranged in a more rational order than that adopted by Aristotle's original editors.)

Physics

ROSS, W. D. Oxford, 1936. (Text, Introduction and Commentary.)
WICKSTEED, P. and CORNFORD, F. M. Loeb Series. London, 1929. 2 vols. (Text, Translation, Introduction.)

Poetic

BYWATER, I. Oxford, 1909. (Text, Commentary and Translation.)
BUTCHER, S. H. Aristotle's Theory of Poetry and Fine Art. 4th Edition. London, 1927. (Text, Translation and Essays.)

Politics

BARKER, E. The Politics of Aristotle. Oxford, 1948. (Translation, introduction, notes and appendices.)
NEWMAN, W. L. 4 vols. Oxford, 1887-1902. (Text, Commentary, Essays.)
SUSEMIHL, F. and HICKS, R. D. London, 1894. (Text, Introduction and Commentary Books, 1-5 only.)

B. *Modern Works*

ALLAN, D. J. The Philosophy of Aristotle. London, 1952.
HAMELIN, O. Le Systeme d'Aristote. Ed. L. Robin. Paris, 1920.
JÆGER, W. Aristotle. Fundamentals of the History of His Development. 2nd Edition revised and enlarged. English Trans. by R. ROBINSON. Oxford, 1948.
ROBIN, L. Aristote, Paris, 1944.
ROSS, W. D. Aristotle. Revised Edition. London, 1930.
STOCKS, J. L. Aristotelianism. Our Debt to Greece and Rome. 1925.
TAYLOR, A. E. Aristotle. 2nd Edition. London, 1919.

VI. CYNICS AND EARLY STOICS

A. *Collections of Fragments*

VON ARNIM, J. Stoicorum Veterum Fragmenta. Vols. I-III. Leipzig, 1903-5. Vol. IV. Indices by M. Adler. Leipzig, 1924.
PEARSON, A. C. The Fragments of Zeno and Cleanthes. London, 1891. (With Introduction and Notes.)

B. *Modern Works*

BARTH, P. Die Stoa. 6th Edition revised by A. GOEDECKEMEYER. Stuttgart, 1946.
BEVAN, E. R. Stoics and Sceptics. Oxford, 1913.
BRÉHIER, E. Chrysippe. Paris, 2nd Edition, 1951.
DUDLEY, D. R. History of Cynicism. London, 1937.
HICKS, R. D. Stoic and Epicurean. Cambridge, 1910.
POHLENZ, M. Die Stoa. 2 vols. Gottingen, 1948-9.
ZELLER, E. Stoics, Epicureans and Sceptics. English Translation from Vol. III of Philosophie d. Griechen, by O. Reichel. London, 1880.

VII. EPICUREANS AND SCEPTICS

A. *Translations and Commentaries*

BAILEY, C. Epicurus: the Extant Remains. Oxford, 1926. (Text, Translation, Introduction, Commentary, Appendices.)
BAILEY, C. Lucretius. 3 vols. Oxford, 1947. (Text. Translation, Introduction, Commentary.)
MUNRO, H. A. J. Lucretius. 3 vols. London, 1886. Vol. II. Notes, Rp. with Essay by Prof. Andrade, 1928. (Text, Commentary, Translation.)

B. *Modern Works*

BAILEY, C. The Greek Atomists and Epicurus. London, 1928.
BROCHARD, V. Les Sceptiques Grecs. Paris. 1887. (Rp. 1923.)
FESTUGIÈRE, A. J. Epicure et Ses Dieux. Paris, 1946.
HICKS, R. D. See VI. B.
MASSON, J. Lucretius: Epicurean and Poet. 2 vols. London, 1908-9.
MASSON, J. Atomic Theory of Lucretius. London, 1884.
ZELLER, E. See VI. B.

VIII. LATER STOICS AND MIDDLE PLATONISTS

A. *Translations and Commentaries*

Text and Translations of Seneca, Epictetus, Marcus Aurelius, and Plutarch's Essays (Moralia, in progress) in Loeb Series; translations of Epictetus and a selection of Plutarch's Essays in the Oxford Library of Translations.

FARQUHARSON, A. S. L. The Meditations of the Emperor Marcus Antoninus. 2 vols. Oxford, 1944. (Text, Introduction, Translation, Commentary.)

LUCK, G. Der Akademiker Antiochos. Berne, 1952.

VAN STRAATEN. M. Panétius. Amsterdam, 1946. (3rd revised and enlarged separate edition of fragments. Leiden 1962.)
(Both these works contain collections of fragments.)

B. *Modern Works*

Information on the Middle Platonists is also to be found in works on Neo-Platonism and the early Christian writers.

FONDATION HARDT. Entretiens III. Recherches sur la Tradition Platonicienne. Vandoeuvres—Geneva, 1955. (An important collection of studies in English, French, and German on later Platonism and its influence on Christian and Moslem thought).

MERLAN, P. From Platonism to Neoplatonism. The Hague. 1953.

POHLENZ, M. See VI. B.

THEILER, W. Die Vorbereitung des Neuplatonismus. Berlin, 1930.

WITT, R. E. Albinus, Cambridge, 1937.

ZELLER, E. See VI, B.

IX. PHILO AND THE EARLY CHRISTIAN THEOLOGIANS

A. *Translations*

Text and translation of Philo and of some works of Clement of Alexandria and Tertullian in the Loeb Series. Texts and French translations of the Fathers with valuable introductions and notes are appearing in the collection "Sources Chretiennes" (Paris 1944–). There are three series of translations of the Fathers now being published in English, "The Fathers of the Church" (New York) "Ancient Christian Writers" (Washington and London), "A Library of Christian Classics" (S.C.M. Press). A few notable translations not included in any of these series are listed below.

BUTTERWORTH, G. W. Origen De Principiis. London, 1936. (Translation, introduction and notes.)

CHADWICK, H. Origen Contra Celsum. London, 1953. (Translation, introduction and notes.)

EVANS, E. Tertullian, Treatise against Praxeas. London, 1948. (Text, translation, introduction, commentary.)

LUKYN WILLIAMS. A. Justin Martyr. Dialogue with Trypho. London, 1930.

B. *Modern Works*

ARMSTRONG, A. H. and MARKUS, R. A. Christian Faith and Greek Philosophy. London, 1960. New York, 1964.

BRÉHIER, E. Philon d'Alexandrie. 3rd Edition, Paris, 1950

CADIOU, R. Introduction au Systeme d'Origène. Paris, 1932.

CADIOU, R. La jeunesse d'Origène. Paris, 1935.

CROUZEL, H. Origène et la Philosophie. Paris, 1962.

DANIELOU, J. Origen. Eng. trans. by W. Mitchell. London, 1955.

DANIELOU, J. A History of Early Christian Doctrine before the Council of Nicaea. 3 vols. London, 1964–

DANIELOU, J. and MARROU, H. I. The Christian Centuries. Vol. I. The First Six Hundred years. London, 1964.

FESTUGIÈRE, A–J. L'Ideal religieux des Grecs et L'Evangile. 2nd Edition. Paris, 1931.

FONDATION HARDT, Entretiens III. See VIII B.
GILSON, E. History of Christian Philosophy in the Middle Ages. London, 1955. (Eng. Trans. of 2nd revised edition).
GOODENOUGH, E. R. Introduction to Philo Judaeus. 2nd Edition. 1962.
PRESTIGE, G. L. God in Patristic Thought. London, 1952.
PUECH, A. Les Apologistes grecs. Paris, 1912.
QUASTEN, J. Patrology Vols. I–II. 1950–53.
WOLFSON, H. A. Philo. 2 vols. Cambridge (Mass.) and London, 1947.

X. PLOTINUS AND THE LATER NEO-PLATONISTS

A. *Translations and Commentaries*

ARMSTRONG, A. H. Plotinus. London, 1953, New York, 1962. (Selections in translation with introduction and brief notes.)
ARMSTRONG, A. H. Plotinus Enneads. Loeb Series. London 1966– (Text of the Henry-Schwyzer revised edition with translation, introductions and notes).
BRÉHIER, E. Les Enneades de Plotin. 6 Vols. Bude Series. Paris, 1924–36. (Text, French trans., Introductions to the several Treatises and Notes.)
CHAIGNET, A. E. Damascius. Paris, 1903. (French Translation.)
DODDS, E. R. Proclus. The Elements of Theology. 2nd Edition, Oxford, 1963. (Text, Translation, Introduction, Commentary.)
HARDER, R. Leipzig, 1930–37 (German trans.). Re-issue with Greek text and critical notes. Hamburg, 1956–
KLIBANSKY, R. and LABOWSKY, L. Plato Latinus Vol. III. Parmenides. London, 1953. (Contains an English translation of the last and most philosophically important—hitherto unpublished—part of Proclus's Commentary on the Parmenides).
MACKENNA, S. Plotinus. The Enneads. Third Edition revised by B. S. PAGE. Foreword by E. R. DODDS. Introduction by P. HENRY. London, 1962. (Translation).
O'NEILL, W. Proclus, Commentary on the First Alcibiades of Plato. The Hague, 1965. (Translation with introduction and notes).
SAFFREY, P. and WESTERINK, L. G. Proclus. In Platonis Theologiam. Paris, 1966– (Critical text with French translation, introduction and notes).

B. *Modern Works*

ARMSTRONG, A. H. Architecture of the Intelligible Universe in the Philosophy of Plotinus. Cambridge, 1940.
ARNOU, R. Le desir de Dieu dans la philosophie de Plotin. Paris, 1931.
BRÉHIER, E. La Philosophie de Plotin. 2nd Edition, Paris, 1961.
FONDATION HARDT. Entretiens V, Les Sources de Plotin. Vandoeuvres-Genève, 1960. (A most important collection of essays and discussions on the thought of Plotinus and his relationship to his predecessors).
DE GANDILLAC. M. La Sagesse de Plotin. Paris, 1952.
HADOT, P. Plotin. Paris, 1963.
HENRY, P. Plotin et l'Occident. Louvain, 1934.
INGE. R. The Philosophy of Plotinus. 2 vols. 3rd Edition. London. 1929. (reprinted 1948).
DE LABRIOLLE, P. La reaction paienne. Paris, 1934.
RIST, J. M. Eros and Psyche. Studies in Plato, Plotinus and Origen. Toronto, 1964.
ROSAN, L. J. The Philosophy of Proclus. New York, 1949.
SAMBURSKY, S. The Physical World of Late Antiquity. London, 1962.
TROUILLARD, J. La Procession Plotinienne. Paris, 1955.
TROUILLARD, J. La Purification Plotinienne. Paris, 1955.
WHITTAKER, T. The Neo-Platonists. 2nd Edition, Cambridge, 1928.

XI. S. AUGUSTINE

A. *Translations*

Latin texts and French translation, with introductions and notes, are appearing in the series *Bibliotheque Augustinienne*. (Paris, 1949–). Translations of a number of S. Augustine's works are appearing in all three series of modern English translations of the Fathers (see IX A.). Text and translation of the *Confessions* and a volume of *Select Letters* in the Loeb series. There are many translations of the *Confessions*, notably those of Tobie Mathew, Watts and Pusey, which have often been reprinted; only those editions which include the last three books are much use for the study S. Augustine's thought.

HEALEY, J. The City of God. 1610. Latest reprint. London, 1943.

PRZYWARA, E. An Augustine Synthesis. (Translations of selected passages giving a survey of S. Augustine's thought.) London, 1936.

SHEED, F. J. The Confessions. London, 2nd Edition, 1951.

B. *Modern Works*

AUGUSTINUS MAGISTER. 3 vols. Paris, 1954. (The proceedings of the International Augustinian Congress. Contains essays and discussions in all the principal European languages covering every aspect of S. Augustine's thought and the whole range of modern Augustinian scholarship.)

BONNER, G. Augustine of Hippo. London, 1963.

BOURKE, V. J. Augustine's Quest of Wisdom. Milwaukee, 1945.

COURCELLE, P. Recherches sur les Confessions de S. Augustin. Paris, 1950.

GILSON, E. Introduction a l'Etude de S. Augustin. 3rd edition, Paris, 1949. (English translation, London, 1961).

HENRY, P. See X. B.

HENRY, P. La Vision d'Ostie. Paris, 1938.

MARROU, H-I. S. Augustin et la fin de la culture antique. 2nd edition with "Retractatio", 2 vols. Paris, 1949.

O'MEARA, J. J. The young Augustine. London, 1954.

A MONUMENT TO S. AUGUSTINE (various authors). London, 1930.

INDEX